A Certain Scientific Accelerator 12

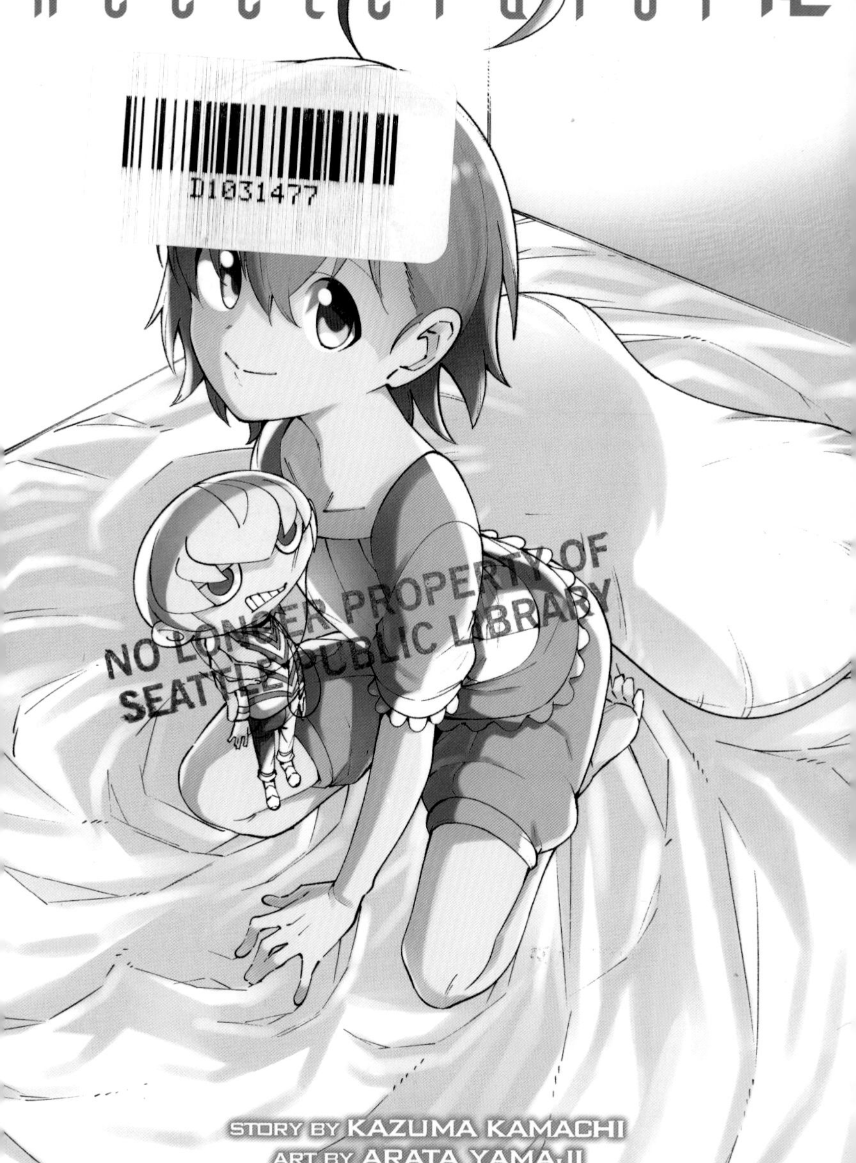

STORY BY KAZUMA KAMACHI
ART BY ARATA YAMAJI
CHARACTER DESIGN BY KIYOTAKA HAIMURA & ARATA YAMAJI

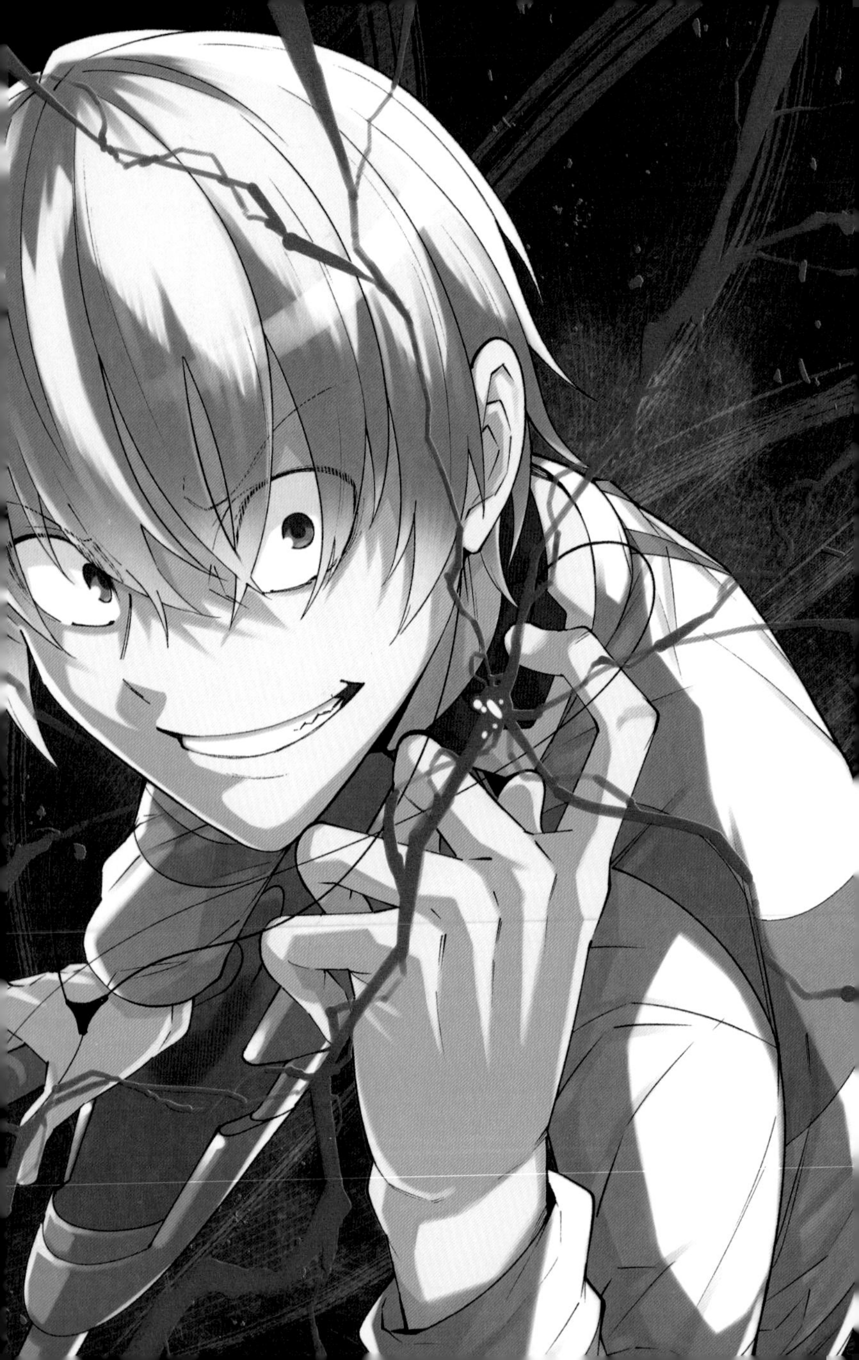

CHAPTER 59

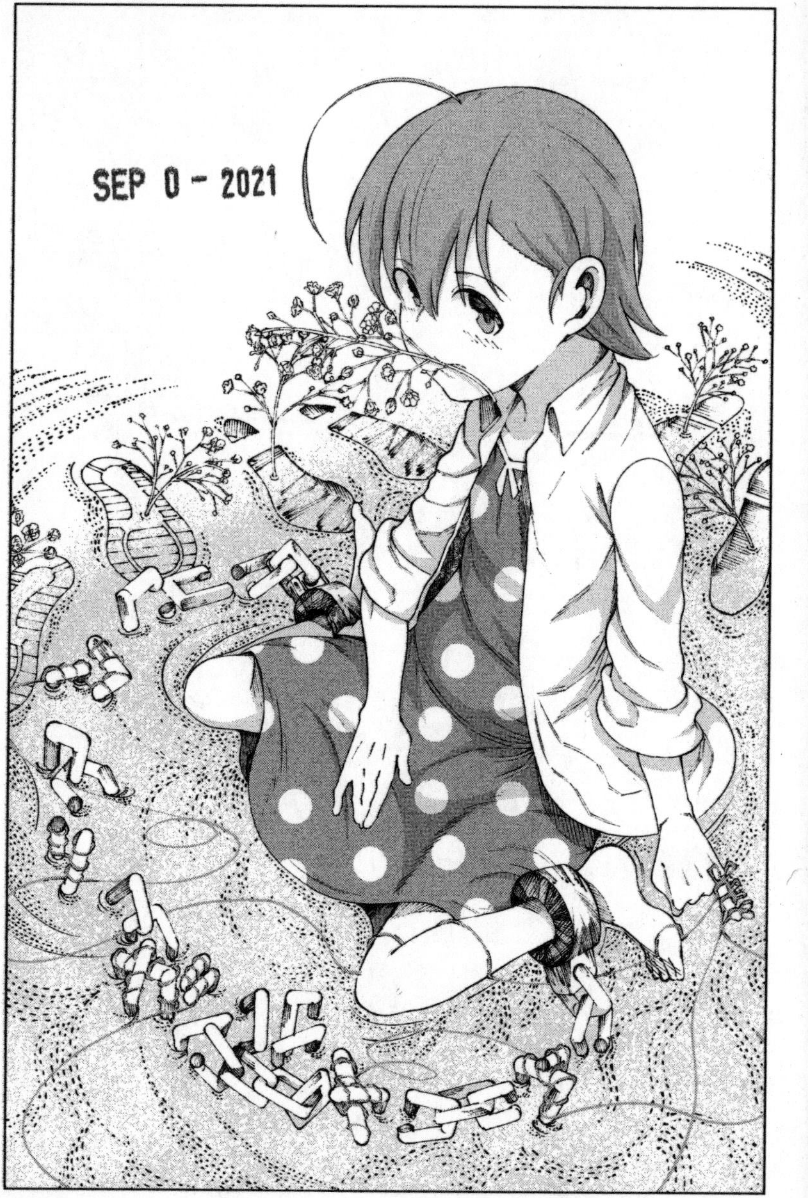

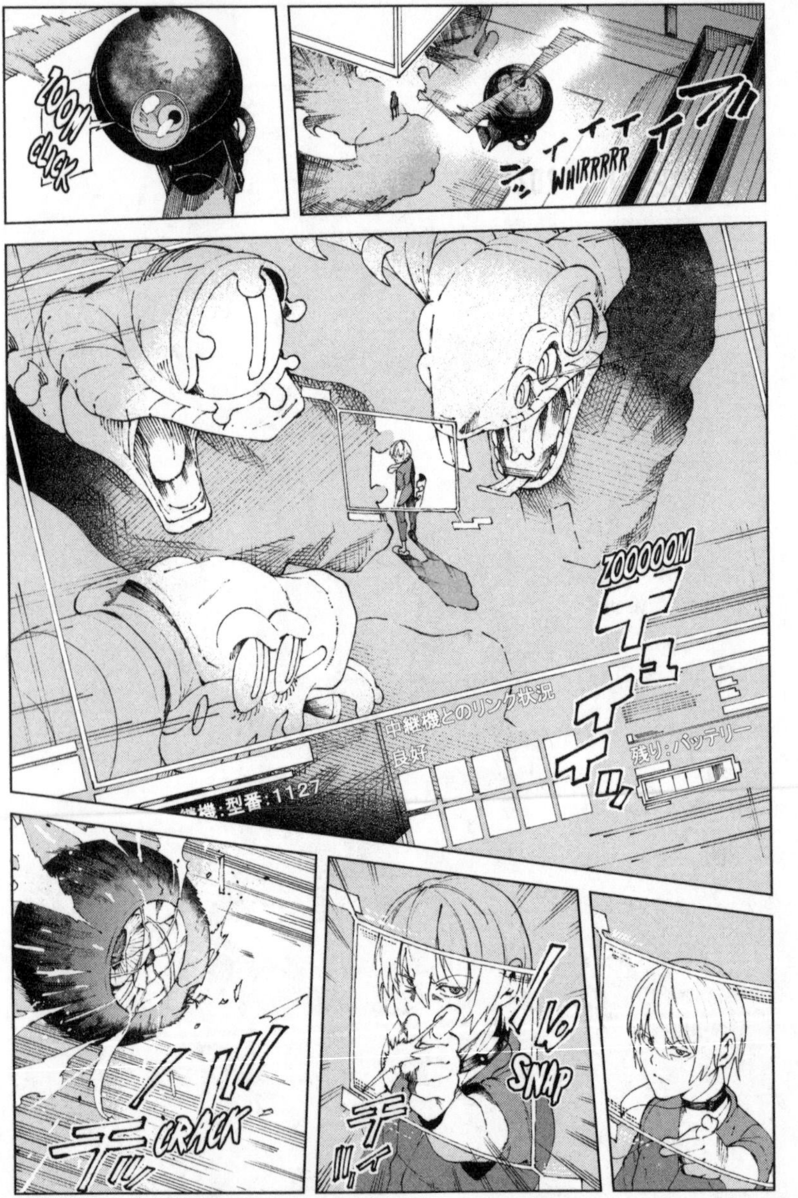
WHIRRRRR
ZOOM
CLICK
ZOOOOOM
中継機とのリンク状況
良好
残り：バッテリー
機：型番：1127
SNAP
CRACK

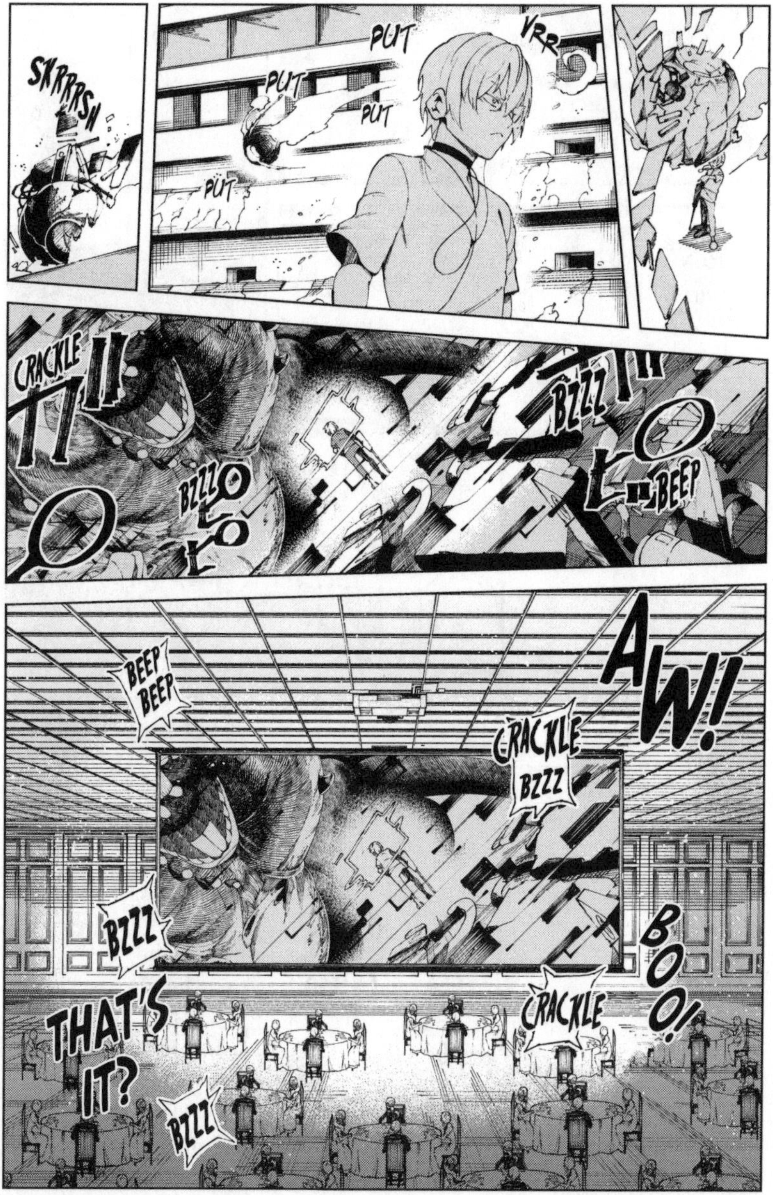
VRR
PUT
PUT
PUT
PUT
SKRRRSH
BZZZ
BEEP
CRACKLE
BZZZ
AW!
CRACKLE
BZZZ
BEEP BEEP
BOO!
CRACKLE
BZZZ
THAT'S IT?
BZZZ

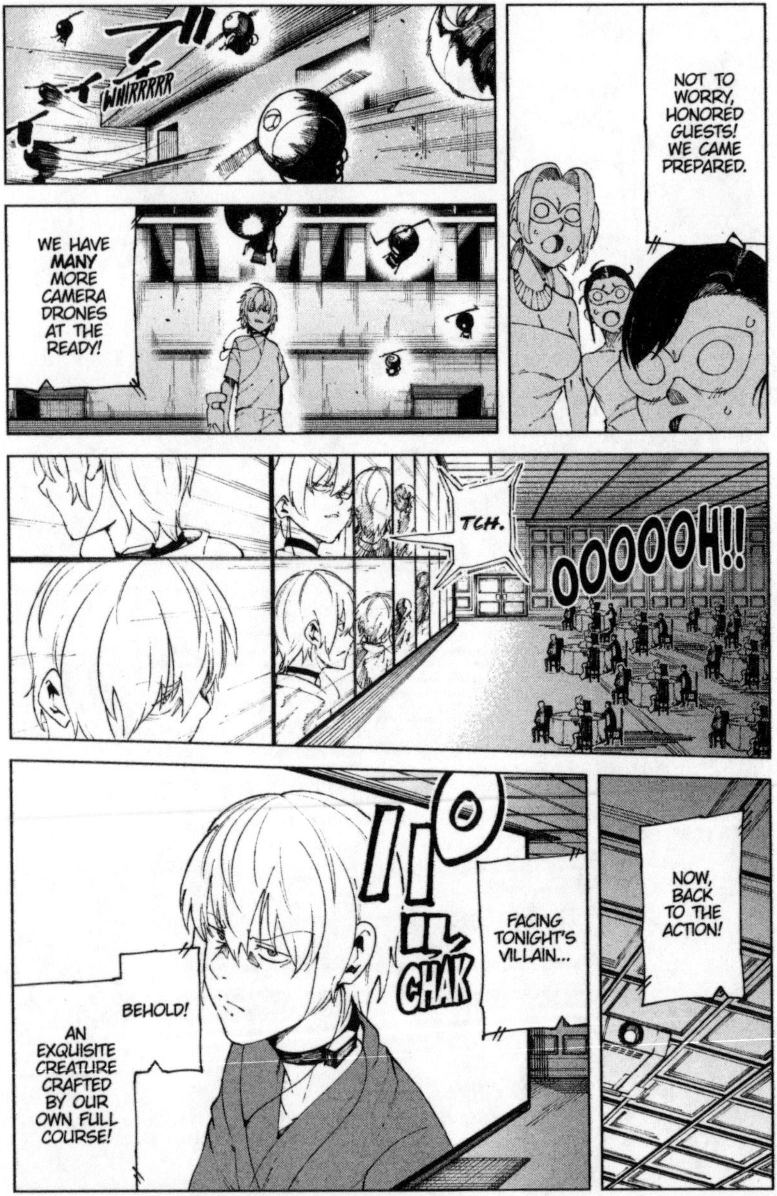
NOT TO WORRY, HONORED GUESTS! WE CAME PREPARED.
WWIRRRRR
WE HAVE MANY MORE CAMERA DRONES AT THE READY!
OOOOOOH!!
TCH.
NOW, BACK TO THE ACTION!
FACING TONIGHT'S VILLAIN...
CHAK
BEHOLD!
AN EXQUISITE CREATURE CRAFTED BY OUR OWN FULL COURSE!

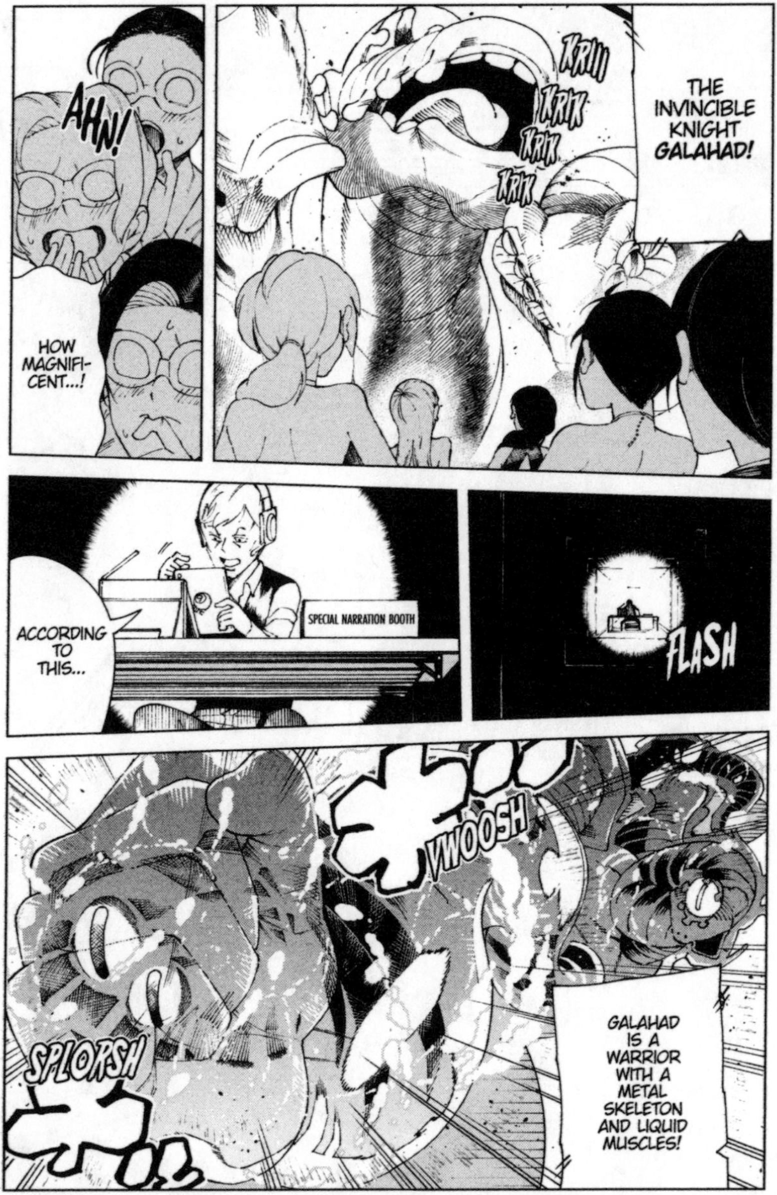
THE INVINCIBLE KNIGHT GALAHAD!
KRIII
KRIK
KRIK
KRIK
AHN!
HOW MAGNIFI-CENT...!
FLASH
SPECIAL NARRATION BOOTH
ACCORDING TO THIS...
VWOOSH
GALAHAD IS A WARRIOR WITH A METAL SKELETON AND LIQUID MUSCLES!
SPLORSH

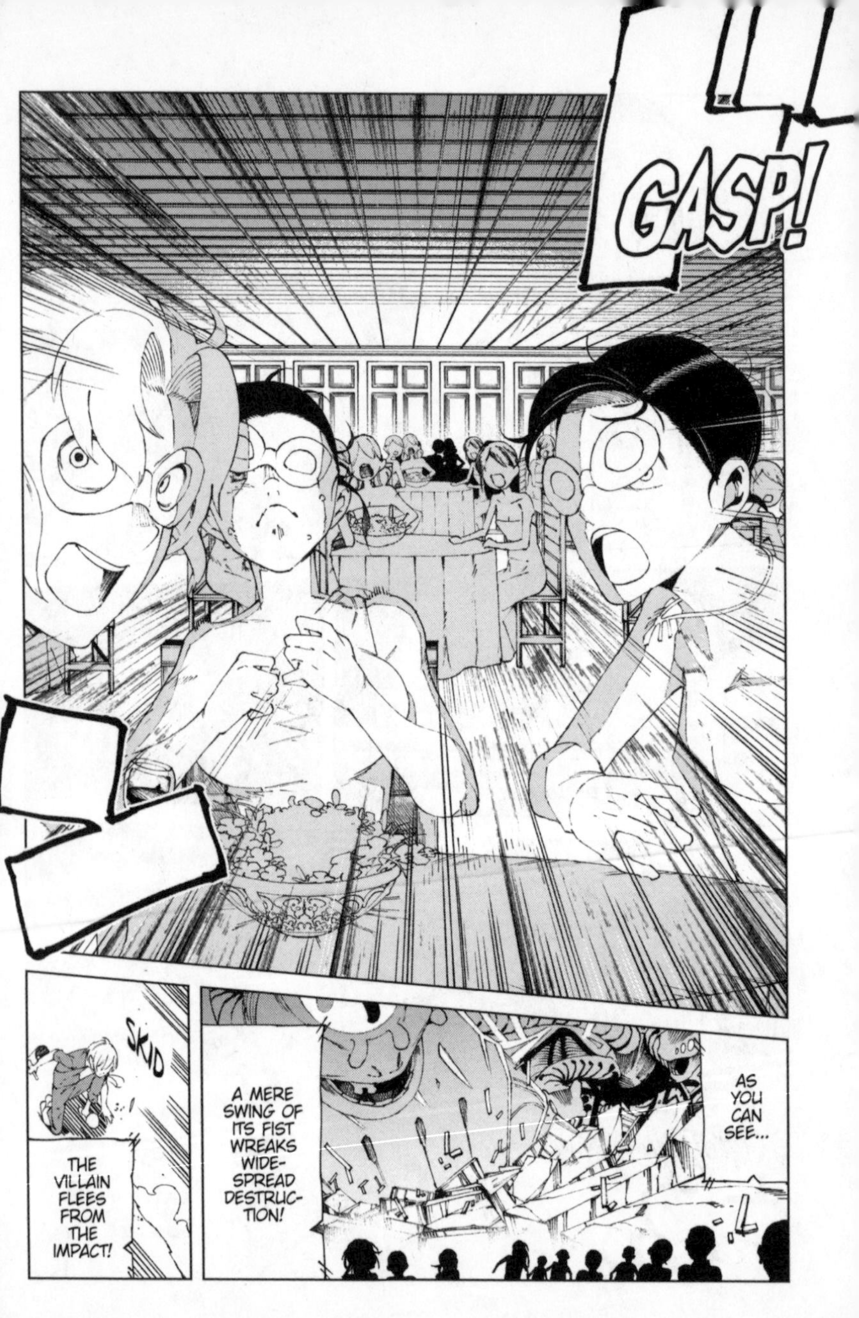
GASP!
AS YOU CAN SEE...
A MERE SWING OF ITS FIST WREAKS WIDE-SPREAD DESTRUC-TION!
SKID
THE VILLAIN FLEES FROM THE IMPACT!

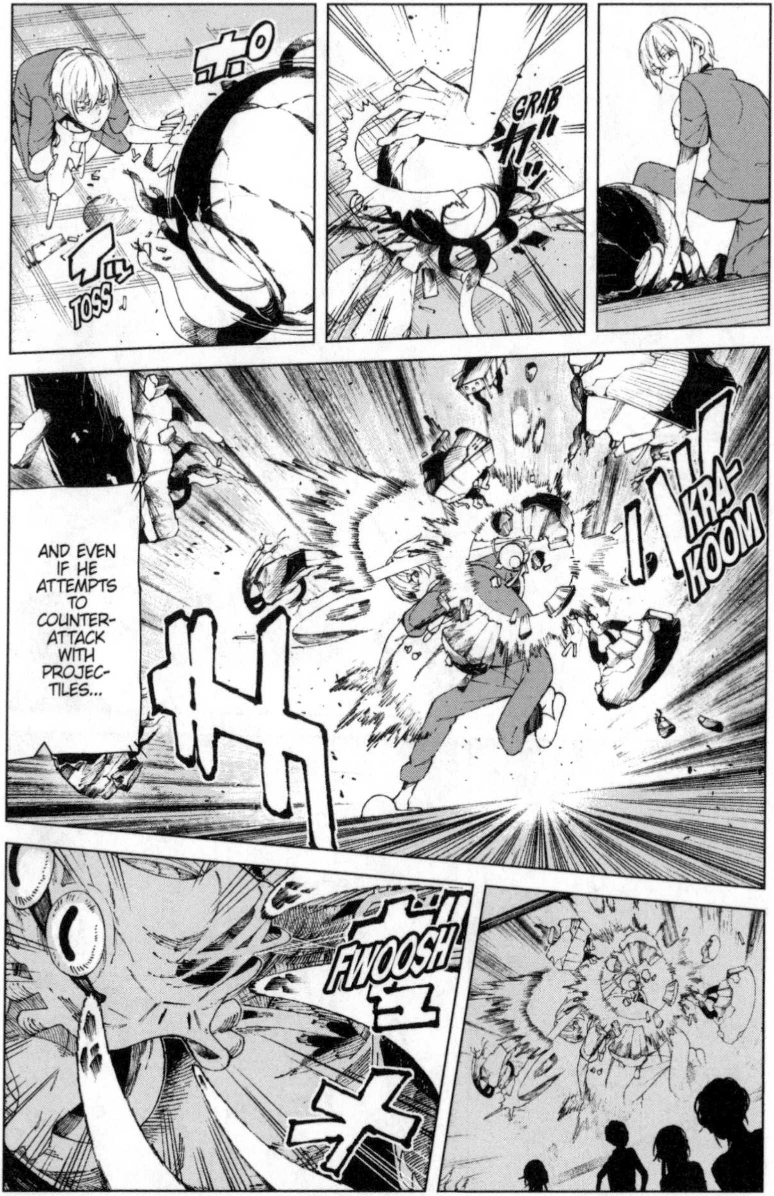
GRAB
TOSS
AND EVEN IF HE ATTEMPTS TO COUNTER-ATTACK WITH PROJEC-TILES...
KRA-KOOM
FWOOSH

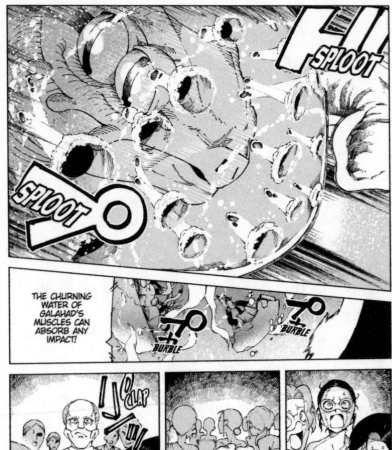

SPLOOT

SPLOOT

THE CHURNING WATER OF GALAHAD'S MUSCLES CAN ABSORB ANY IMPACT!

BURBLE

BURBLE

CLAP

CLAP

CLAP

CLAP

CLAP

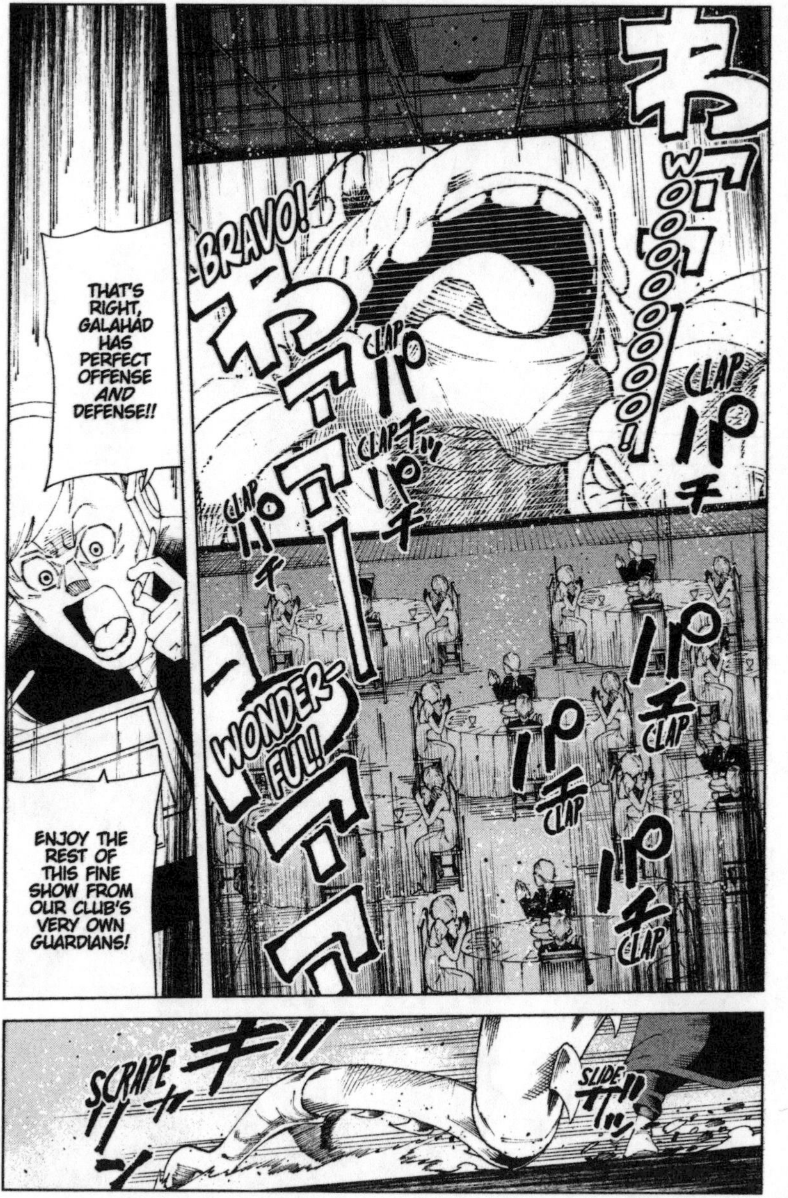
WOOOOOOOOOOO!!
CLAP
BRAVO!
CLAP
CLAP
CLAP
CLAP
CLAP
CLAP
WONDER-FUL!
THAT'S RIGHT, GALAHAD HAS PERFECT OFFENSE AND DEFENSE!!
ENJOY THE REST OF THIS FINE SHOW FROM OUR CLUB'S VERY OWN GUARDIANS!
SLIDE
SCRAPE

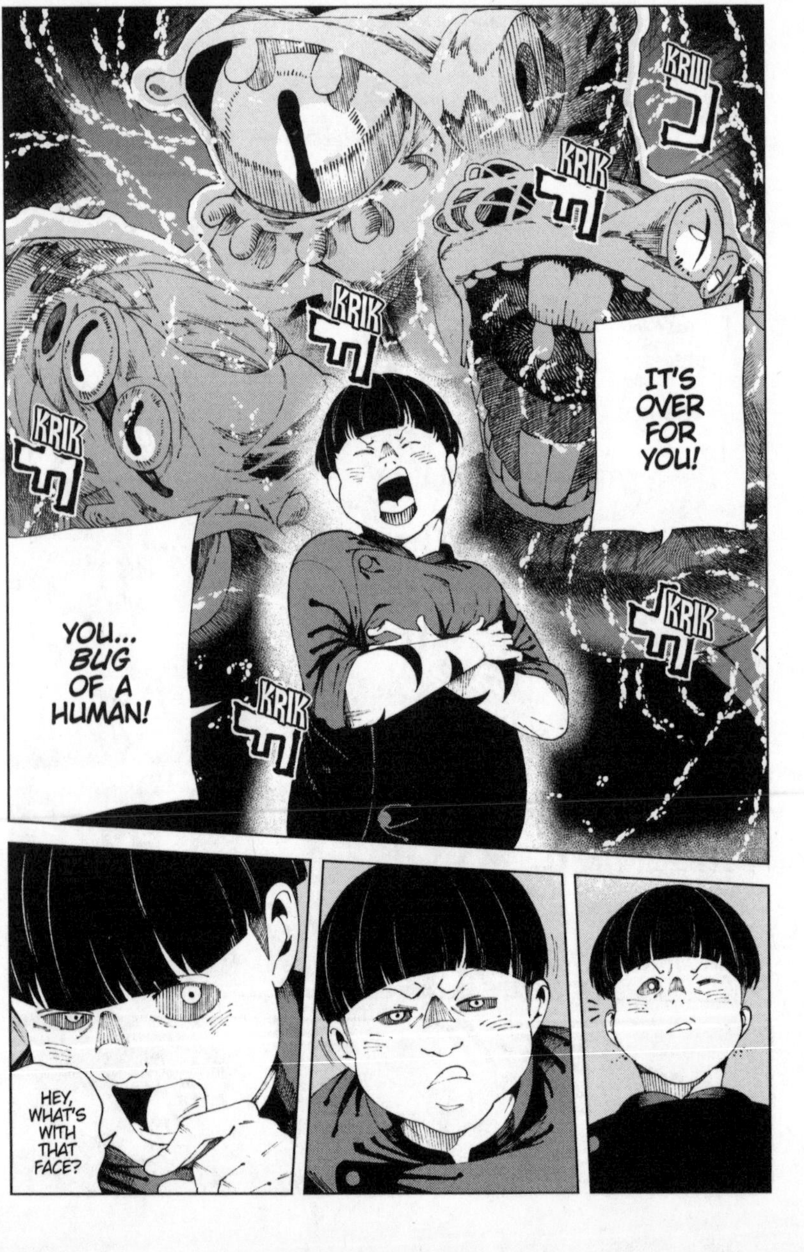
KRIII
KRIK
IT'S OVER FOR YOU!
KRIK
KRIK
KRIK
YOU... BUG OF A HUMAN!
KRIK
HEY, WHAT'S WITH THAT FACE?

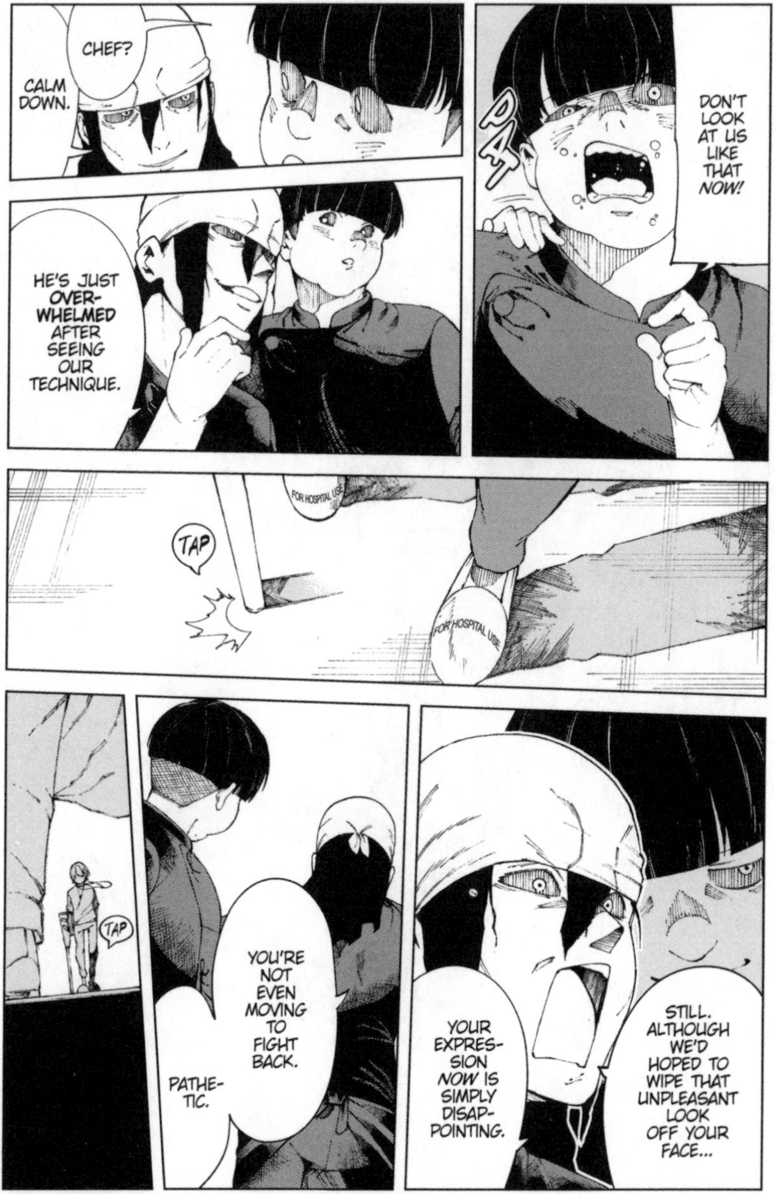
DON'T LOOK AT US LIKE THAT *NOW!*
PAT
CHEF?
CALM DOWN.
HE'S JUST **OVER-WHELMED** AFTER SEEING OUR TECHNIQUE.
FOR HOSPITAL USE
FOR HOSPITAL USE
TAP
STILL. ALTHOUGH WE'D HOPED TO WIPE THAT UNPLEASANT LOOK OFF YOUR FACE...
YOUR EXPRES-SION *NOW* IS SIMPLY DISAP-POINTING.
YOU'RE NOT EVEN MOVING TO FIGHT BACK.
PATHE-TIC.
TAP

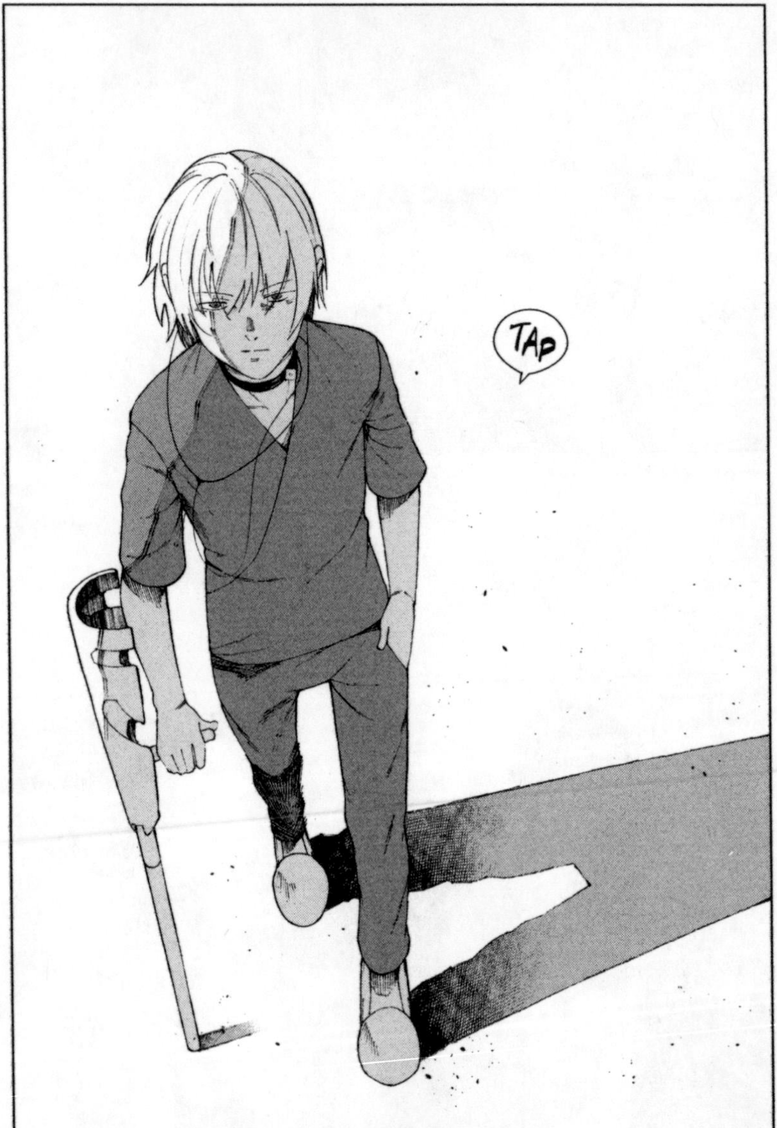
TAP

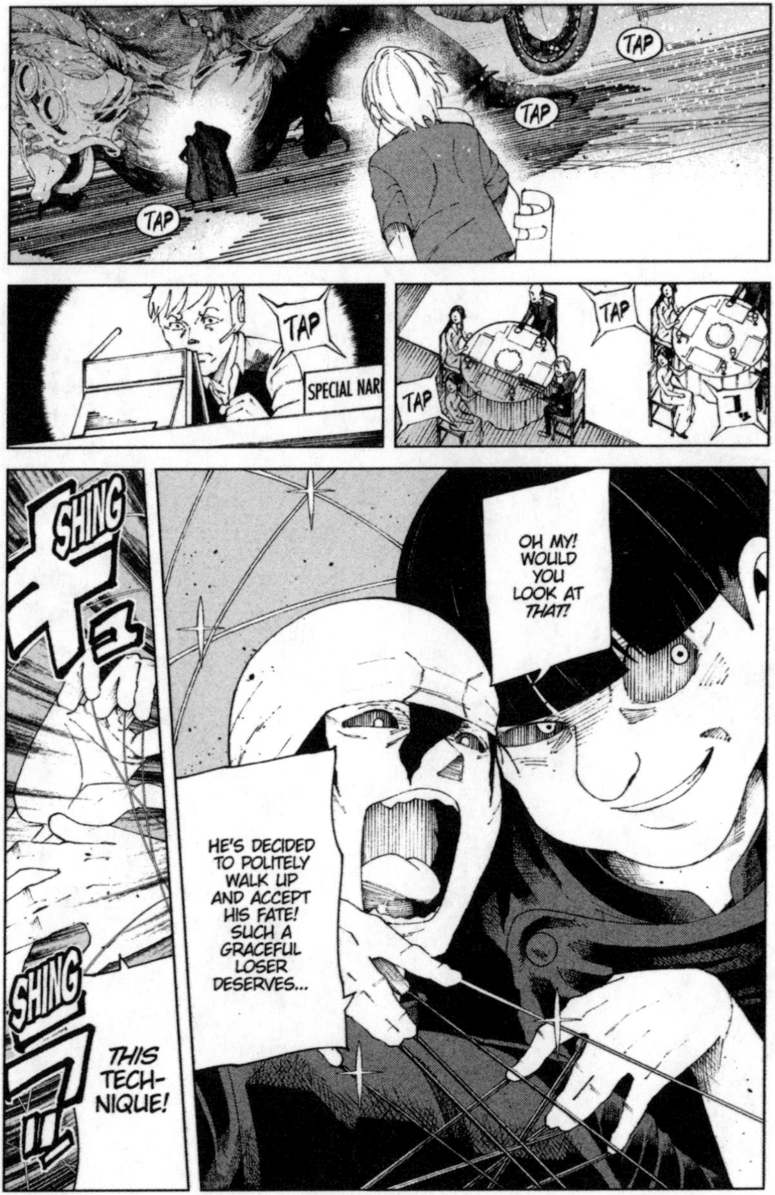
TAP
TAP
TAP
TAP
TAP
TAP
SPECIAL NAR
OH MY! WOULD YOU LOOK AT *THAT!*
HE'S DECIDED TO POLITELY WALK UP AND ACCEPT HIS FATE! SUCH A GRACEFUL LOSER DESERVES...
SHING
SHING
THIS TECH-NIQUE!

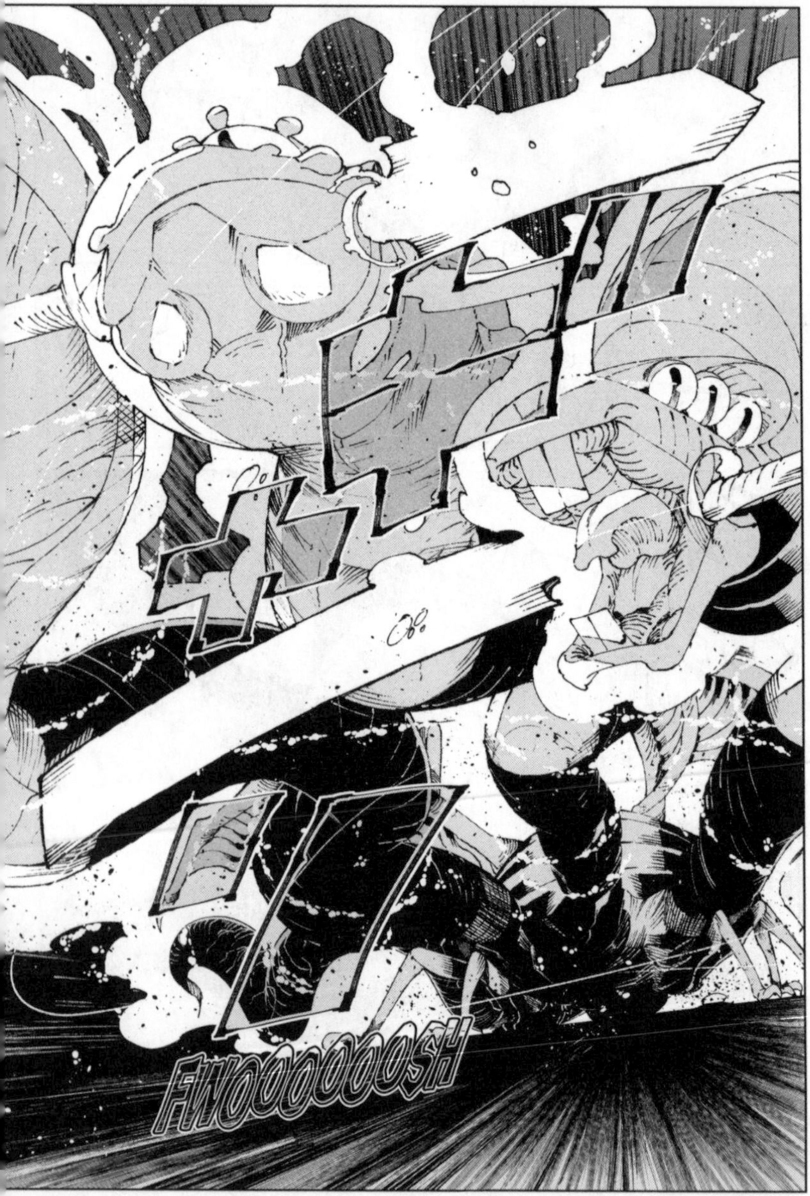
FWOOOOOOOSH

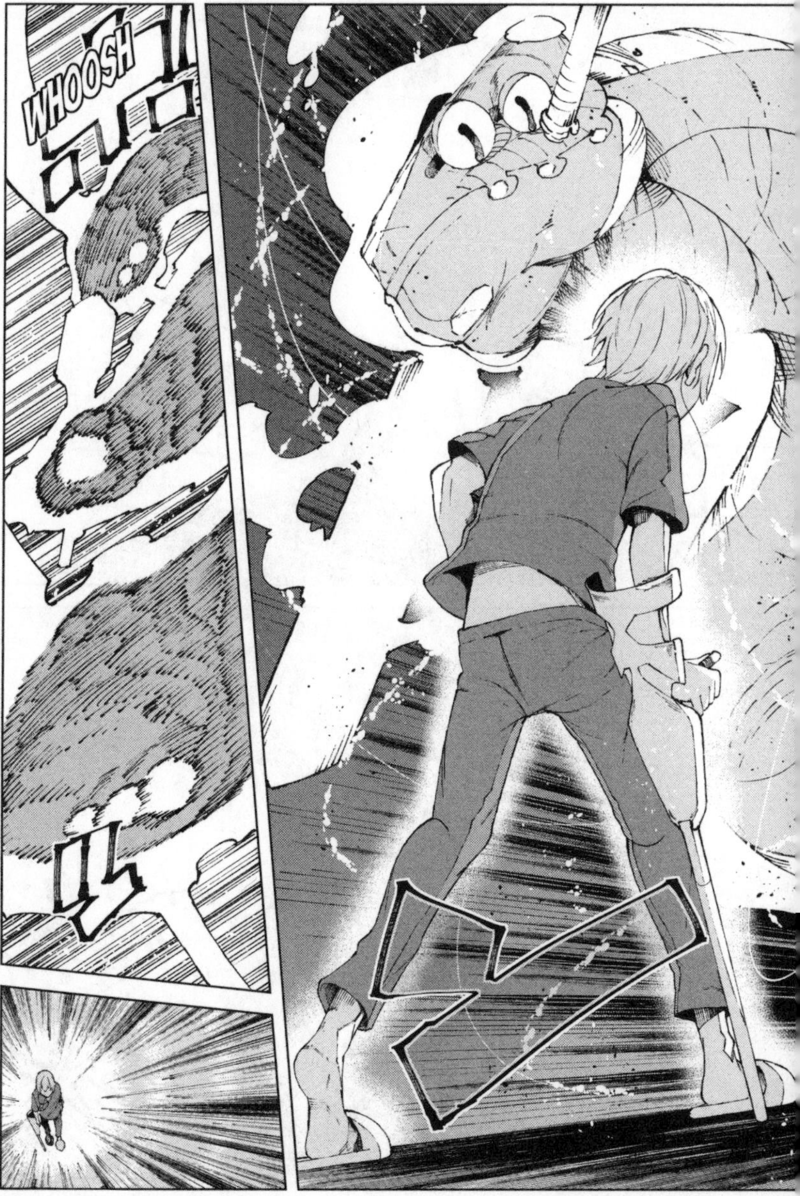
WHOOSH

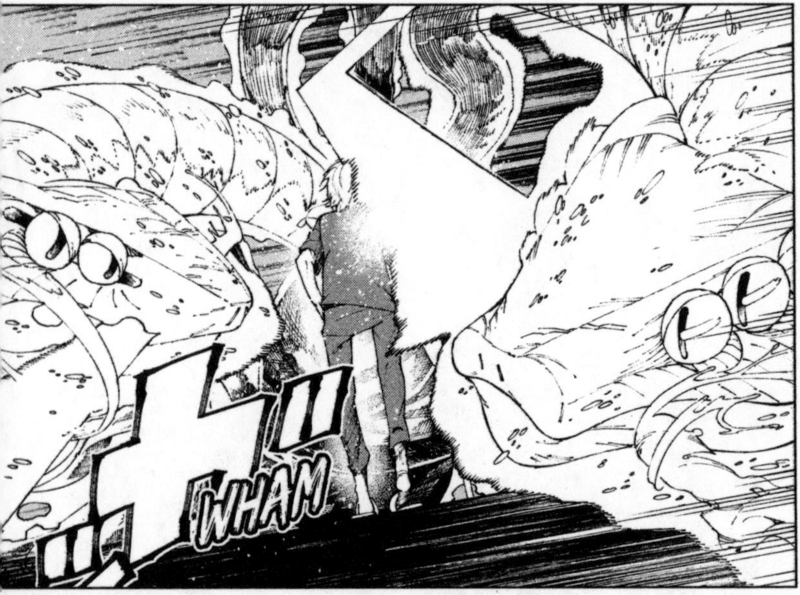
WHAM
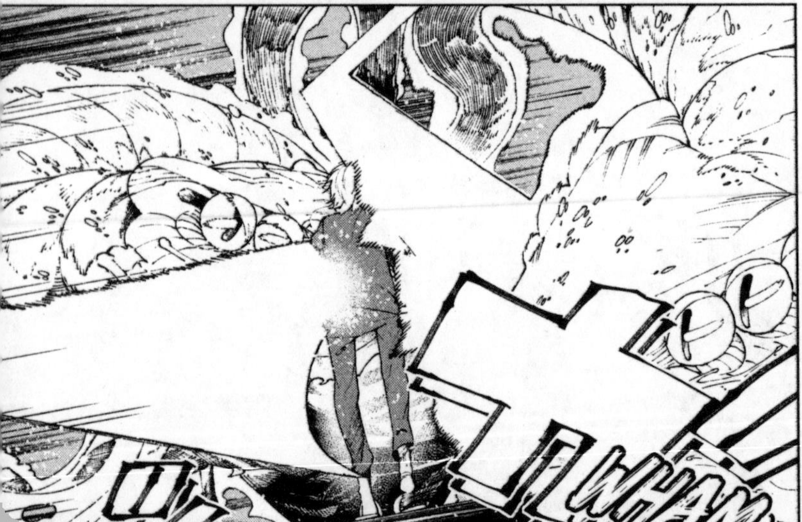
WHAM

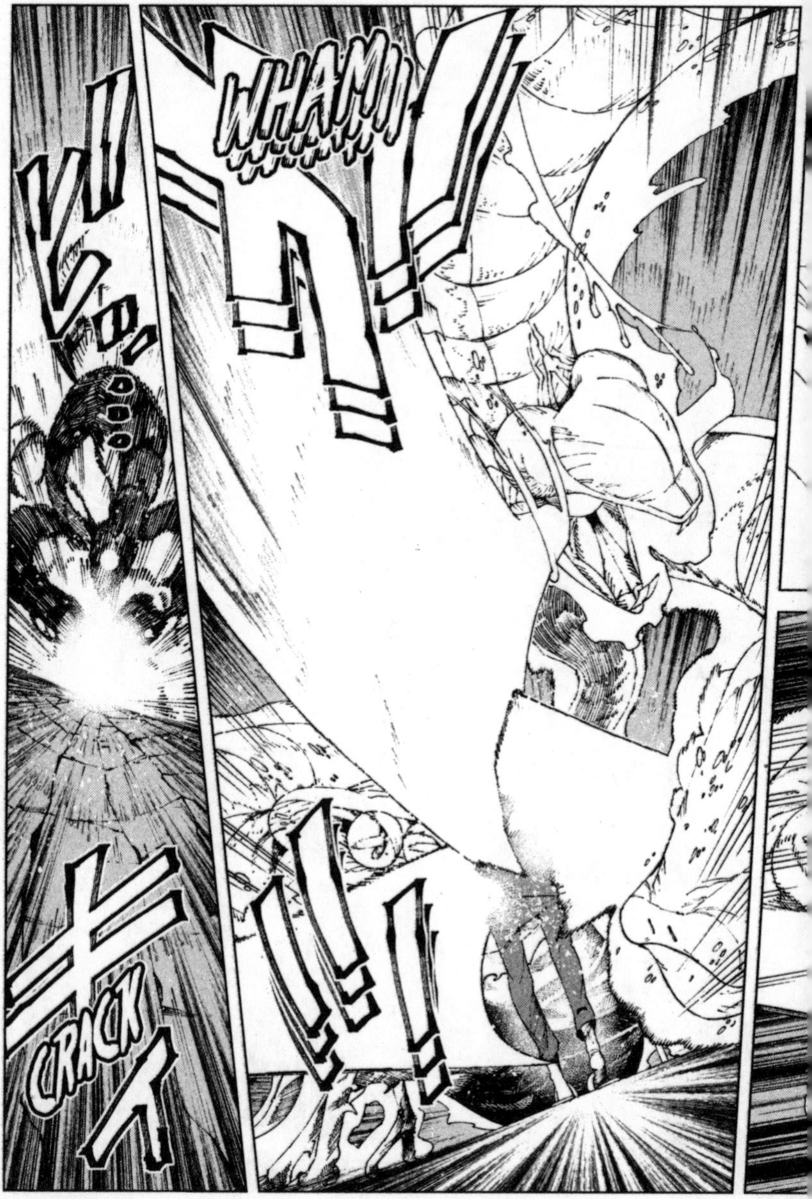
WHAM!!
CRACK

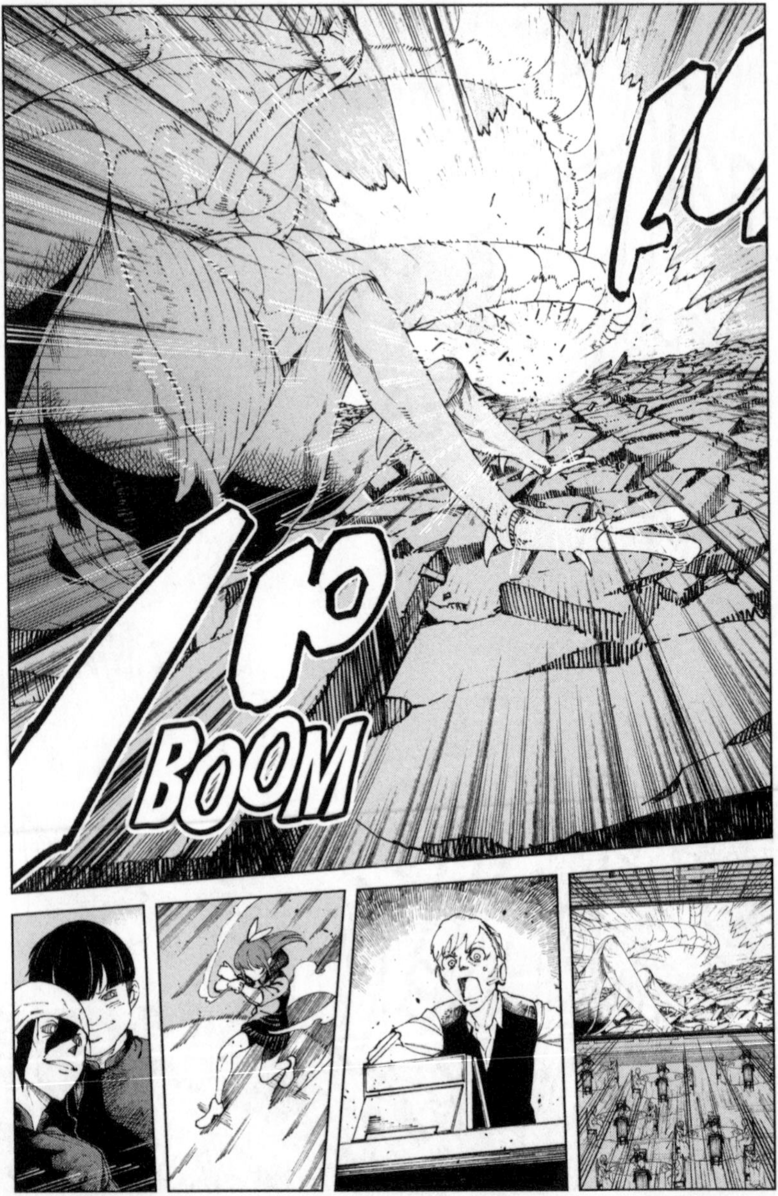
BOOM

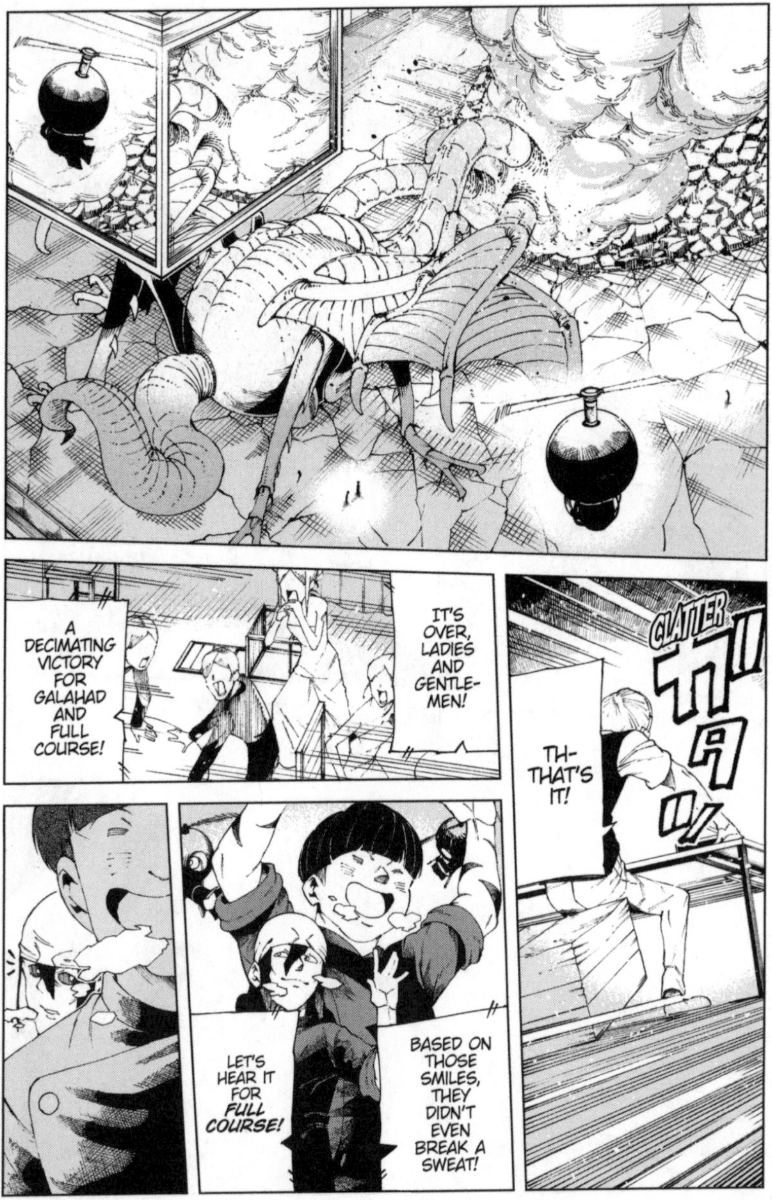
CLATTER
ガタッ!
TH-THAT'S IT!
IT'S OVER, LADIES AND GENTLEMEN!
A DECIMATING VICTORY FOR GALAHAD AND FULL COURSE!
BASED ON THOSE SMILES, THEY DIDN'T EVEN BREAK A SWEAT!
LET'S HEAR IT FOR *FULL COURSE!*

I CAN... SEE HIS BREATH?

CRACK

THAT'S STRANGE. THIS SHIP'S TEMPERATURE IS SUPPOSED TO BE CAREFULLY CONTROLLED.

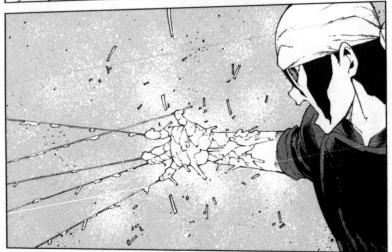

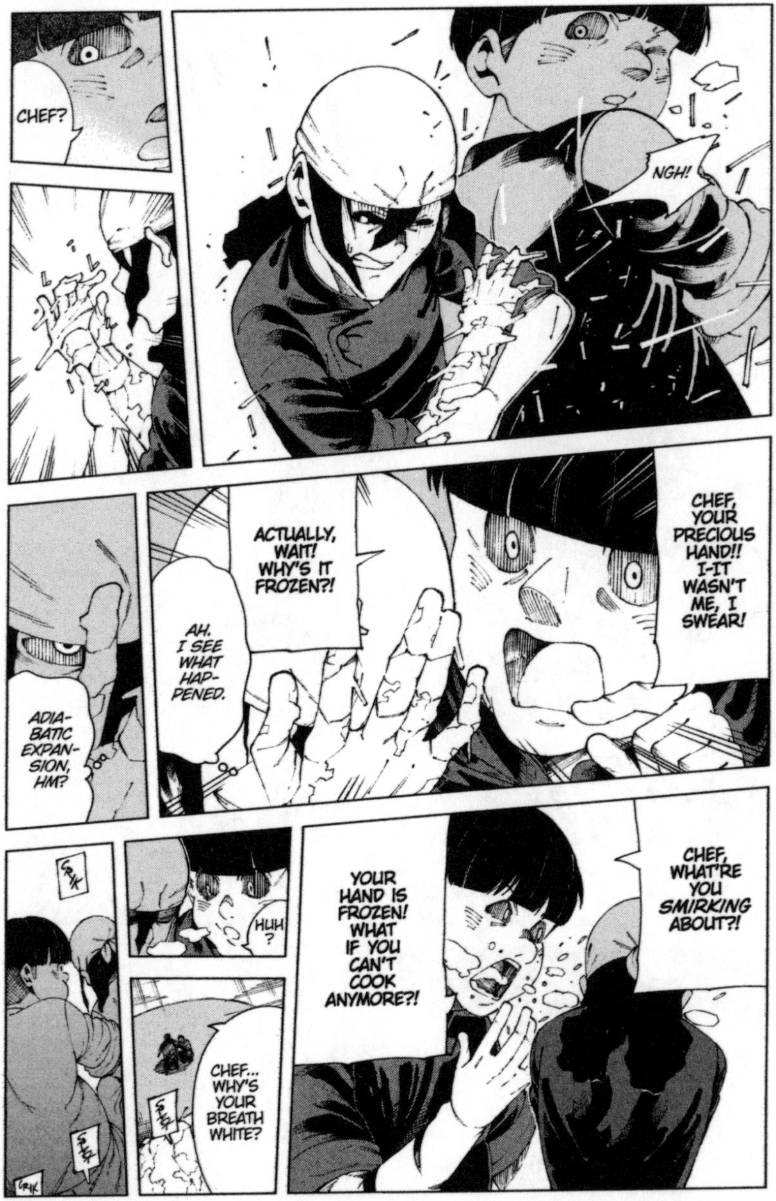
NGH!
CHEF?
CHEF, YOUR PRECIOUS HAND!! I-IT WASN'T ME, I SWEAR!
ACTUALLY, WAIT! WHY'S IT FROZEN?!
AH. I SEE WHAT HAP-PENED.
ADIA-BATIC EXPAN-SION, HM?
CHEF, WHAT'RE YOU SMIRKING ABOUT?!
YOUR HAND IS FROZEN! WHAT IF YOU CAN'T COOK ANYMORE?!
HUH?
CHEF... WHY'S YOUR BREATH WHITE?

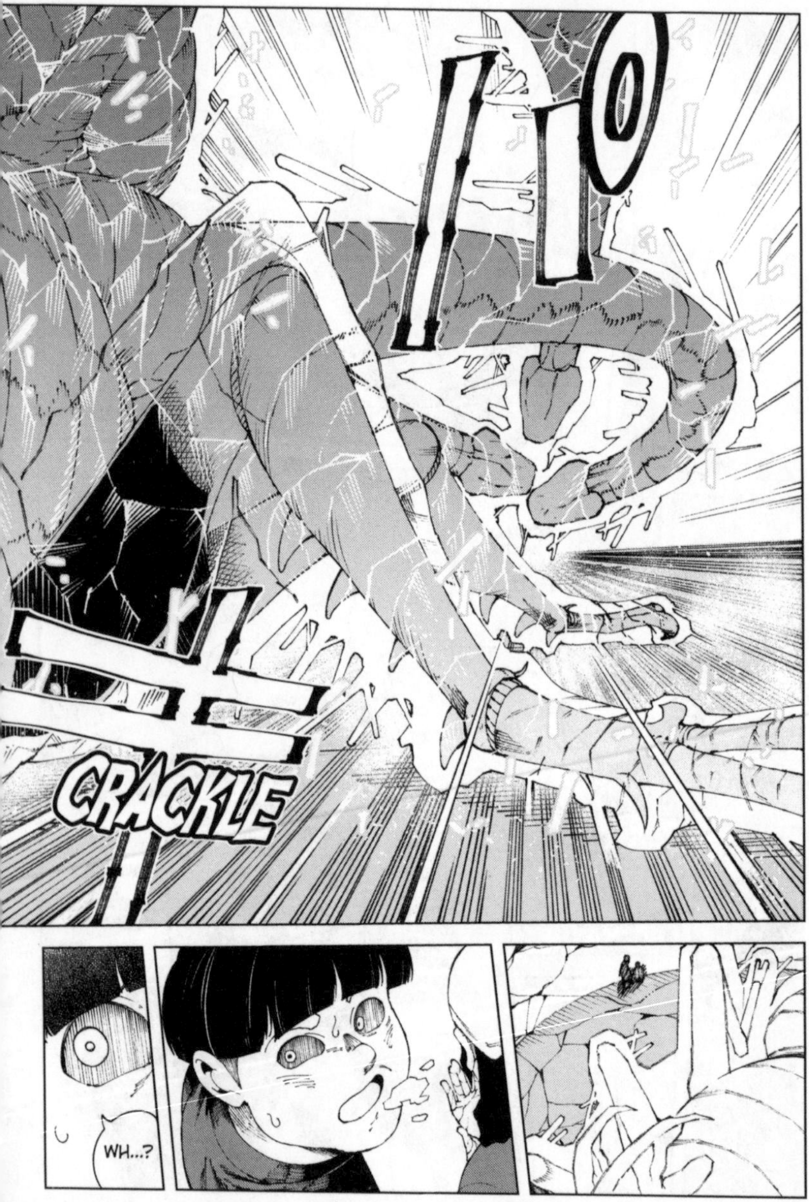
CRACKLE
WH...?

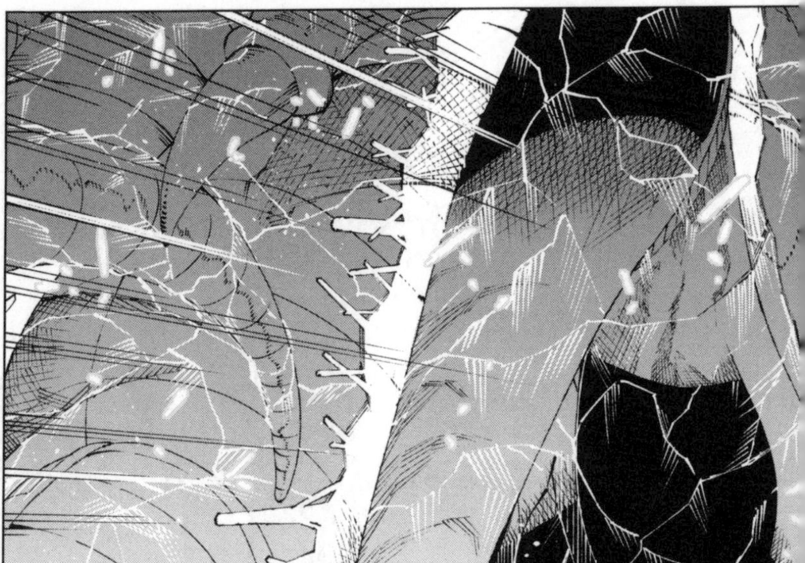
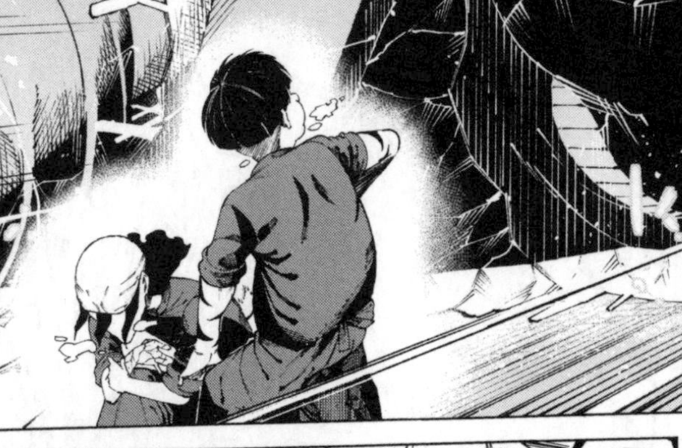
CRACK
CRIK
CRIK
CRIK
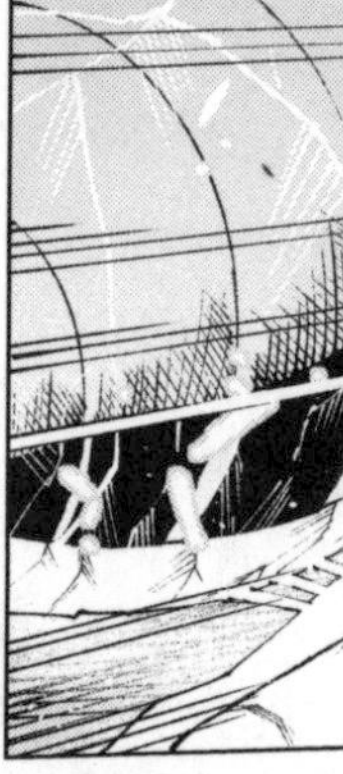
CRACK

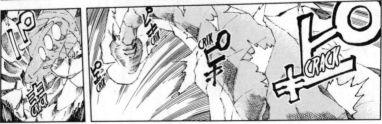

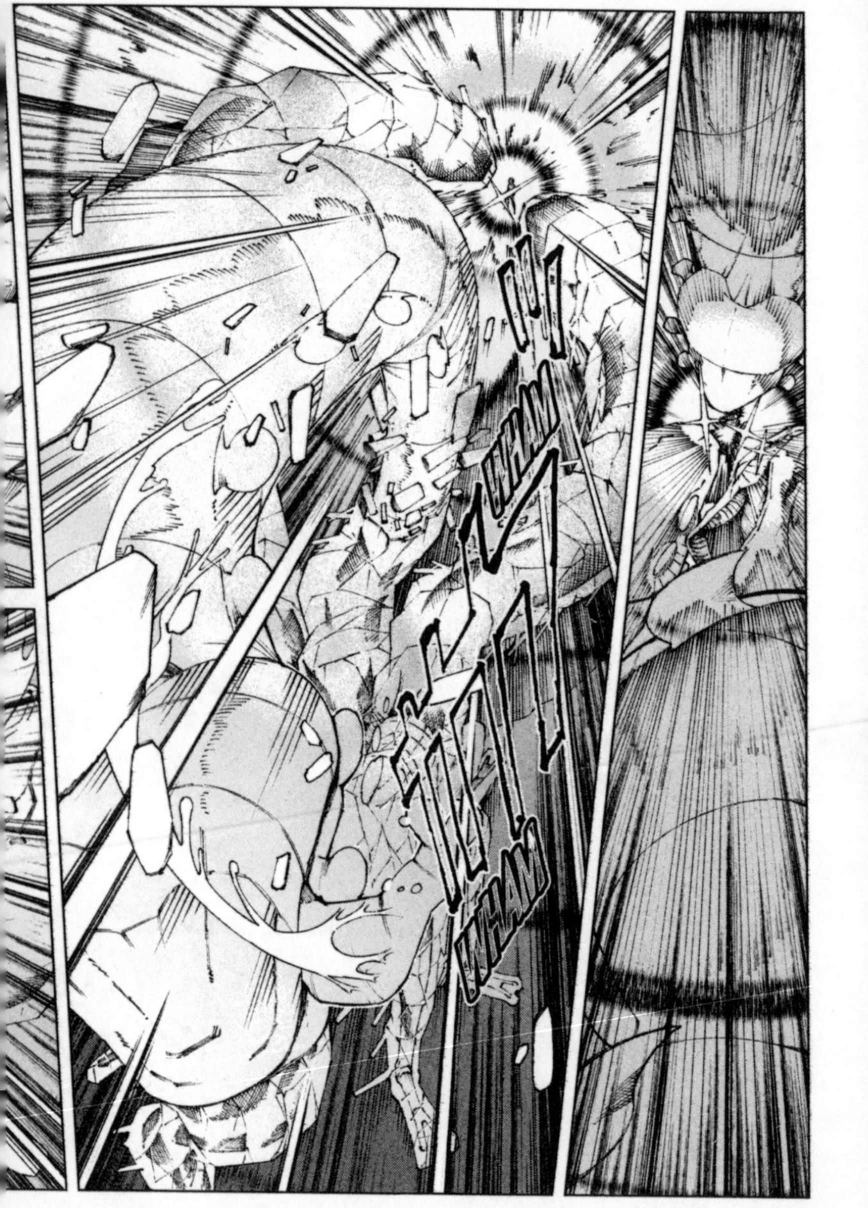
WHAM
WHAM

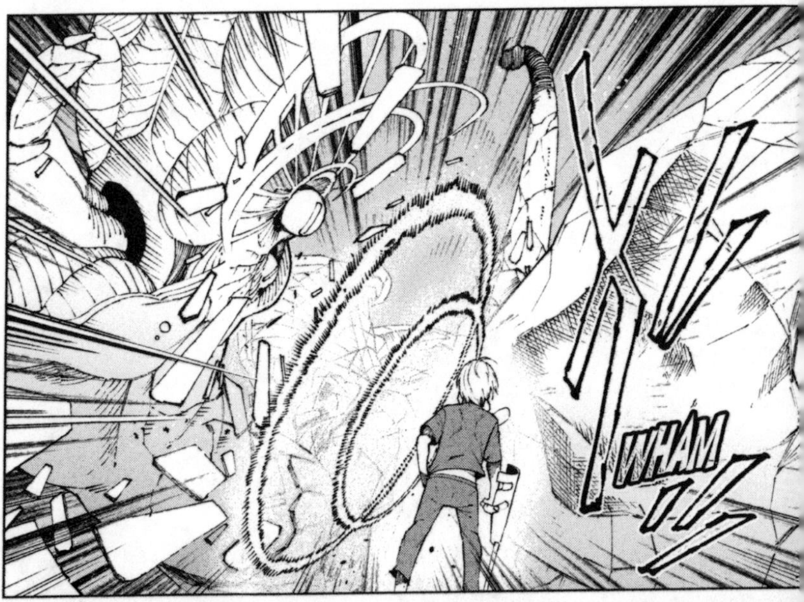
WHAM
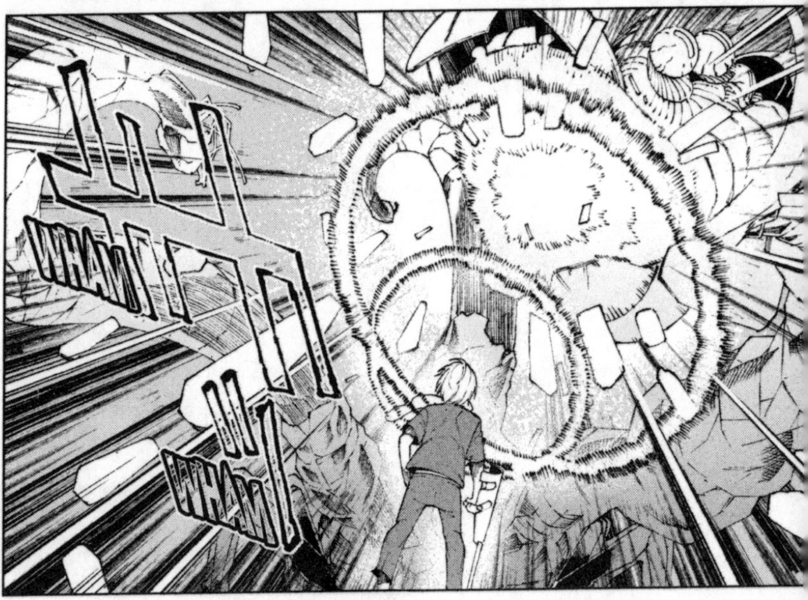
WHAM
WHAM

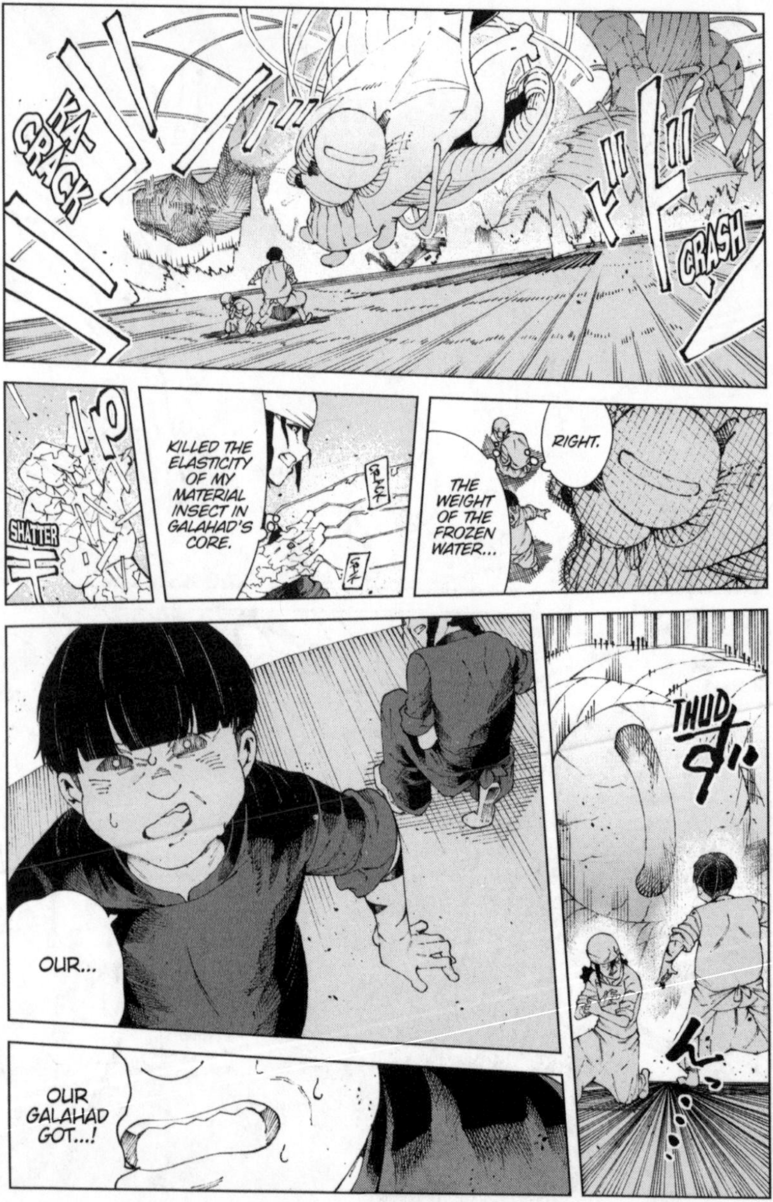
KA-
CRACK
CRASH
RIGHT.
THE WEIGHT OF THE FROZEN WATER...
KILLED THE ELASTICITY OF MY MATERIAL INSECT IN GALAHAD'S CORE.
SHATTER
THUD
OUR...
OUR GALAHAD GOT...!

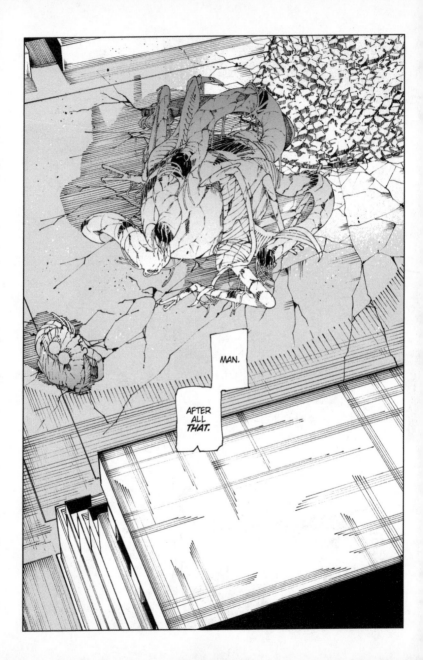

MAN.

AFTER ALL *THAT.*

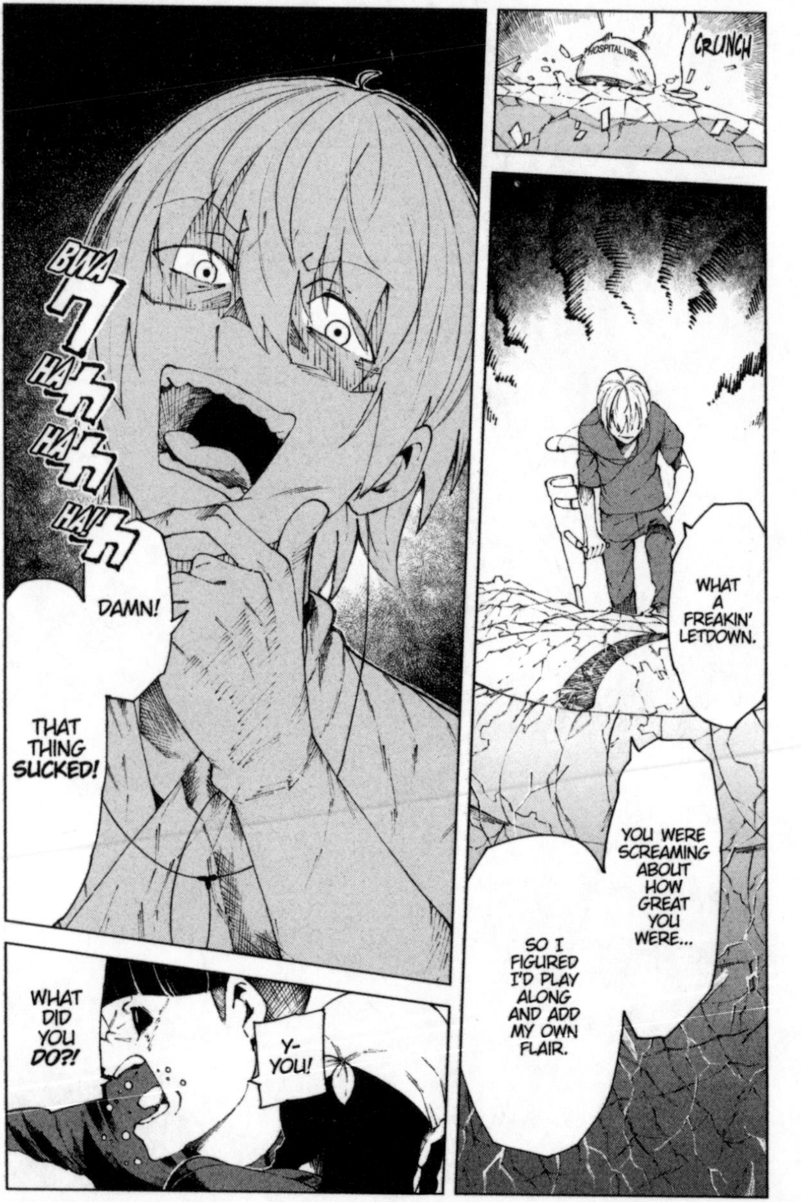
HOSPITAL USE
CRUNCH
WHAT A FREAKIN' LETDOWN.
YOU WERE SCREAMING ABOUT HOW GREAT YOU WERE...
SO I FIGURED I'D PLAY ALONG AND ADD MY OWN FLAIR.
BWA HA HA HA!
DAMN!
THAT THING SUCKED!
Y-YOU!
WHAT DID YOU DO?!

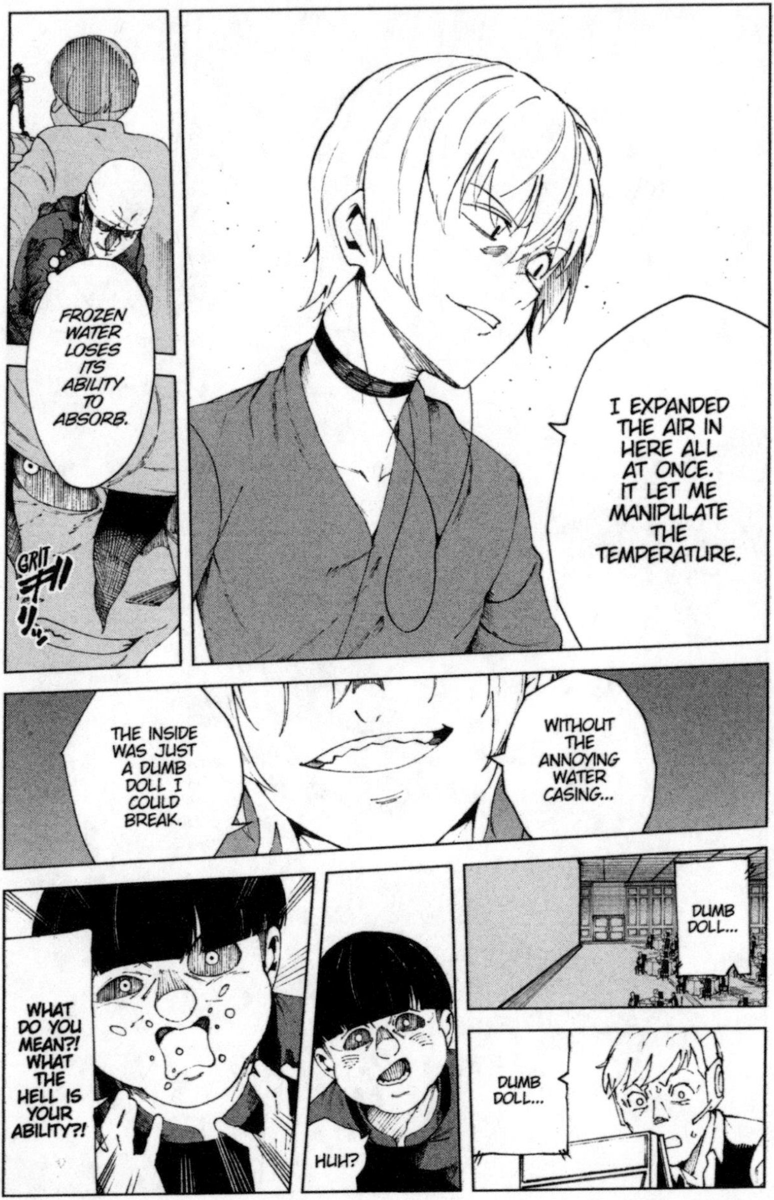
I EXPANDED THE AIR IN HERE ALL AT ONCE. IT LET ME MANIPULATE THE TEMPERATURE.
FROZEN WATER LOSES ITS ABILITY TO ABSORB.
GRIT
WITHOUT THE ANNOYING WATER CASING...
THE INSIDE WAS JUST A DUMB DOLL I COULD BREAK.
DUMB DOLL...
DUMB DOLL...
HUH?
WHAT DO YOU MEAN?! WHAT THE HELL IS YOUR ABILITY?!

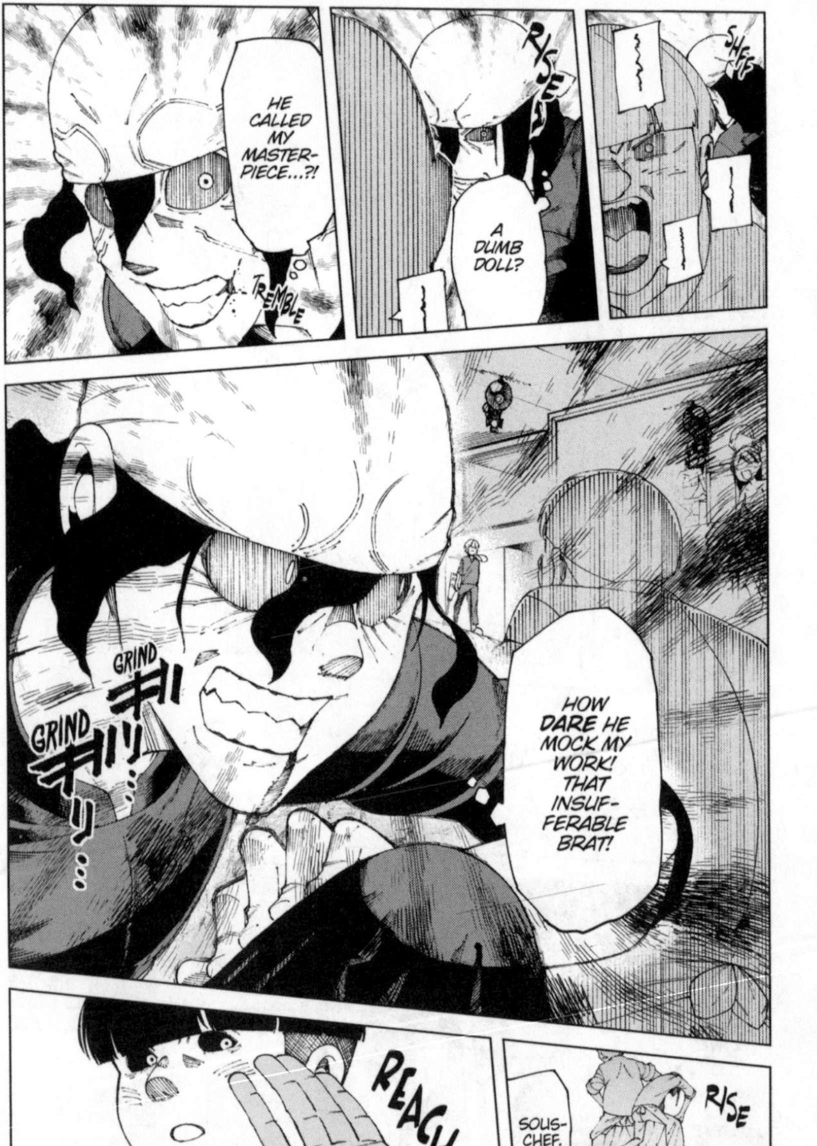
SHFFS
RISE
A DUMB DOLL?
HE CALLED MY MASTERPIECE...?!
TREMBLE
HOW DARE HE MOCK MY WORK! THAT INSUFFERABLE BRAT!
GRIND
GRIND
RISE
SOUS-CHEF.
REACH

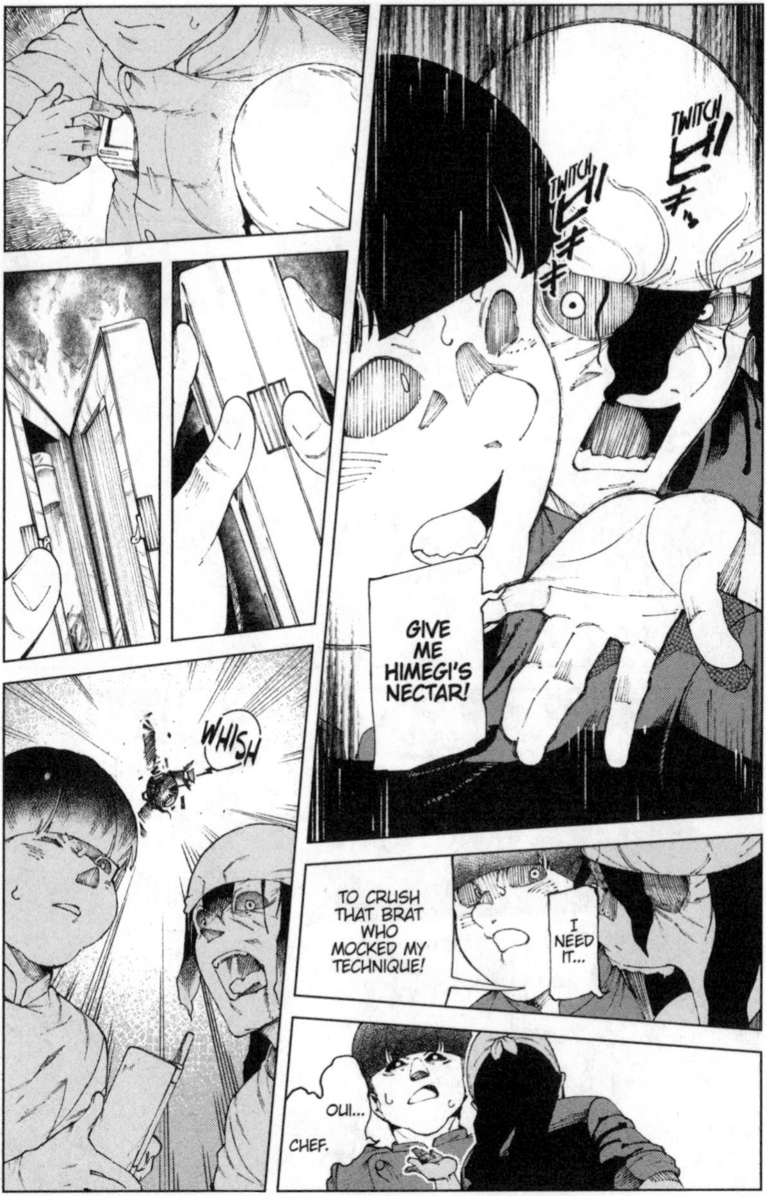
TWITCH
ピキッ
TWITCH
ピキキ
GIVE ME HIMEGI'S NECTAR!
I NEED IT...
TO CRUSH THAT BRAT WHO MOCKED MY TECHNIQUE!
WHISH
OUI...
CHEF.

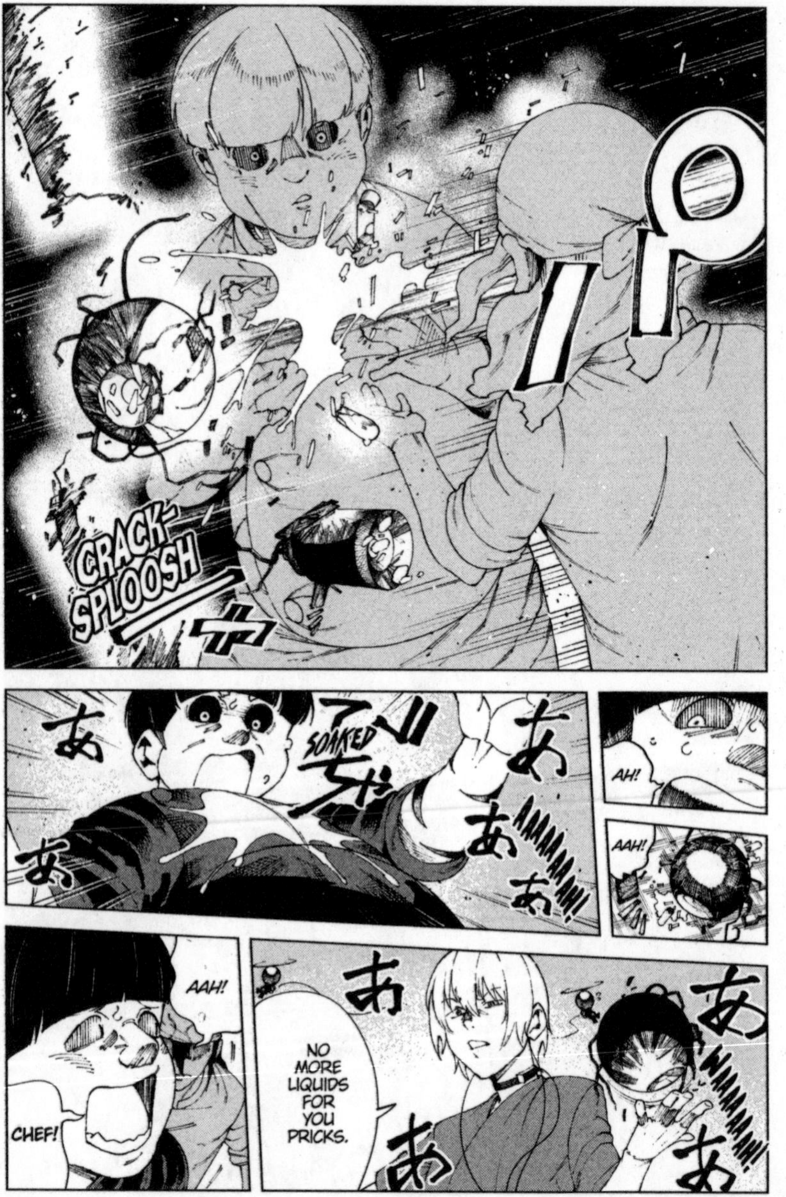

CRACK-SPLOOSH
SOAKED
AH!
AAH!
あ あ あ
AAAAAAAAAH!
あ あ
AAAAAAAAAAH!
NO MORE LIQUIDS FOR YOU PRICKS.
あ あ
AAH!
CHEF!

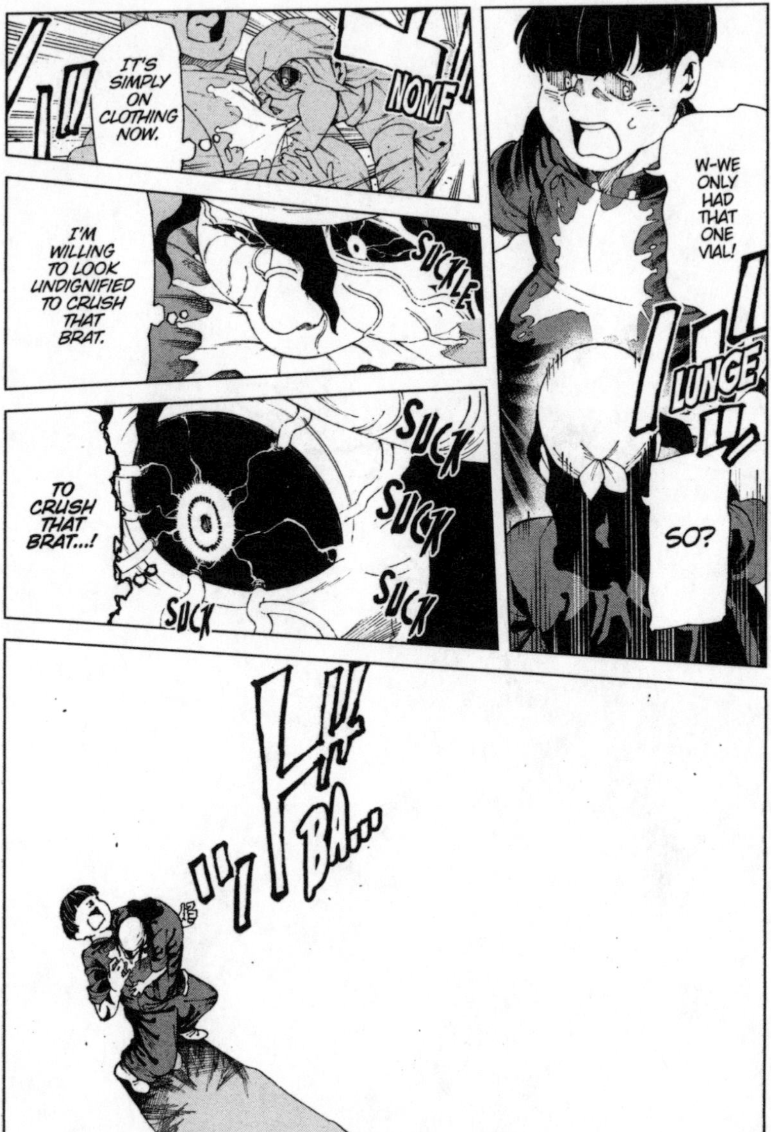
W-WE ONLY HAD THAT ONE VIAL!
LUNGE
SO?
IT'S SIMPLY ON CLOTHING NOW.
NOMF
I'M WILLING TO LOOK UNDIGNIFIED TO CRUSH THAT BRAT.
SUCKLE
TO CRUSH THAT BRAT...!
SUCK
SUCK
SUCK
SUCK
BA...

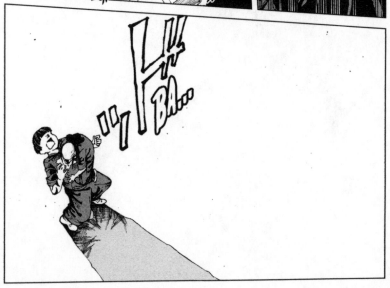

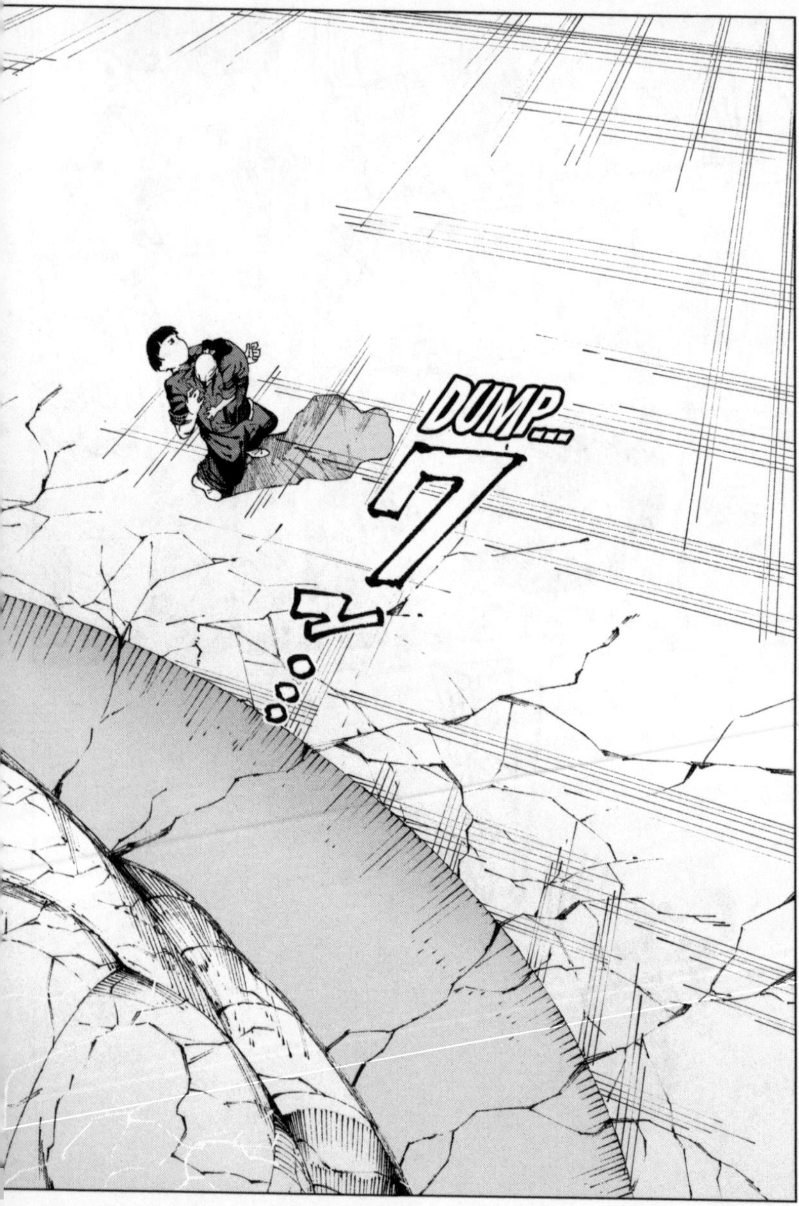
DUMP...

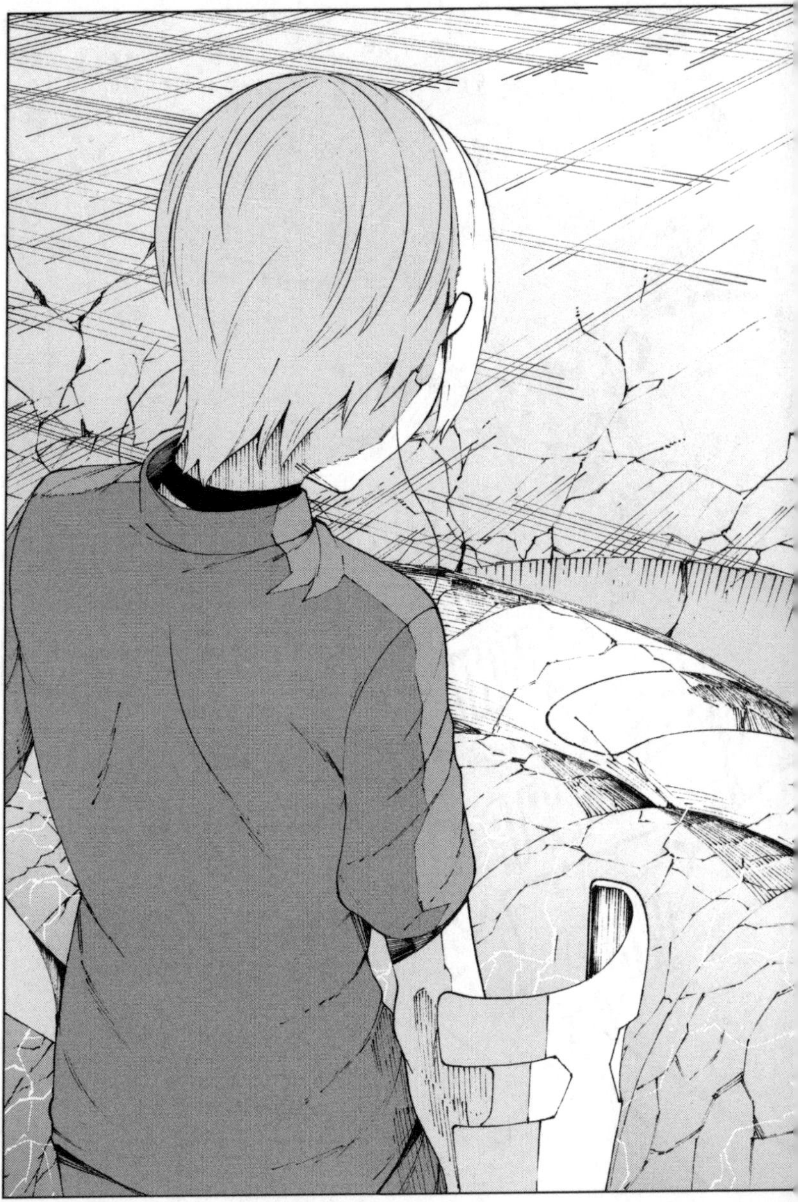

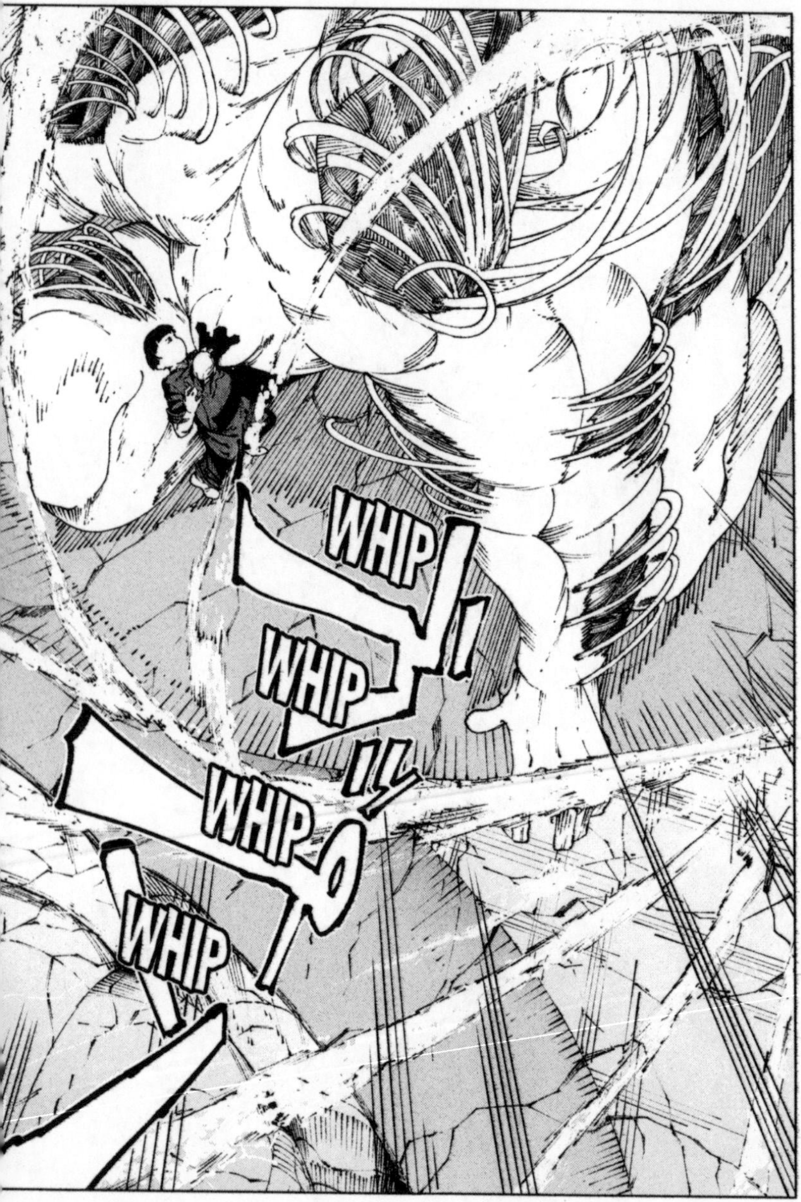
WHIP
WHIP
WHIP
WHIP

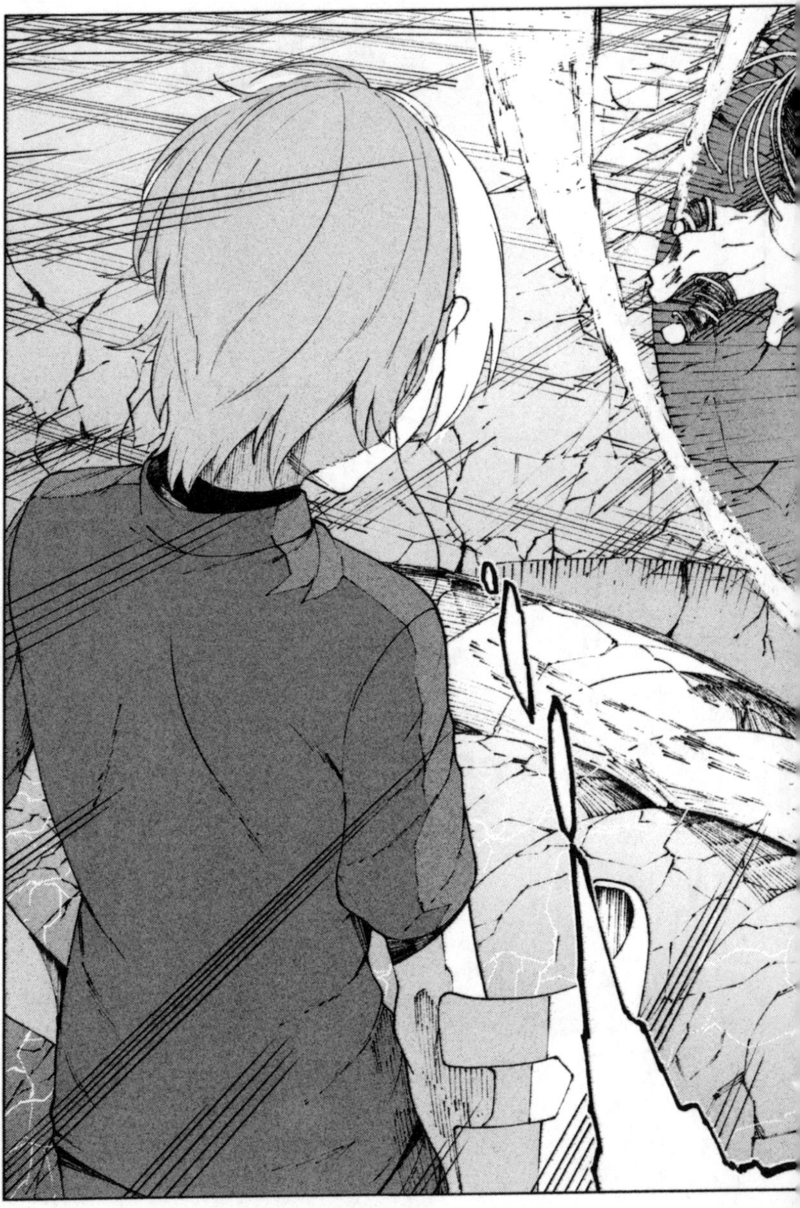

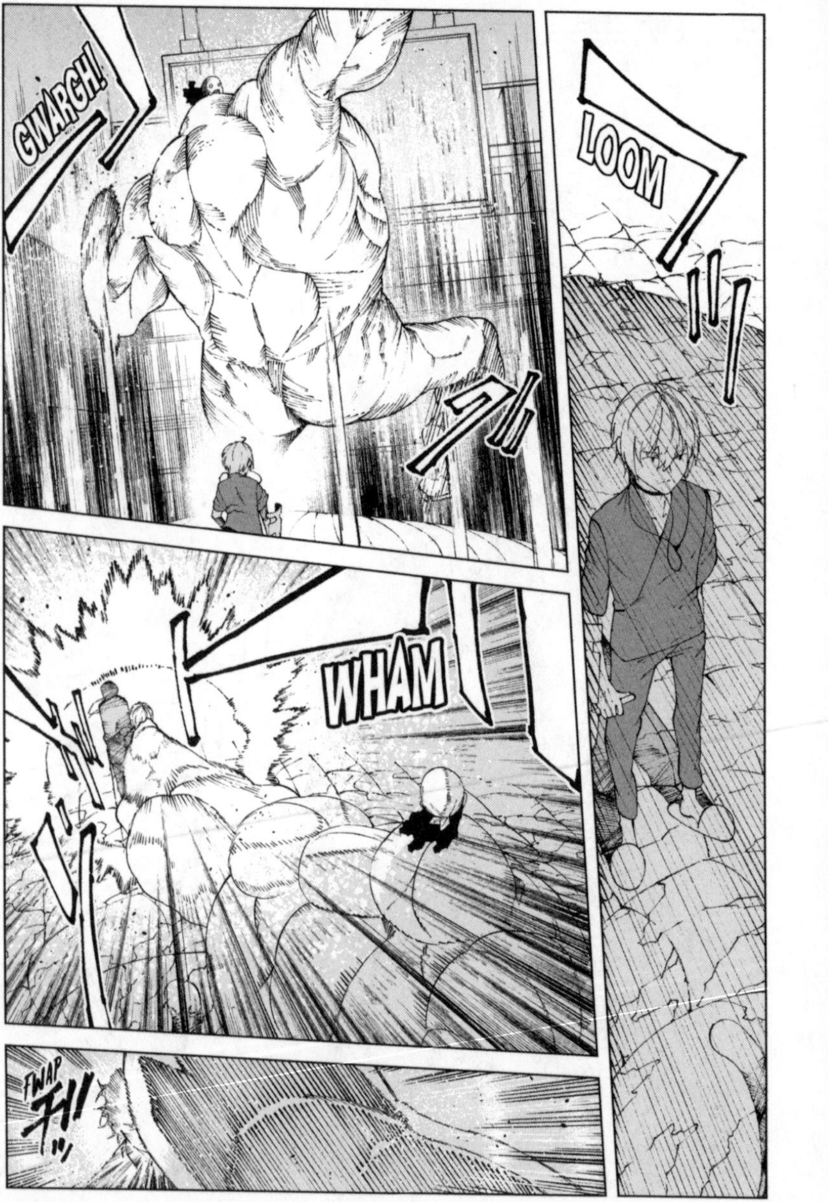
LOOM
GWARCH!
WHAM
FWAP

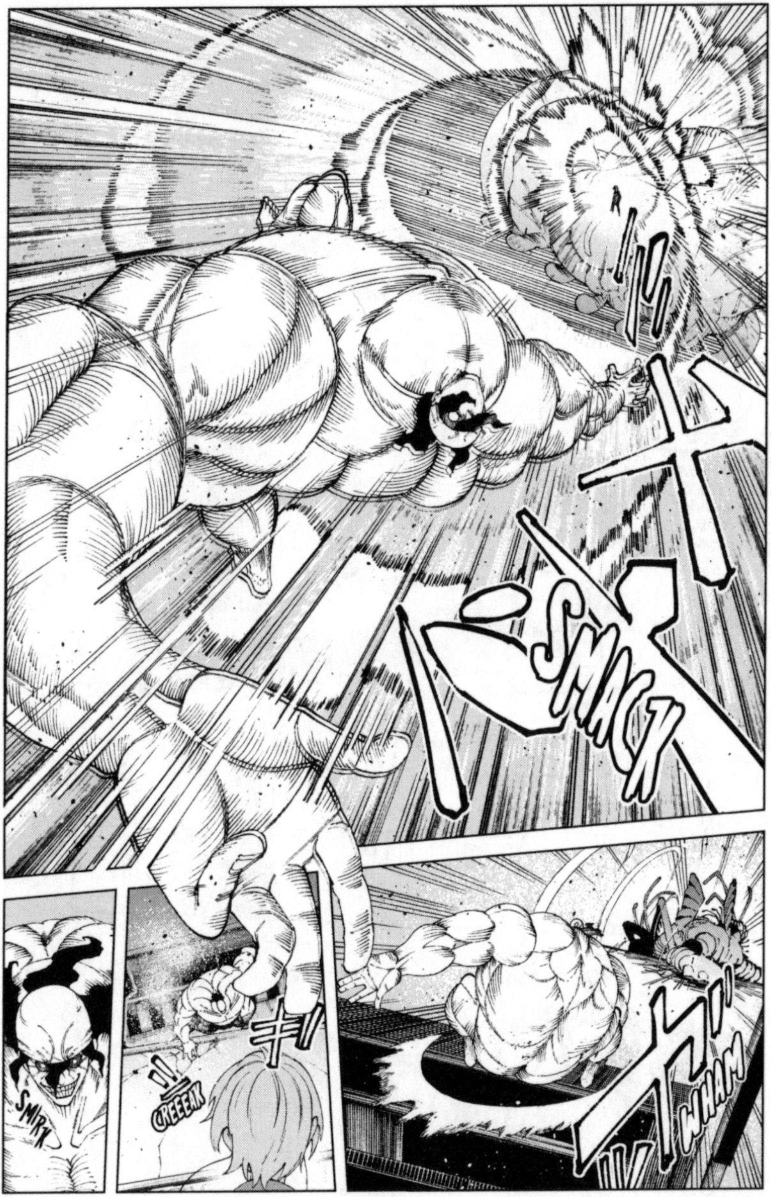
SMACK
WHAM
!!
CREEEAK
SMIRK

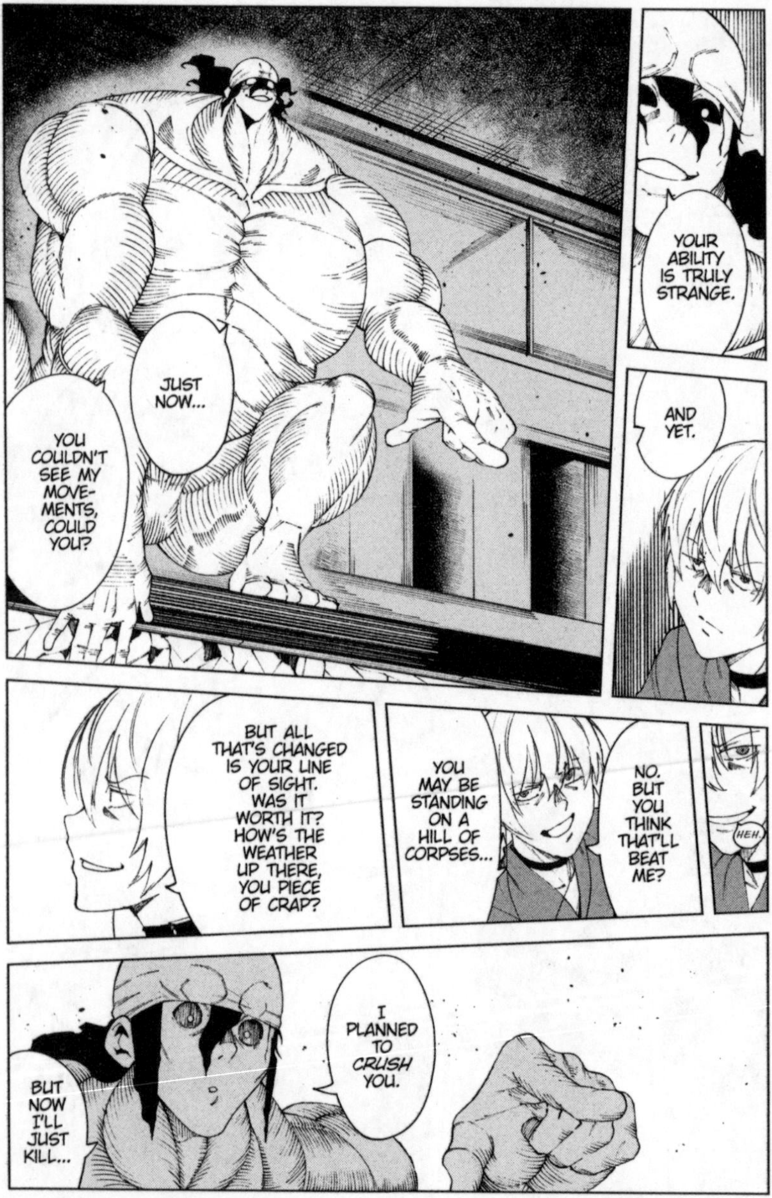
YOUR ABILITY IS TRULY STRANGE.
AND YET.
JUST NOW...
YOU COULDN'T SEE MY MOVEMENTS, COULD YOU?
HEH.
NO. BUT YOU THINK THAT'LL BEAT ME?
YOU MAY BE STANDING ON A HILL OF CORPSES...
BUT ALL THAT'S CHANGED IS YOUR LINE OF SIGHT. WAS IT WORTH IT? HOW'S THE WEATHER UP THERE, YOU PIECE OF CRAP?
I PLANNED TO CRUSH YOU.
BUT NOW I'LL JUST KILL...

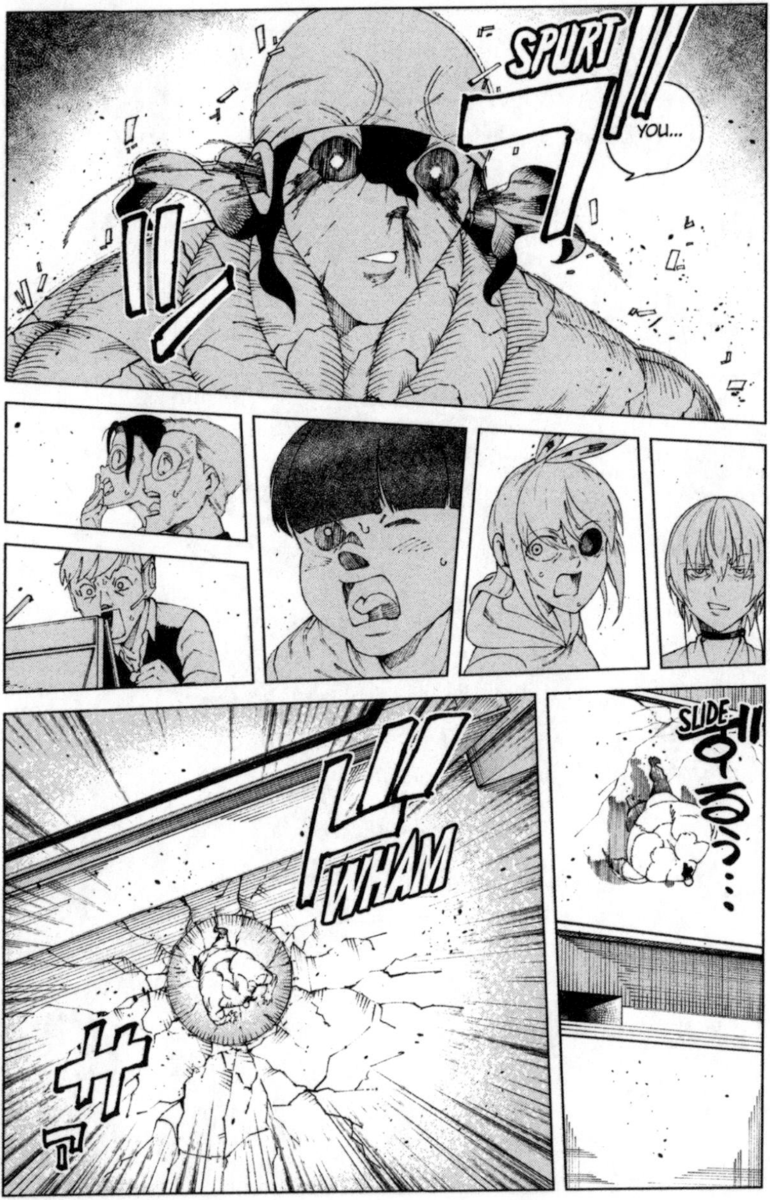
SPURT
YOU...
SLIDE
WHAM

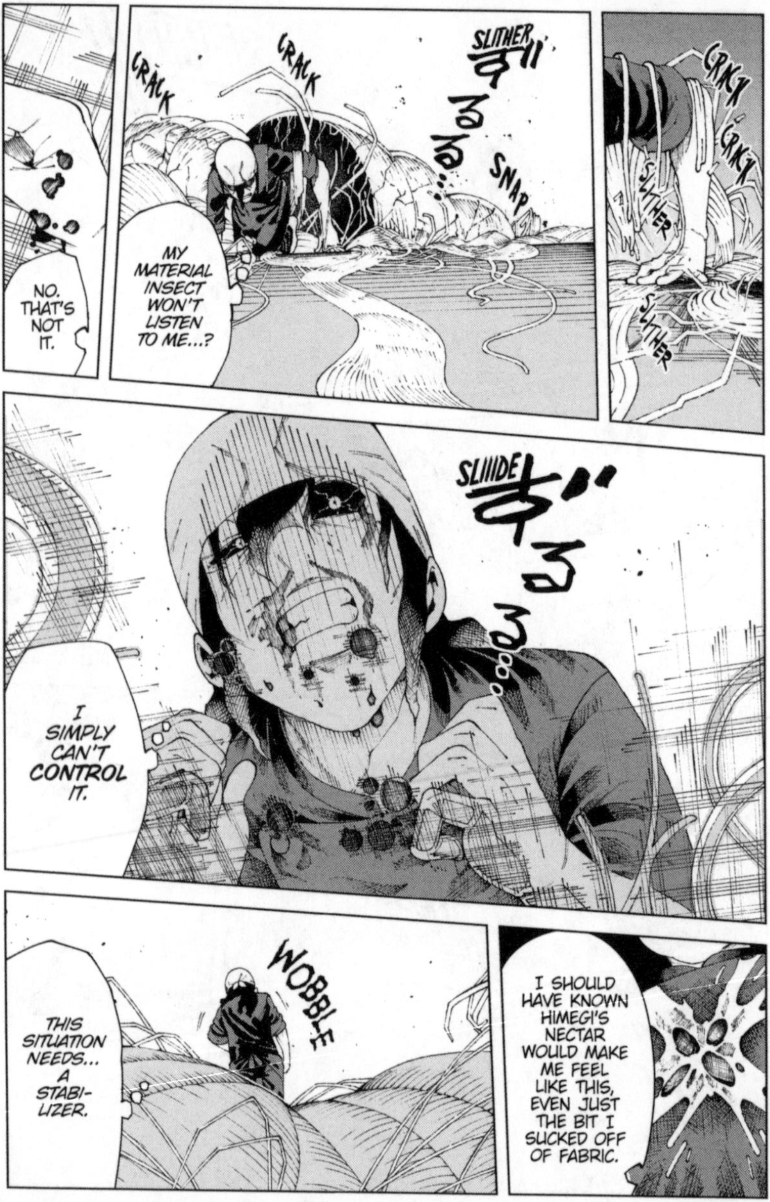
CRACK
CRACK
SLITHER
SLITHER
SLITHER
するる…
CRACK
CRACK
SNAP
MY MATERIAL INSECT WON'T LISTEN TO ME...?
NO. THAT'S NOT IT.
SLIIDE
ずるるる…
I SIMPLY CAN'T CONTROL IT.
I SHOULD HAVE KNOWN HIMEGI'S NECTAR WOULD MAKE ME FEEL LIKE THIS, EVEN JUST THE BIT I SUCKED OFF OF FABRIC.
WOBBLE
THIS SITUATION NEEDS... A STABILIZER.

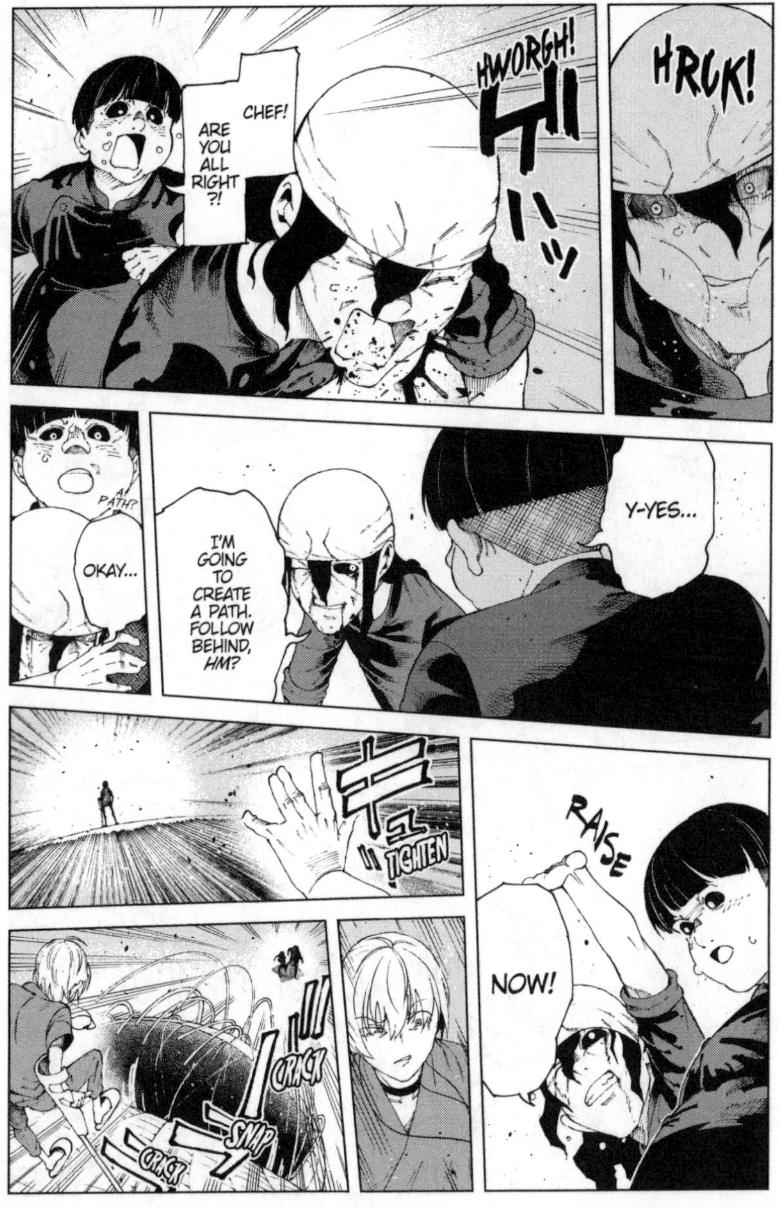
HRCK!
HWORGH!
CHEF!
ARE YOU ALL RIGHT?!
I'M GOING TO CREATE A PATH. FOLLOW BEHIND, HM?
Y-YES...
A PATH?
OKAY...
RAISE
NOW!
TIGHTEN
CRACK
SNAP
CRACK

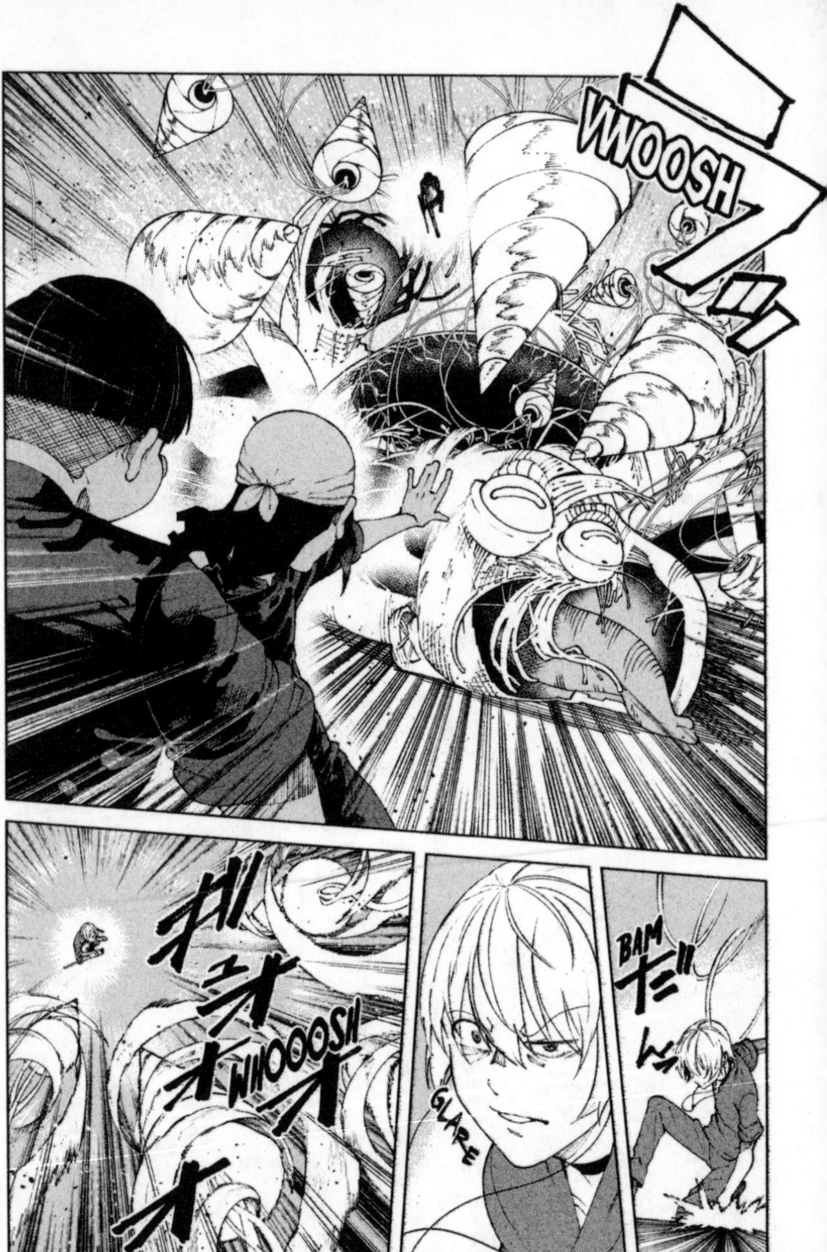
VWOOSH
BAM
GLARE
WHOOOSH

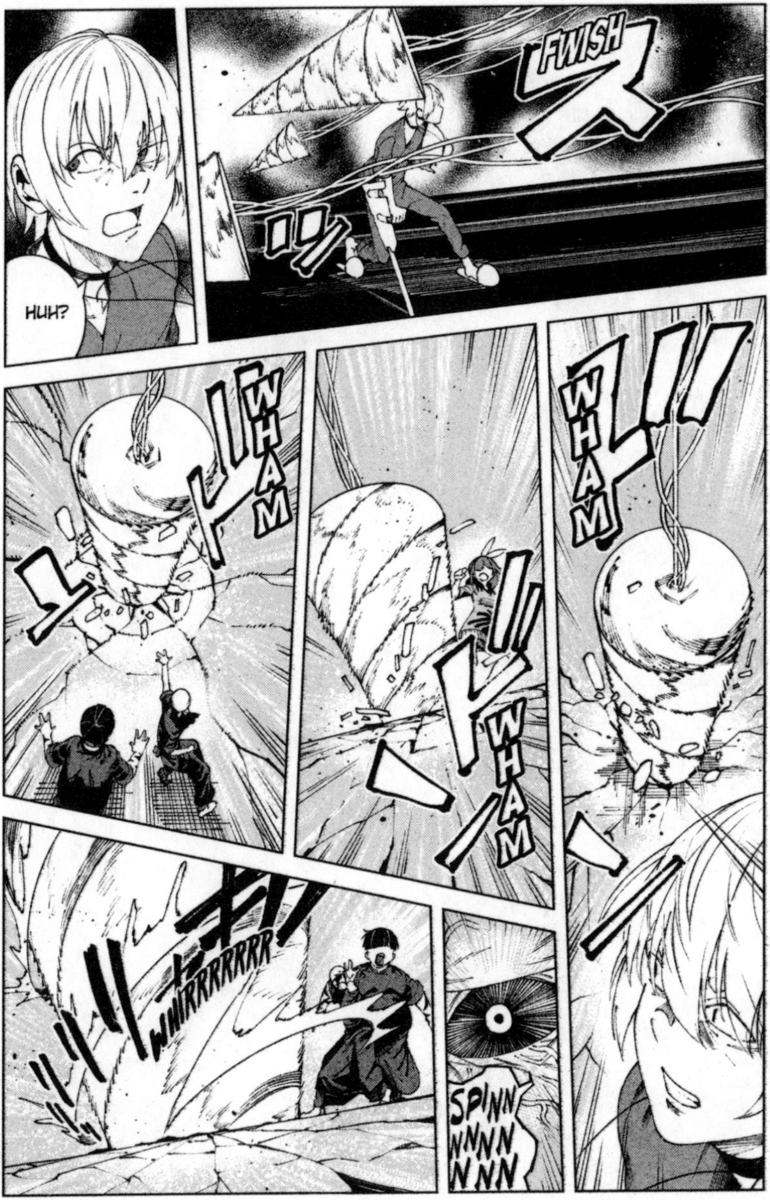
FWISH
HUH?
WHAM
WHAM
WHAM
SPINNNNNNNNNN
WHIRRRRRRR

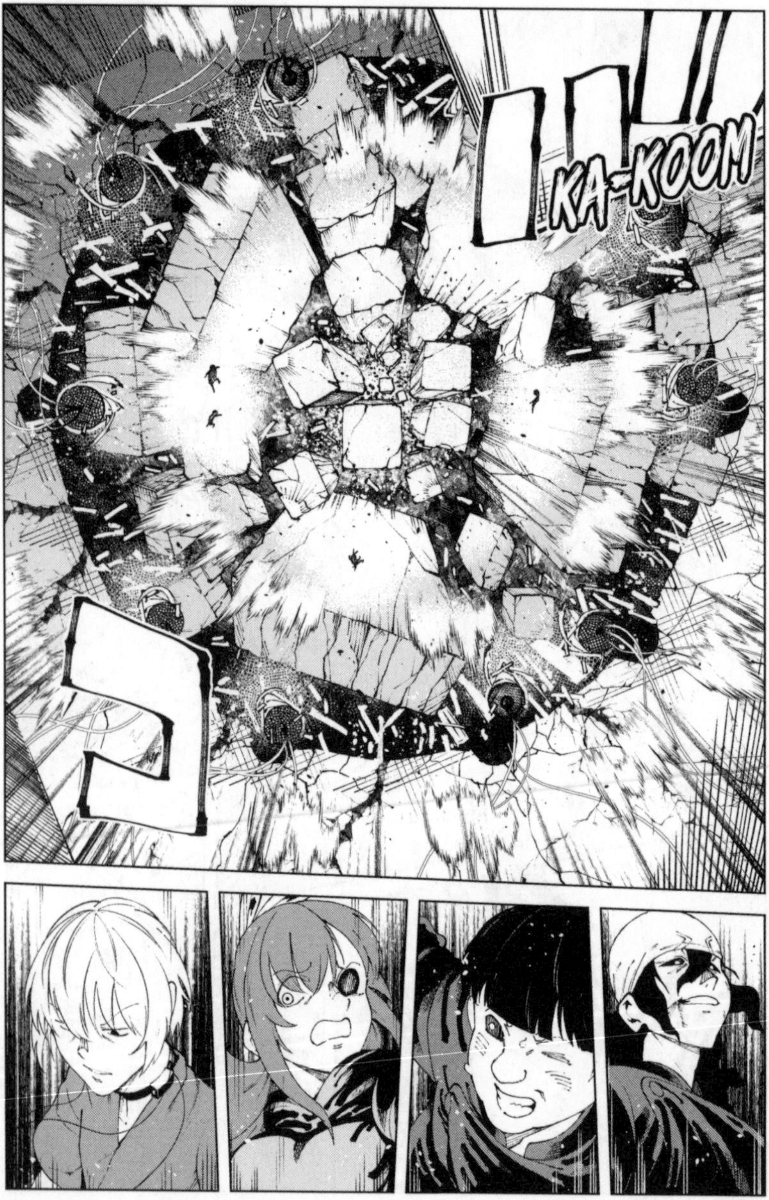
KA-KOOM

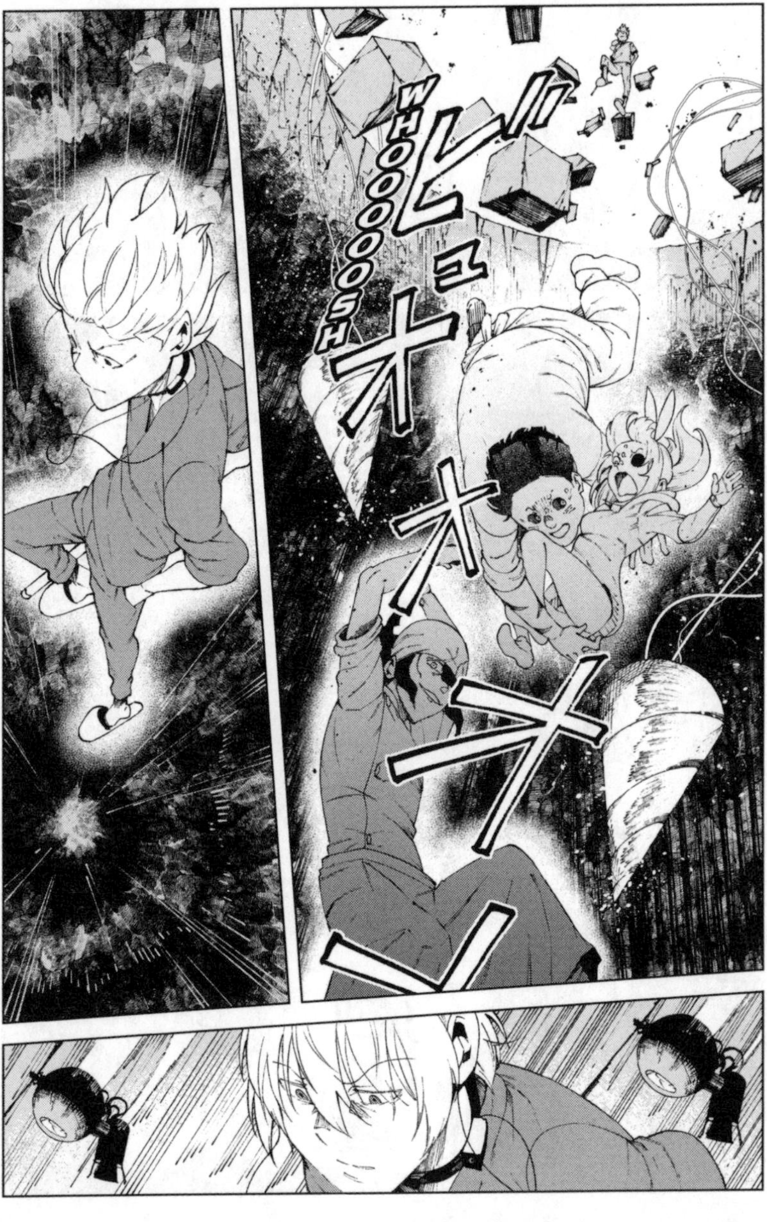
ビュオオオン
WHOOOOOOSH

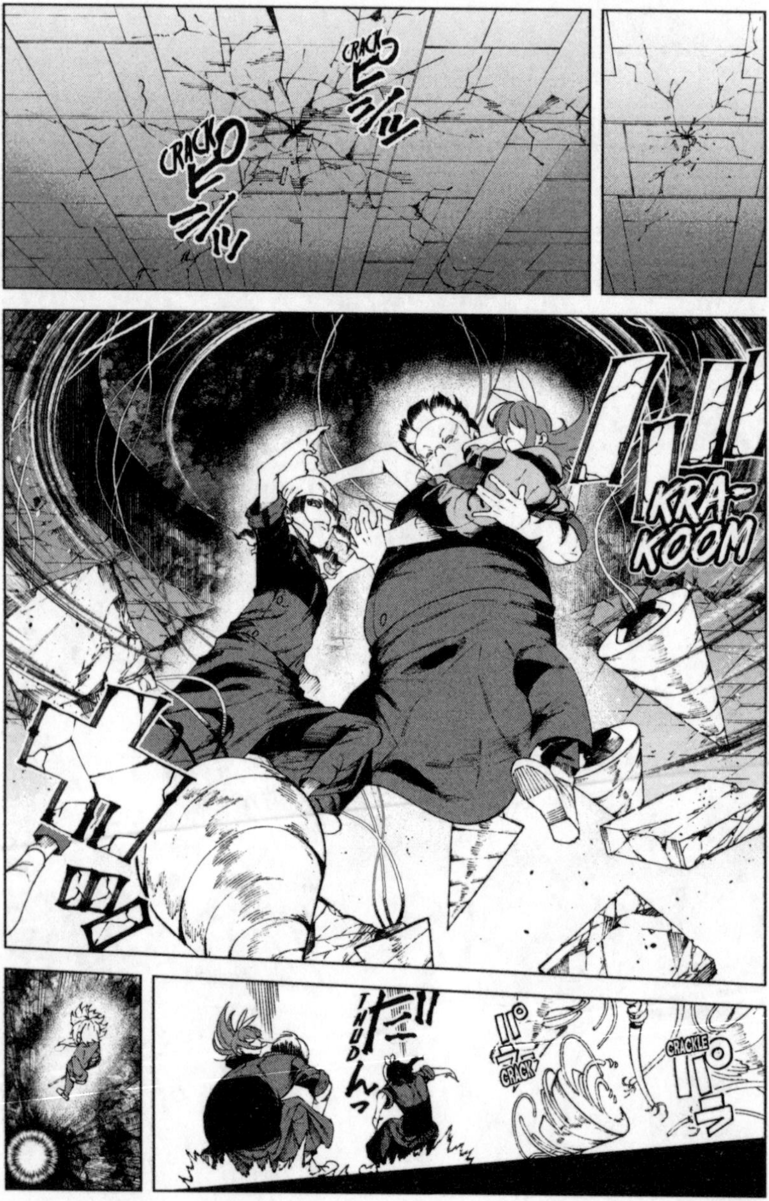
CRACK
CRACK
KRA-KOOM
CRACKLE
CRACK
THUD

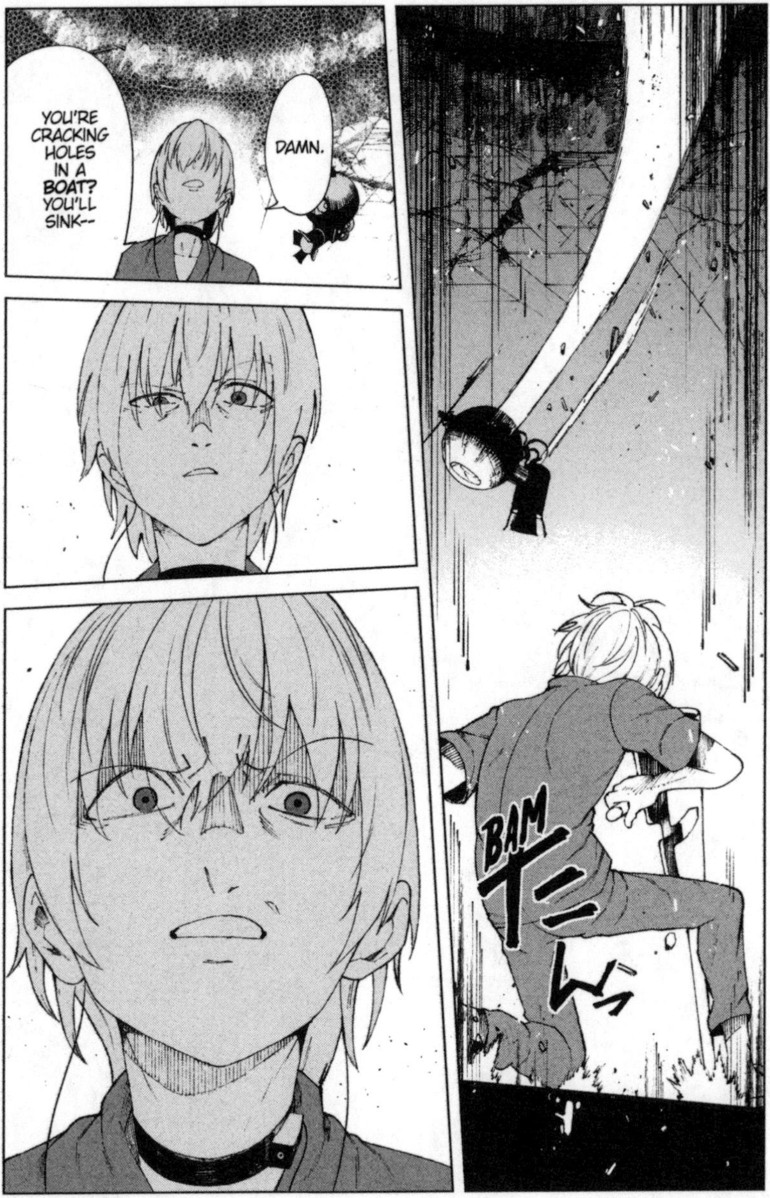
BAM
DAMN.
YOU'RE CRACKING HOLES IN A BOAT? YOU'LL SINK--

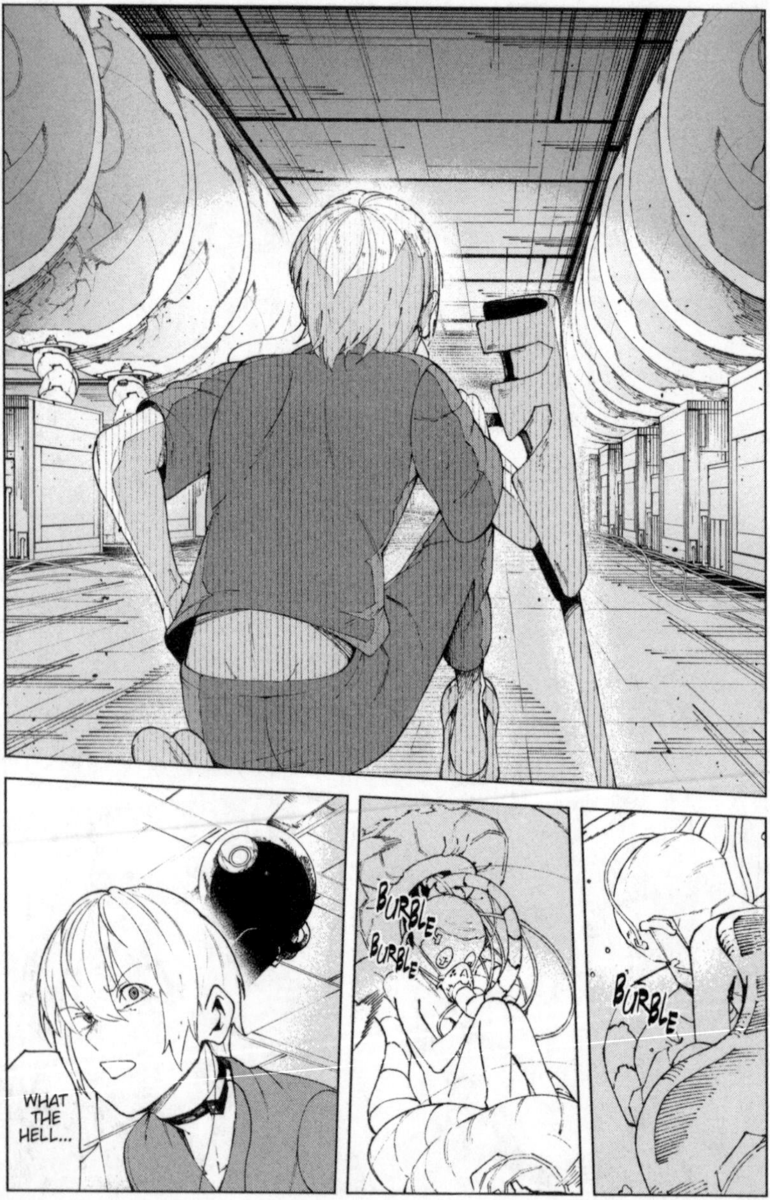
BURBLE
BURBLE BURBLE
WHAT THE HELL...

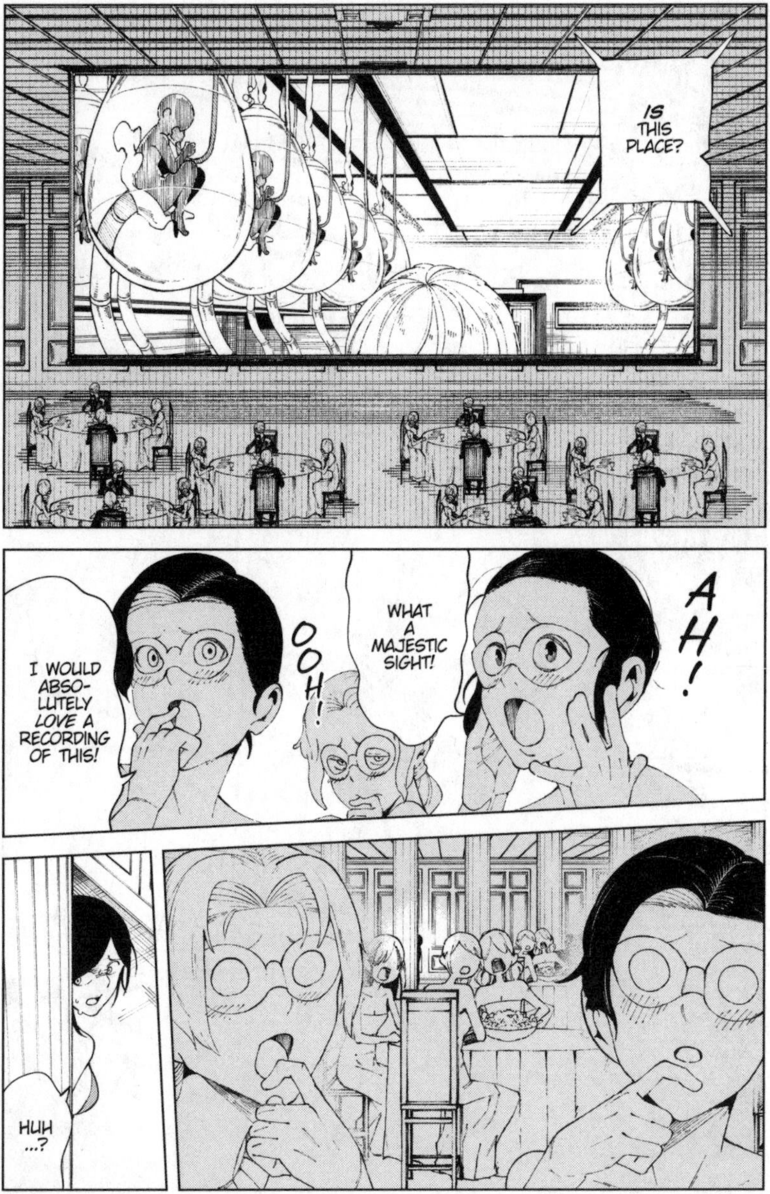
IS THIS PLACE?
AH!
WHAT A MAJESTIC SIGHT!
OOH!
I WOULD ABSO-LUTELY LOVE A RECORDING OF THIS!
HUH ...?

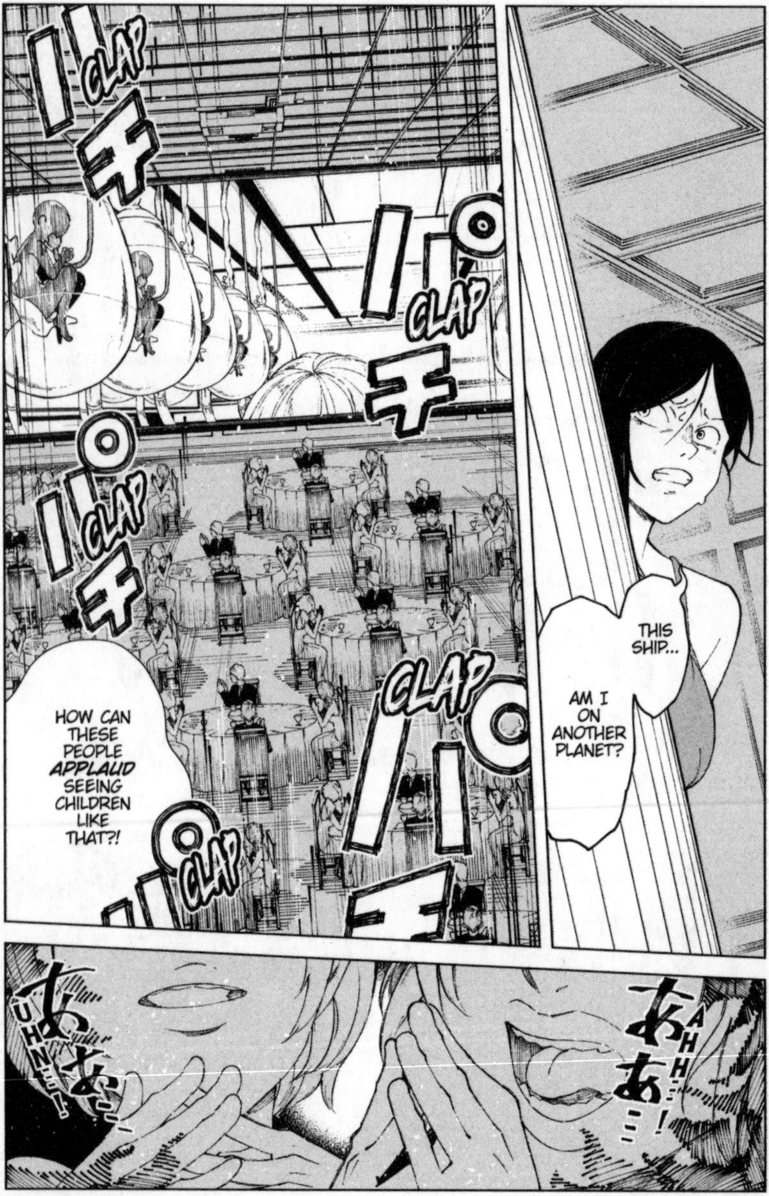
THIS SHIP...
AM I ON ANOTHER PLANET?
CLAP
CLAP
CLAP
CLAP
CLAP
HOW CAN THESE PEOPLE ***APPLAUD*** SEEING CHILDREN LIKE THAT?!
AHH...!
UHN...!

a certain
SCIENTIFIC
ACCELERATOR

とある科学の一方通行 アクセラレータ
とある魔術の禁書目録外伝

CHAPTER 60

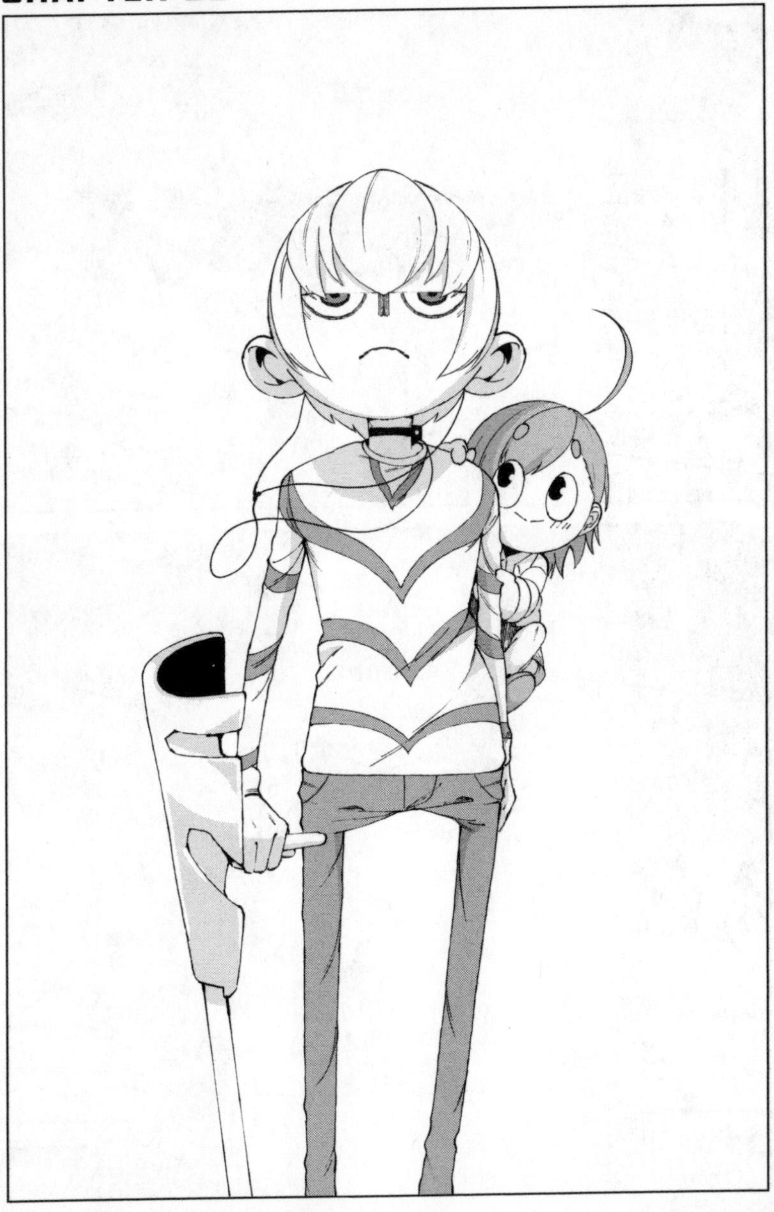

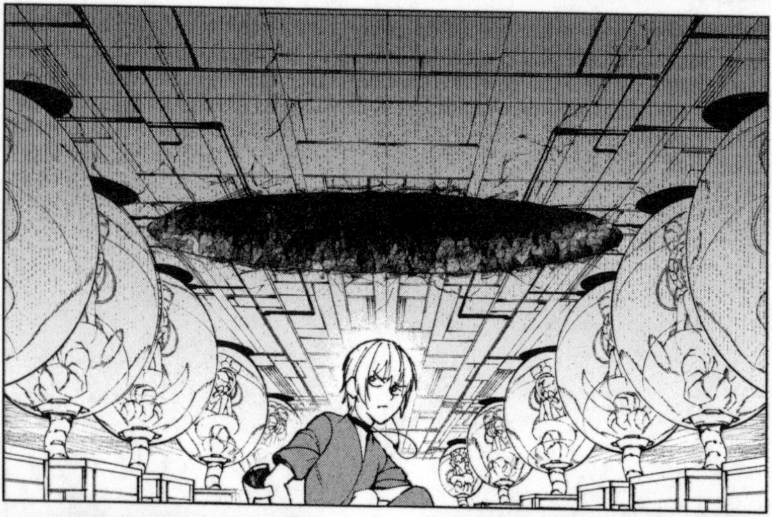

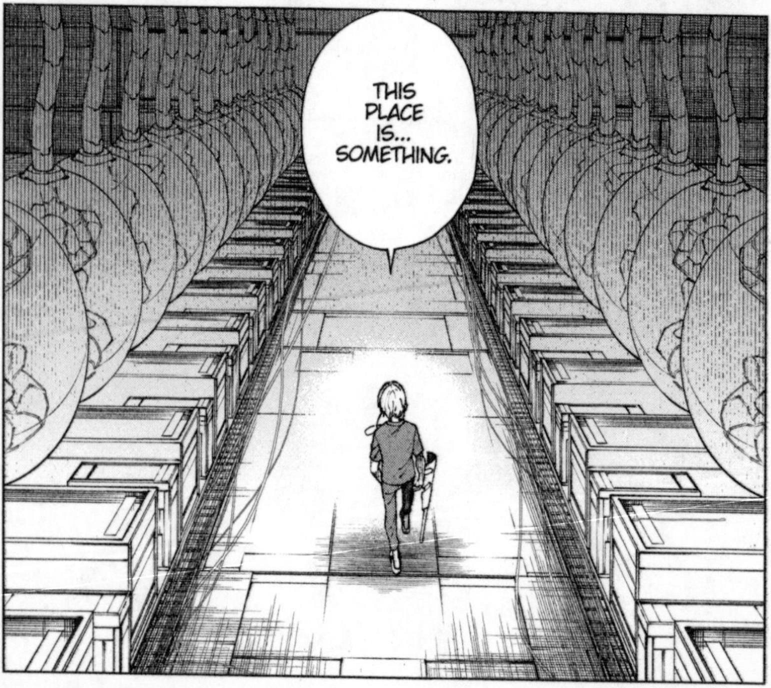
THIS PLACE IS... SOMETHING.

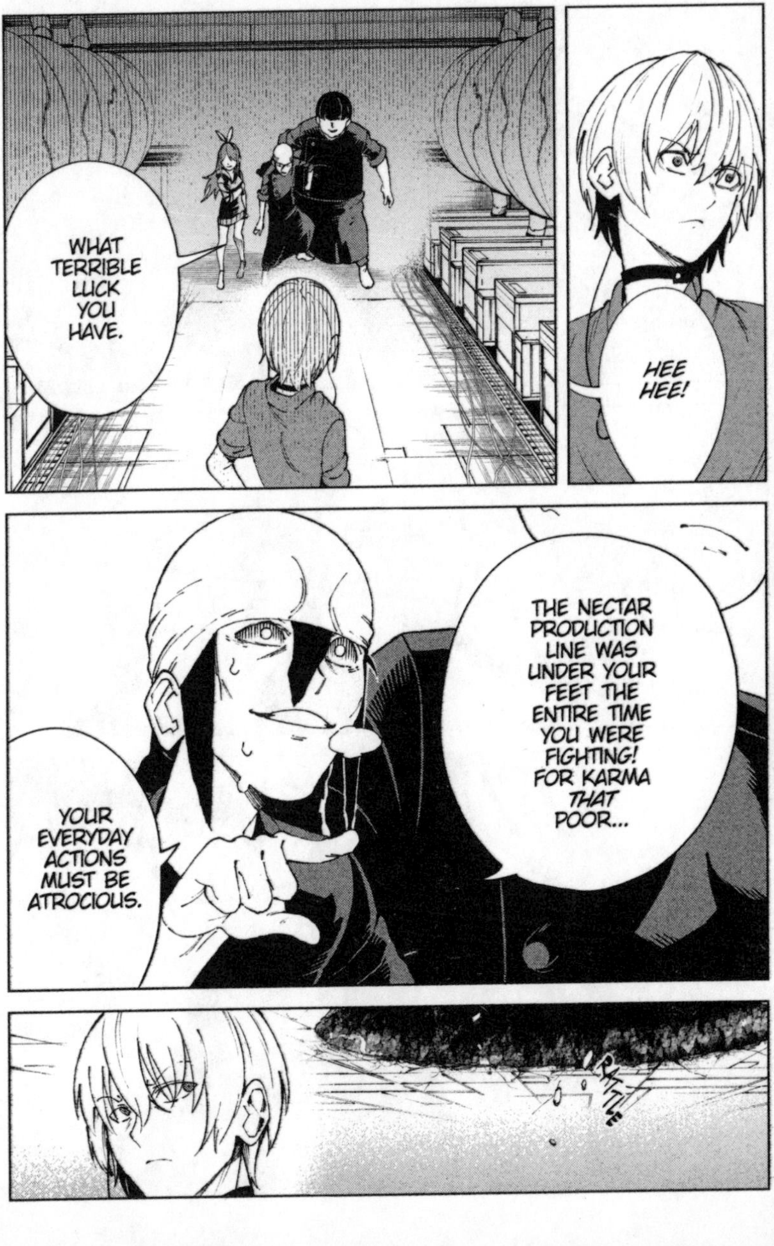
HEE HEE!
WHAT TERRIBLE LUCK YOU HAVE.
THE NECTAR PRODUCTION LINE WAS UNDER YOUR FEET THE ENTIRE TIME YOU WERE FIGHTING! FOR KARMA *THAT* POOR...
YOUR EVERYDAY ACTIONS MUST BE ATROCIOUS.
RATTLE

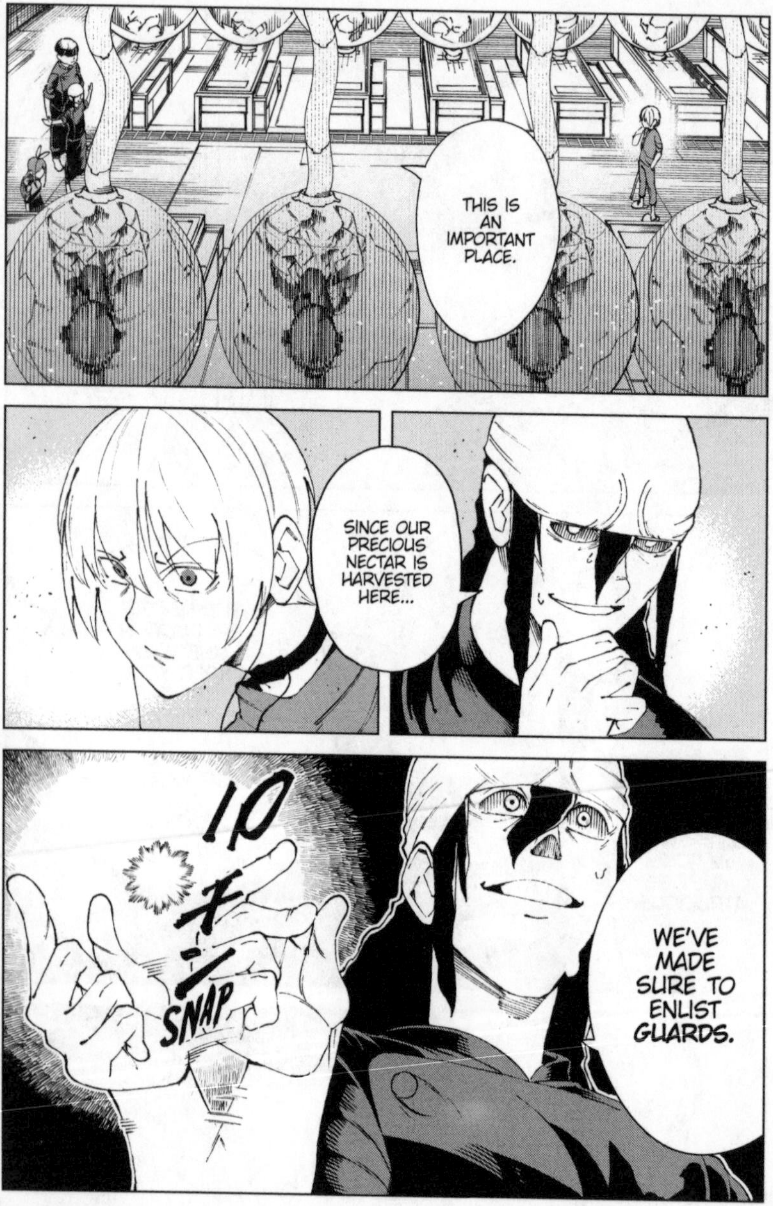
THIS IS AN IMPORTANT PLACE.
SINCE OUR PRECIOUS NECTAR IS HARVESTED HERE...
WE'VE MADE SURE TO ENLIST GUARDS.
SNAP

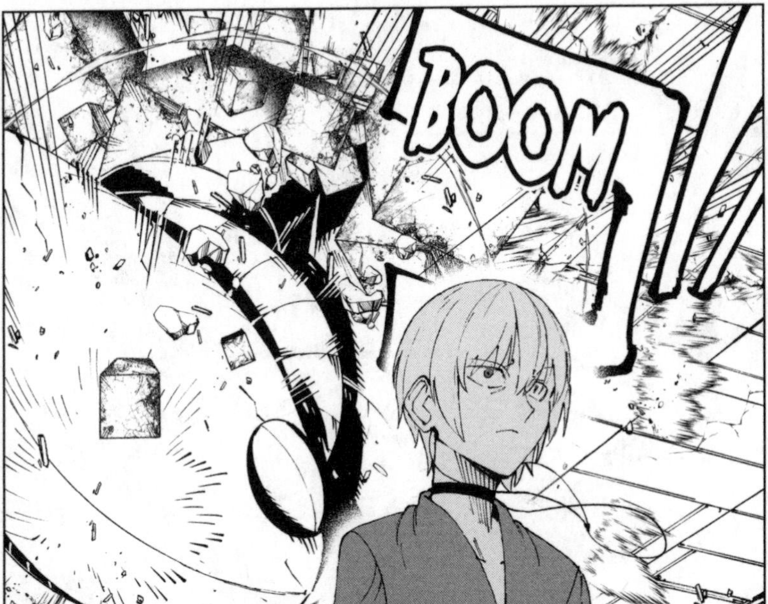
BOOM

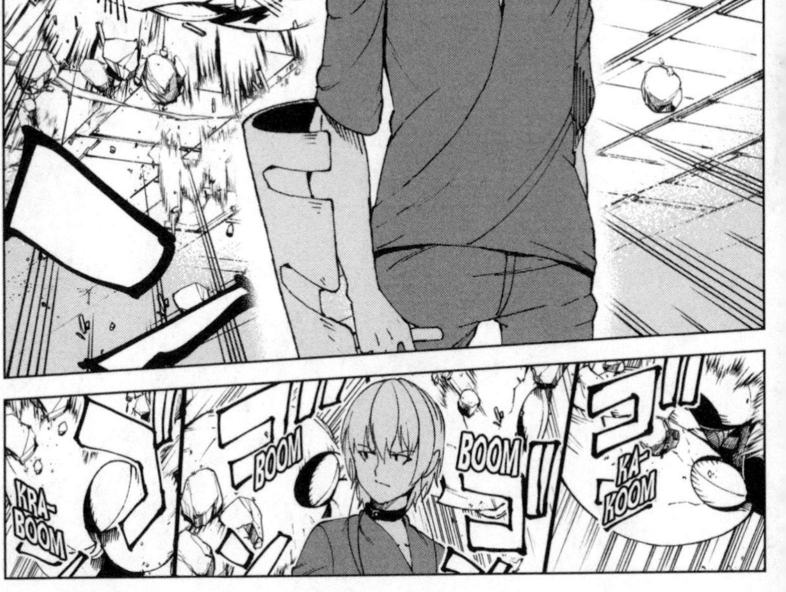
KA-KOOM
BOOM
BOOM
KRA-BOOM

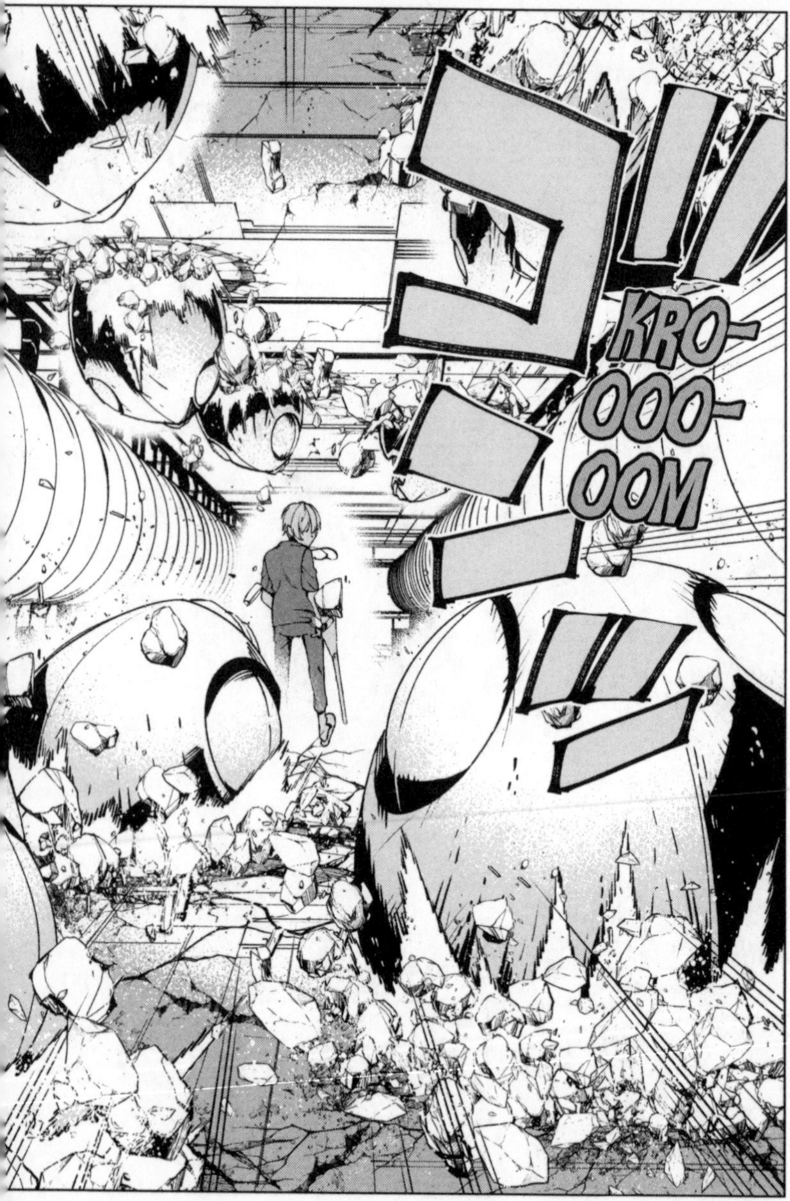
KRO-OOO-OOM

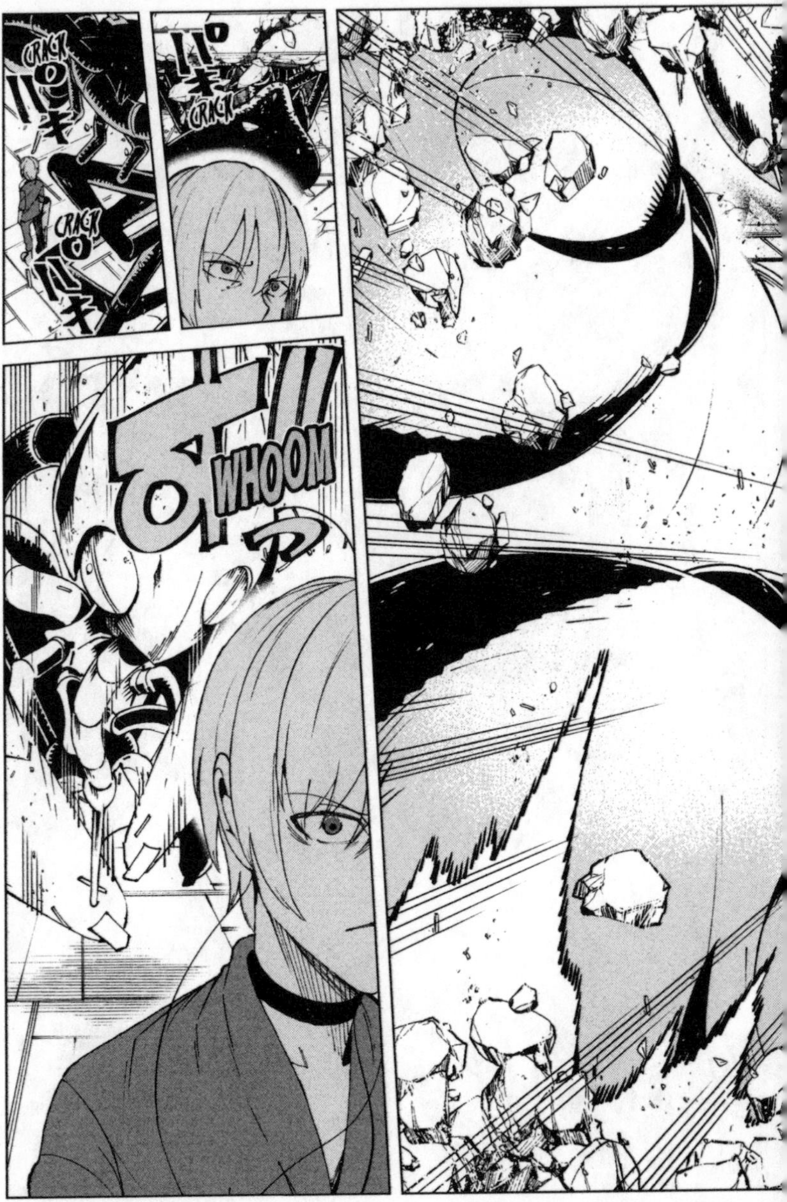
CRACK
CRACK
CRACK
WHOOM

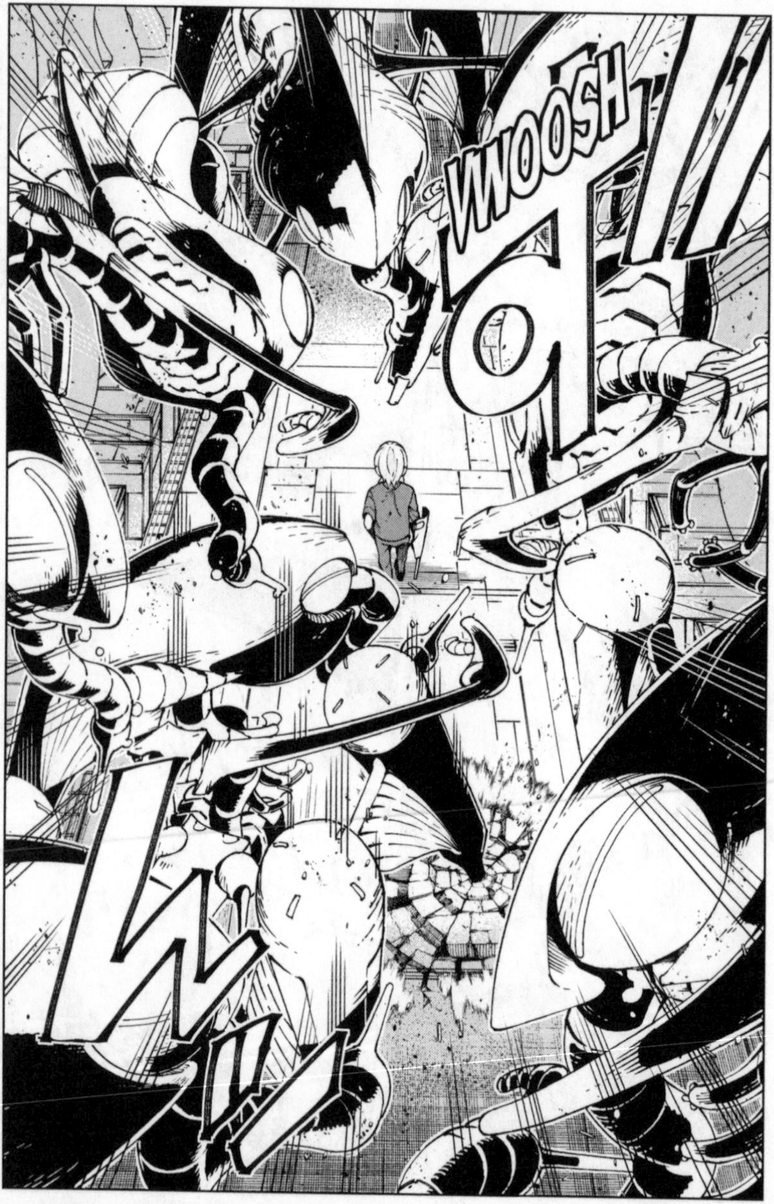
VWOOSH

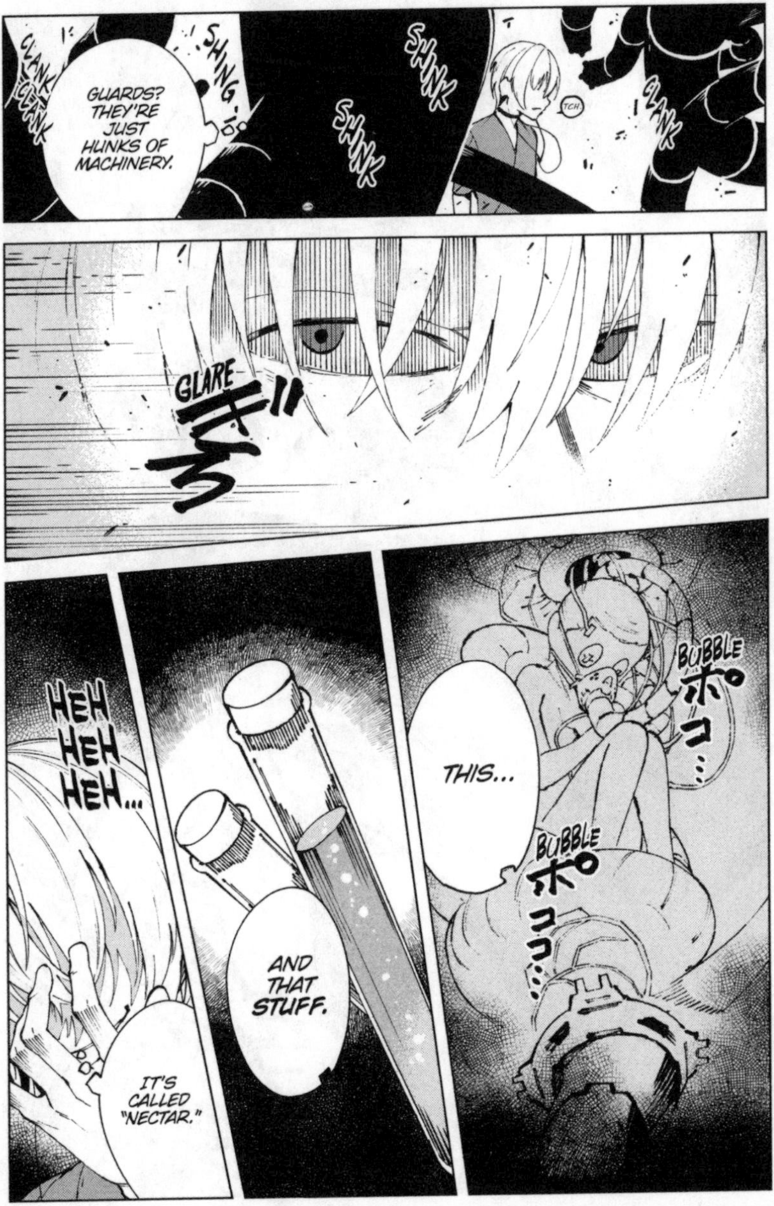
TCH
CLANK
SHINK
SHINK
SHING
GUARDS? THEY'RE JUST HUNKS OF MACHINERY.
CLANK CLANK
GLARE
BUBBLE
BUBBLE
THIS...
AND THAT STUFF.
HEH HEH HEH...
IT'S CALLED "NECTAR."

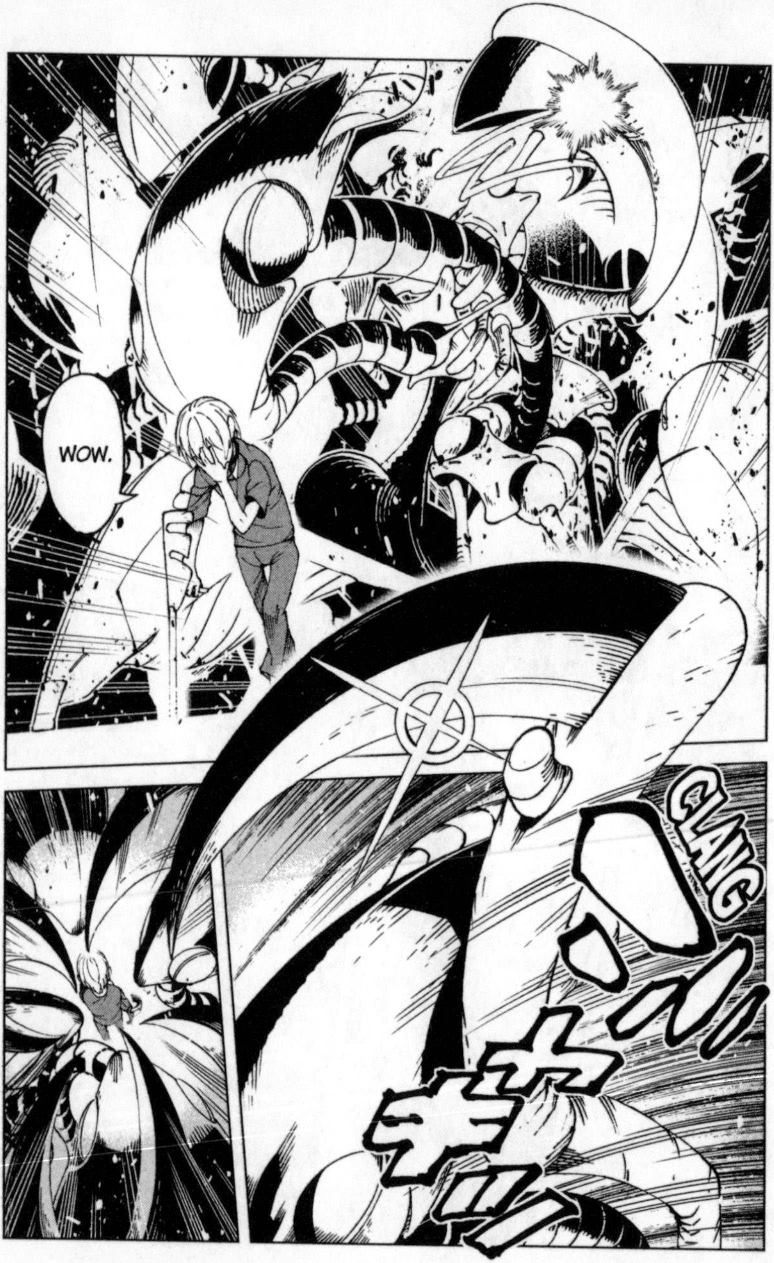
WOW.
CLANG

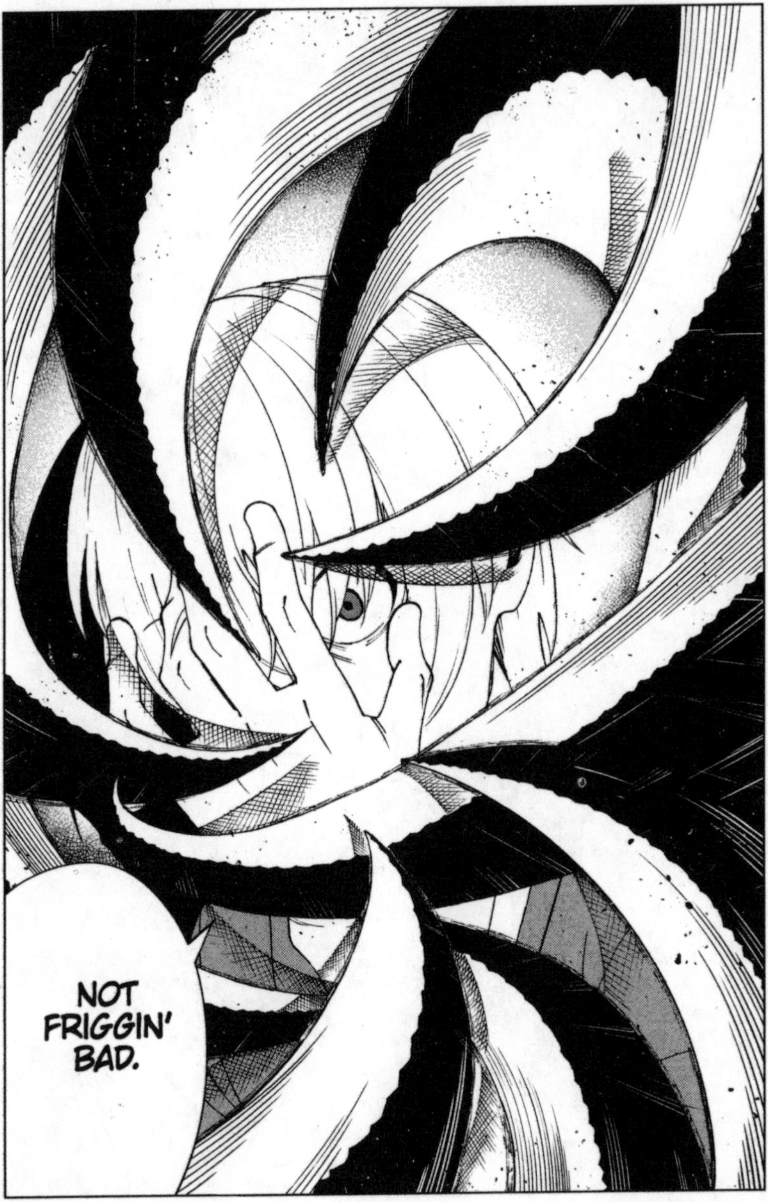
NOT FRIGGIN' BAD.

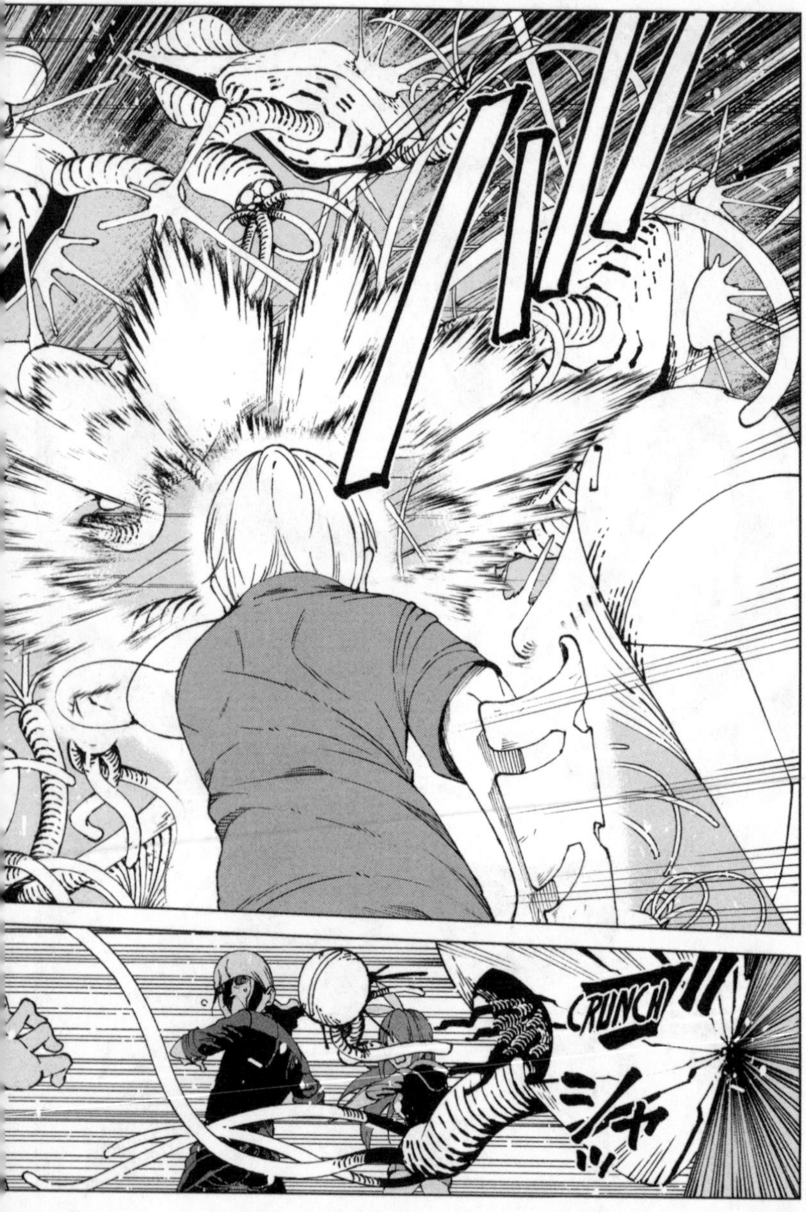
CRUNCH
ミシャッ

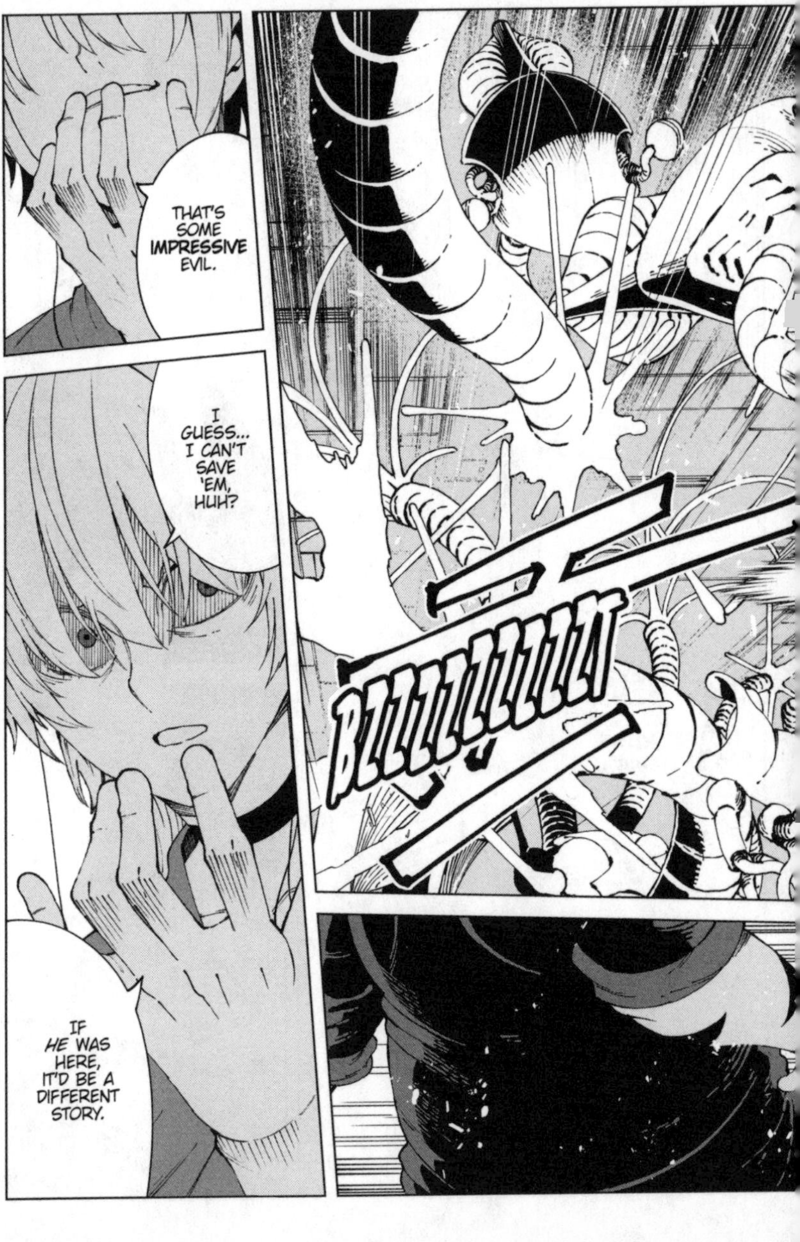
BZZZZZZZZZT
THAT'S SOME IMPRESSIVE EVIL.
I GUESS... I CAN'T SAVE 'EM, HUH?
IF *HE* WAS HERE, IT'D BE A DIFFERENT STORY.

MAYBE I CAN'T DO THAT, BUT I CAN...

SHFF
すラ...

FINE.

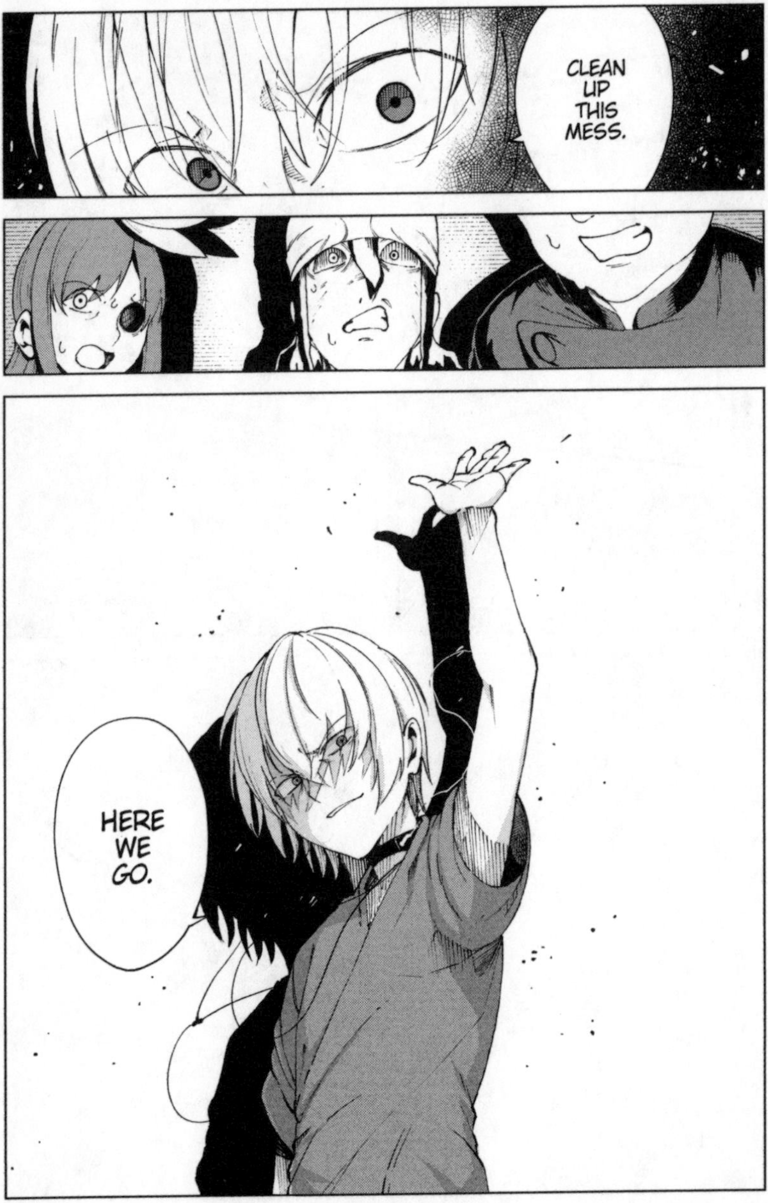
CLEAN UP THIS MESS.
HERE WE GO.

YUM!

WHA?

HEY...

WHOA, DO YOU SEE THAT?

HUH?

LOOK...!

CHATTER

CHATTER

CHATTER

GAH! WH-WHAT THE HECK IS THAT?!

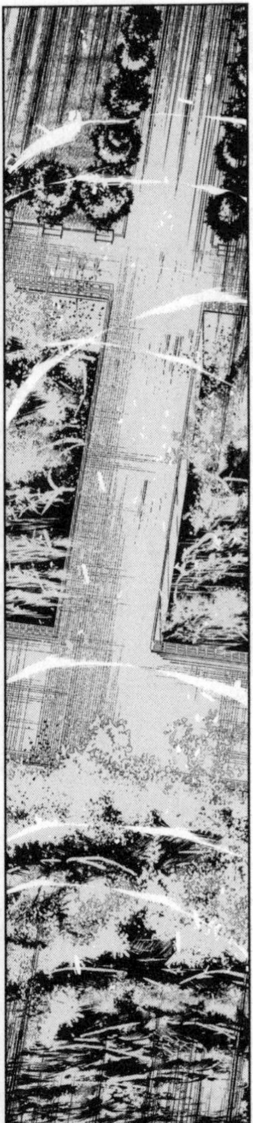
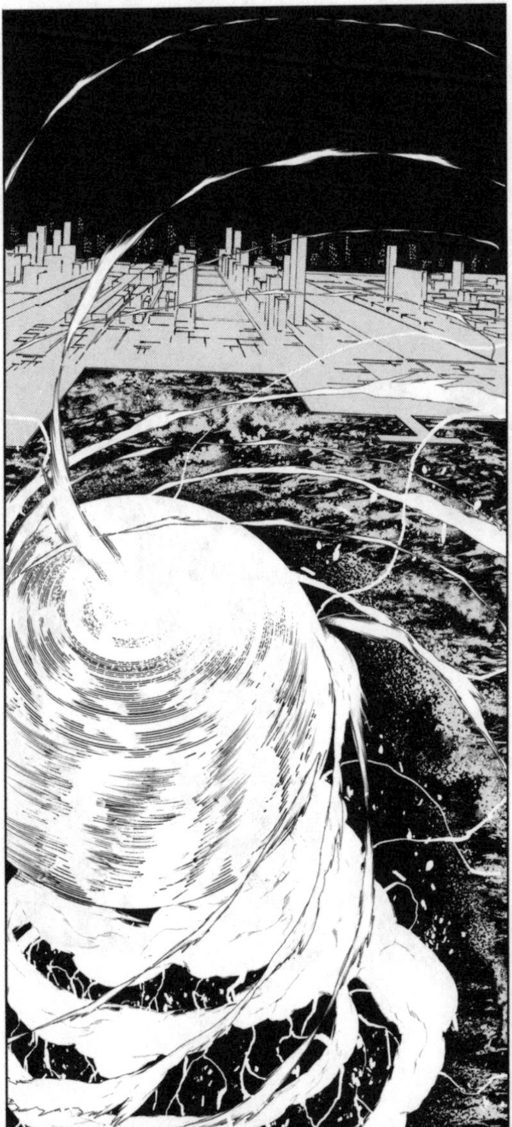

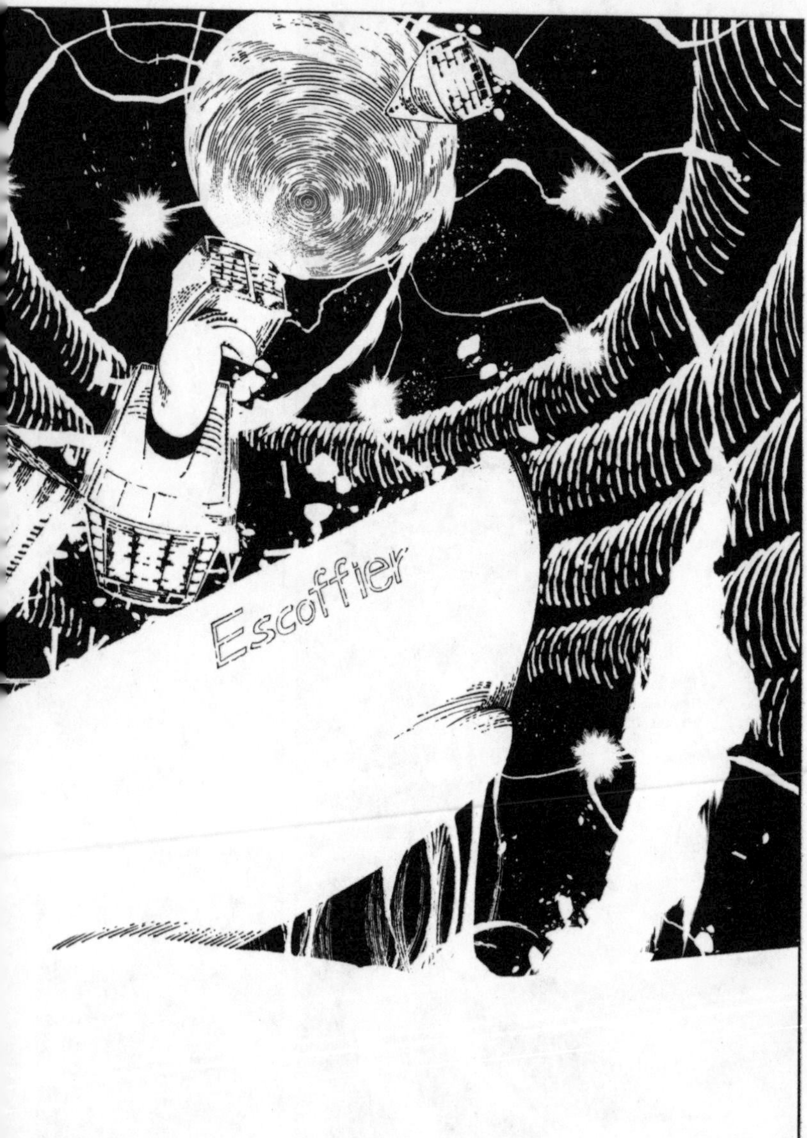
Escoffier

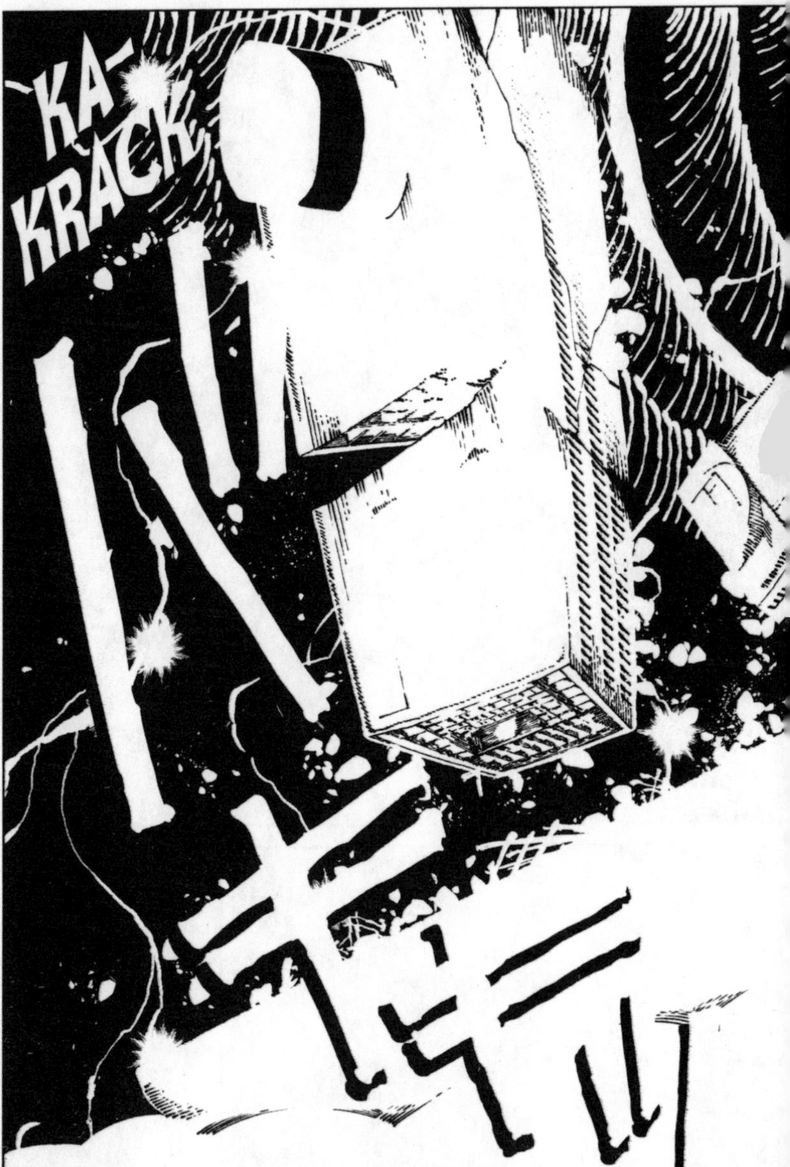
KA-KRACK

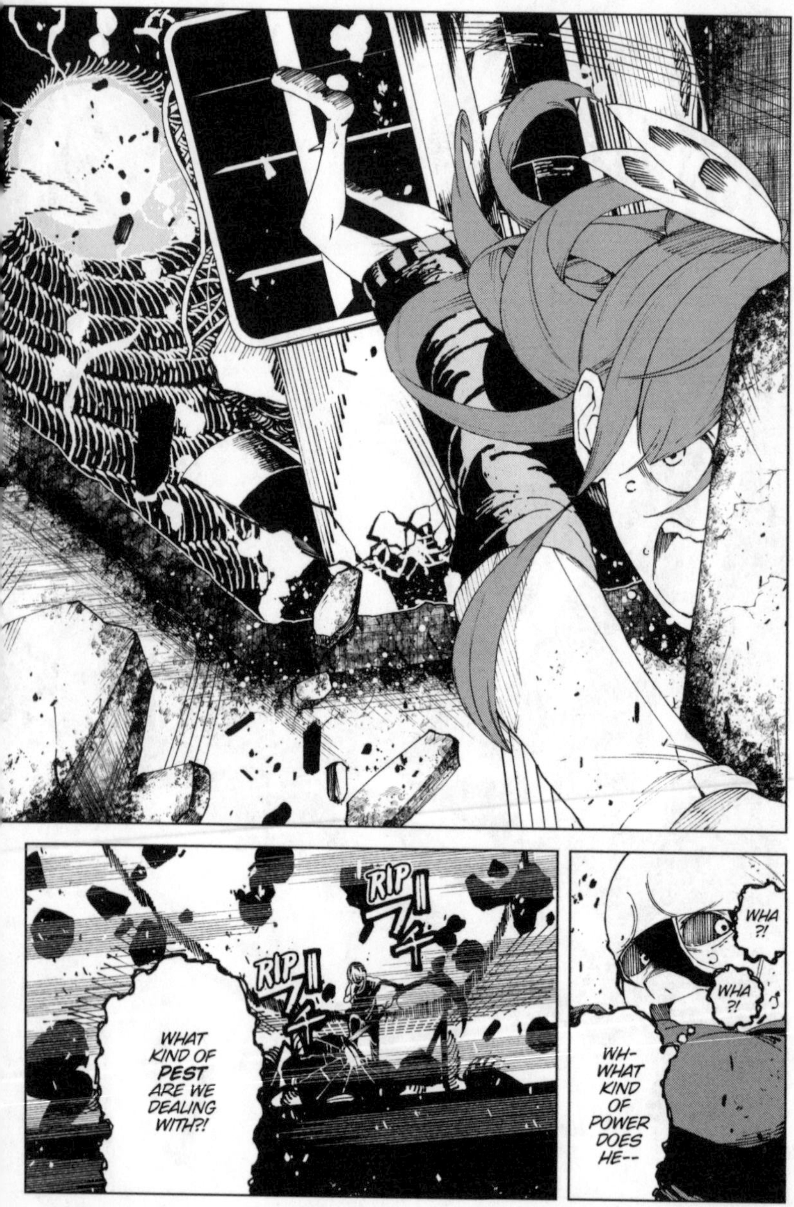
WHA?!
WHA?!
WH-WHAT KIND OF POWER DOES HE--
RIP
RIP
WHAT KIND OF PEST ARE WE DEALING WITH?!

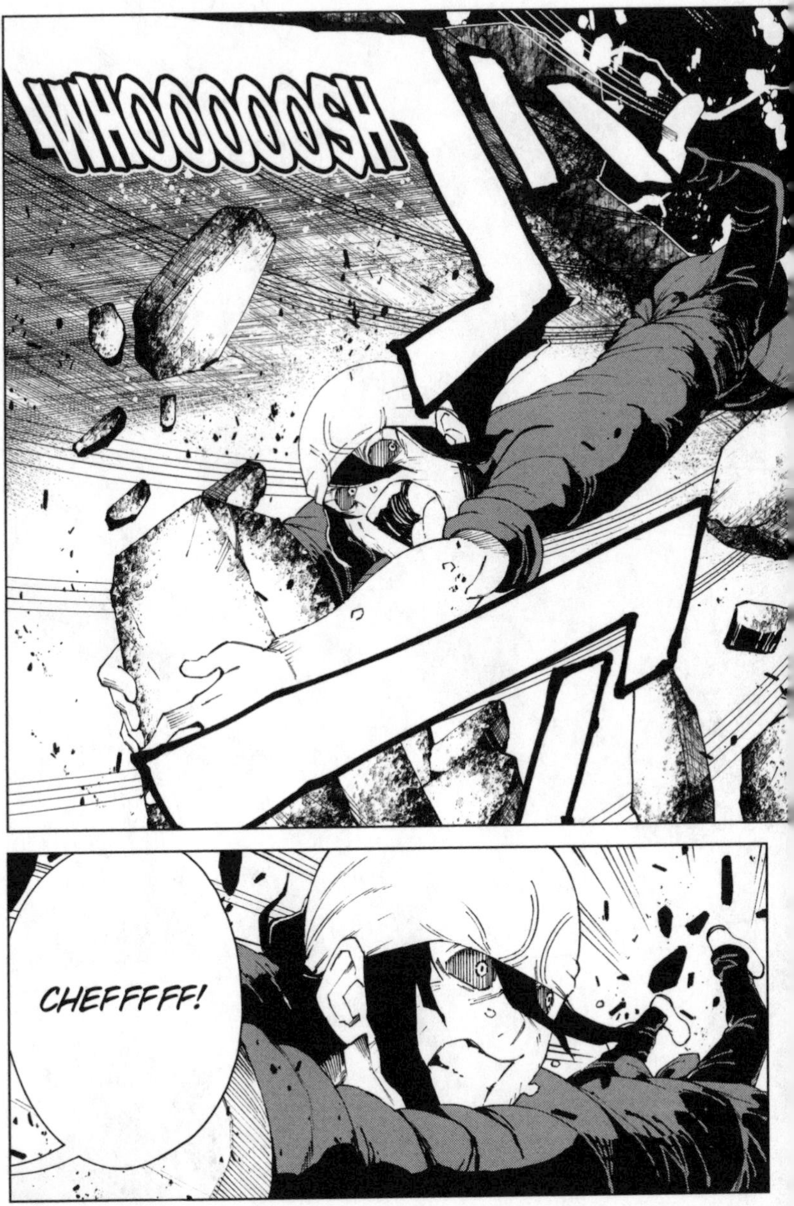
WHOOOOOSH
CHEFFFFF!

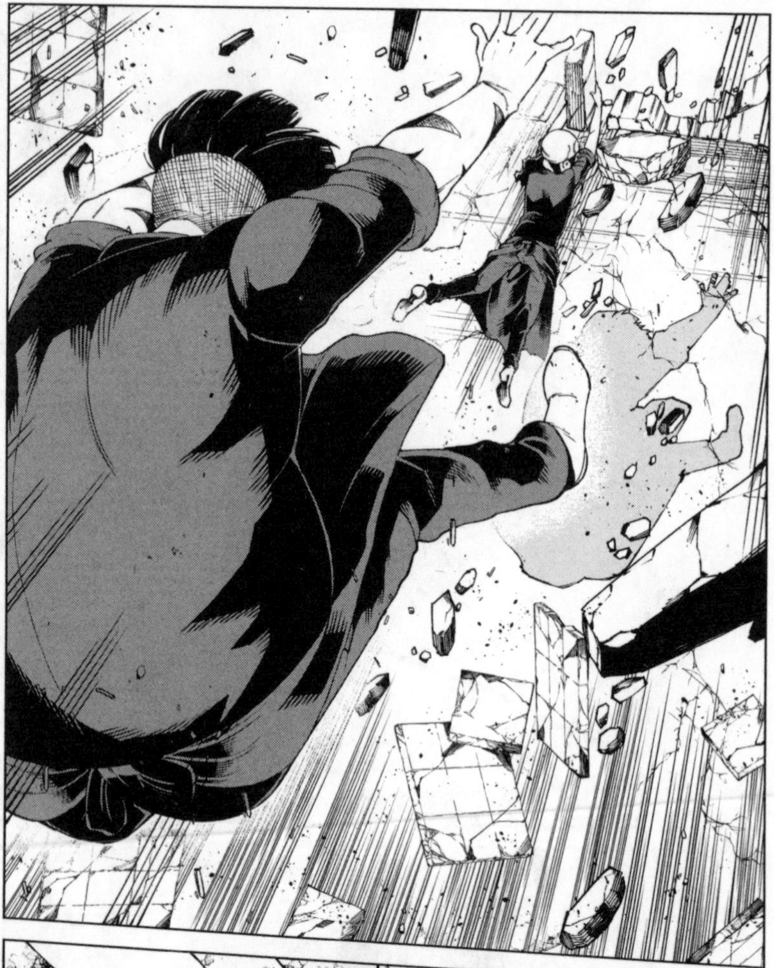
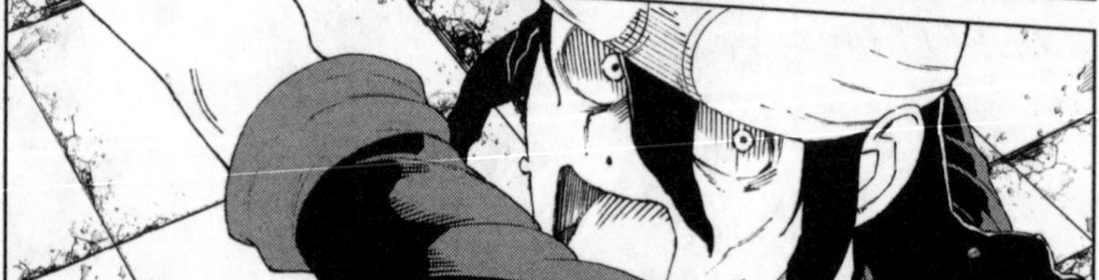

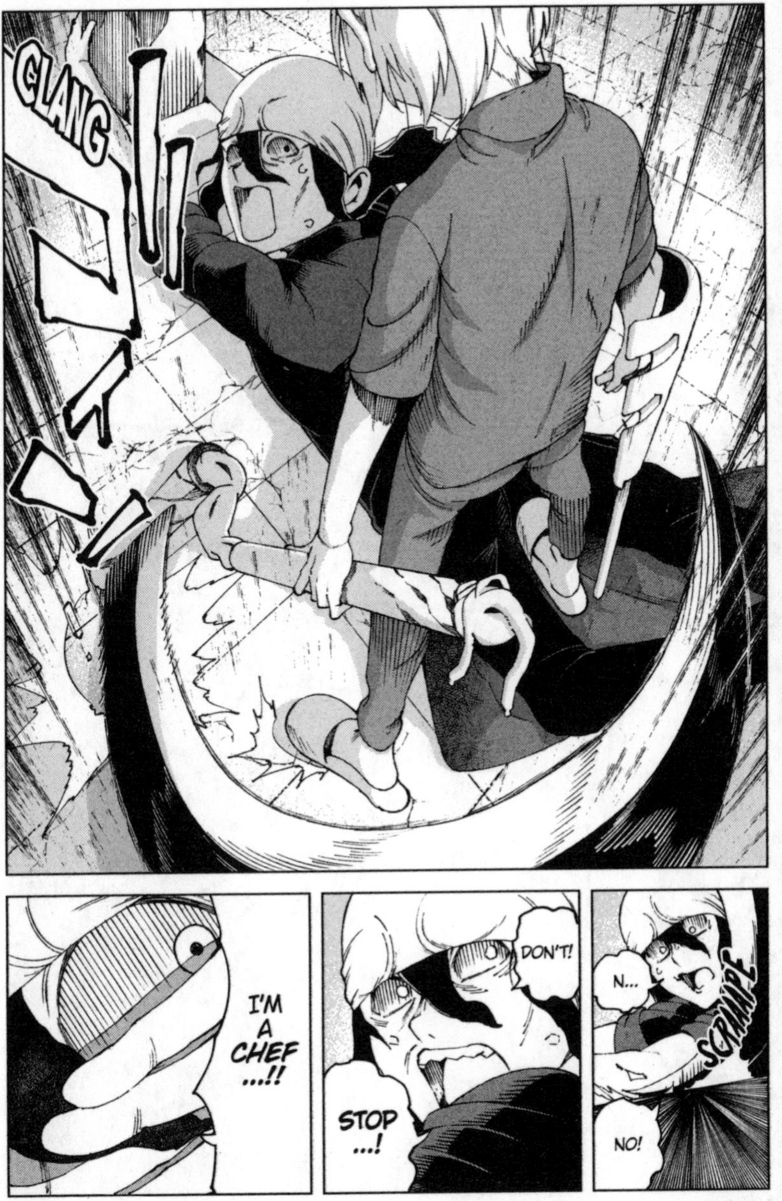
CLANG
N...
SCRAAPE
NO!
DON'T!
STOP ...!
I'M A CHEF ...!!

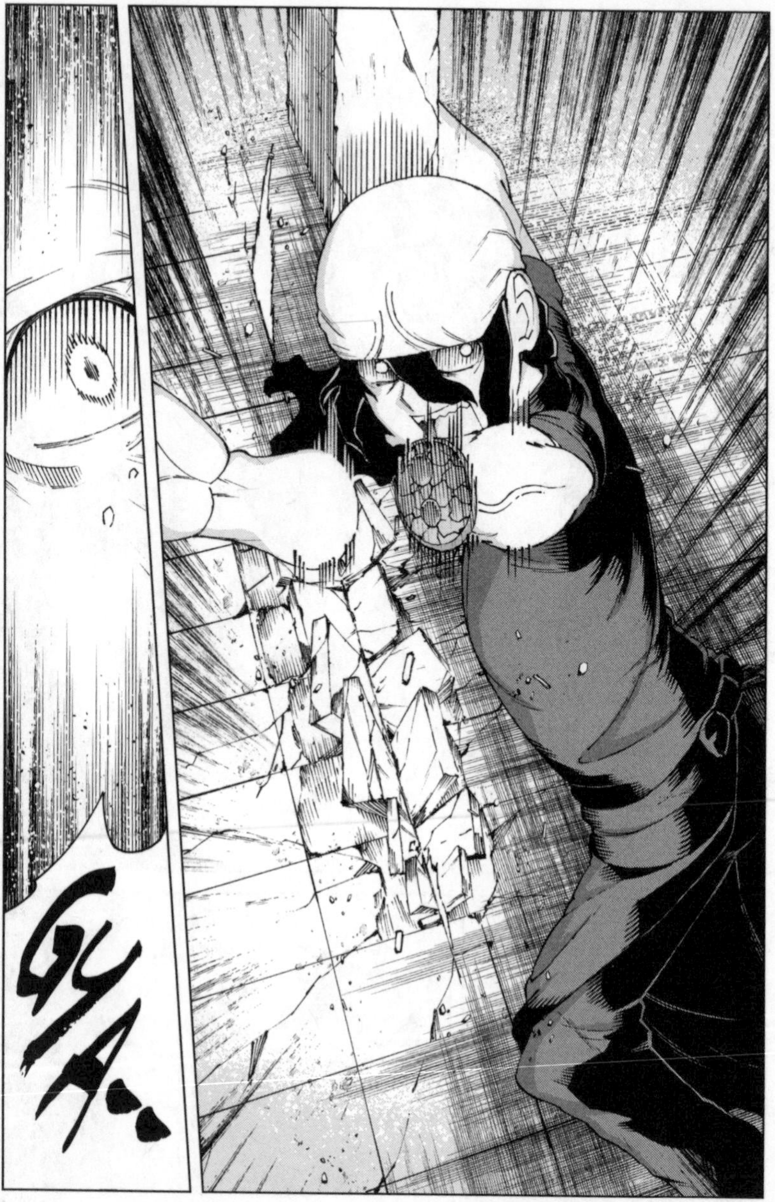
GUA...

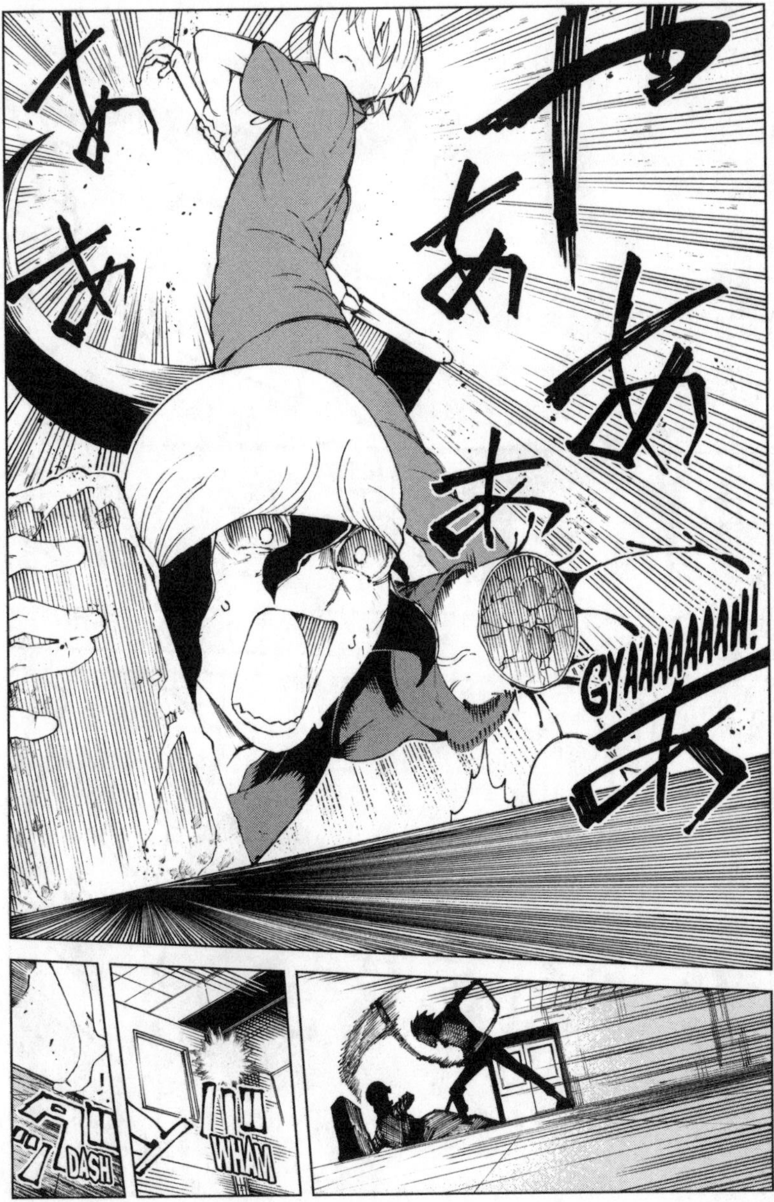
GYAAAAAAH!
WHAM
DASH

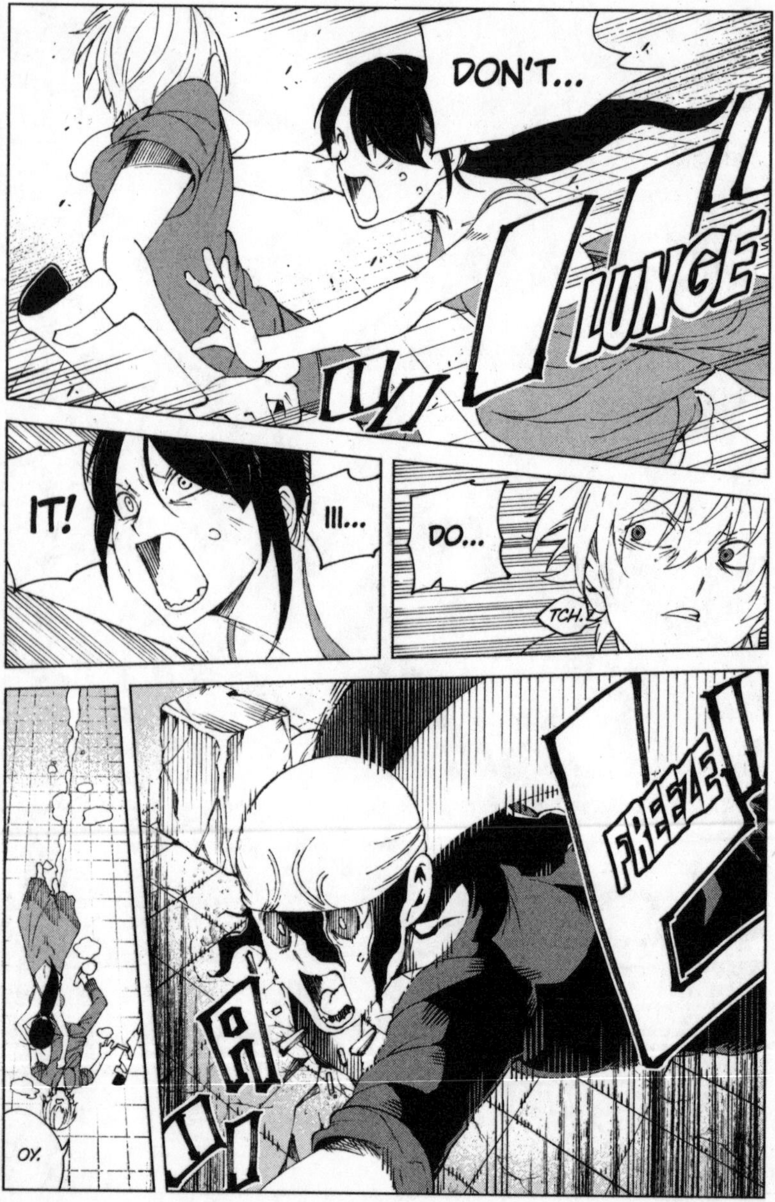
DON'T...
LUNGE
DO...
TCH.
III...
IT!
FREEZE
OY.

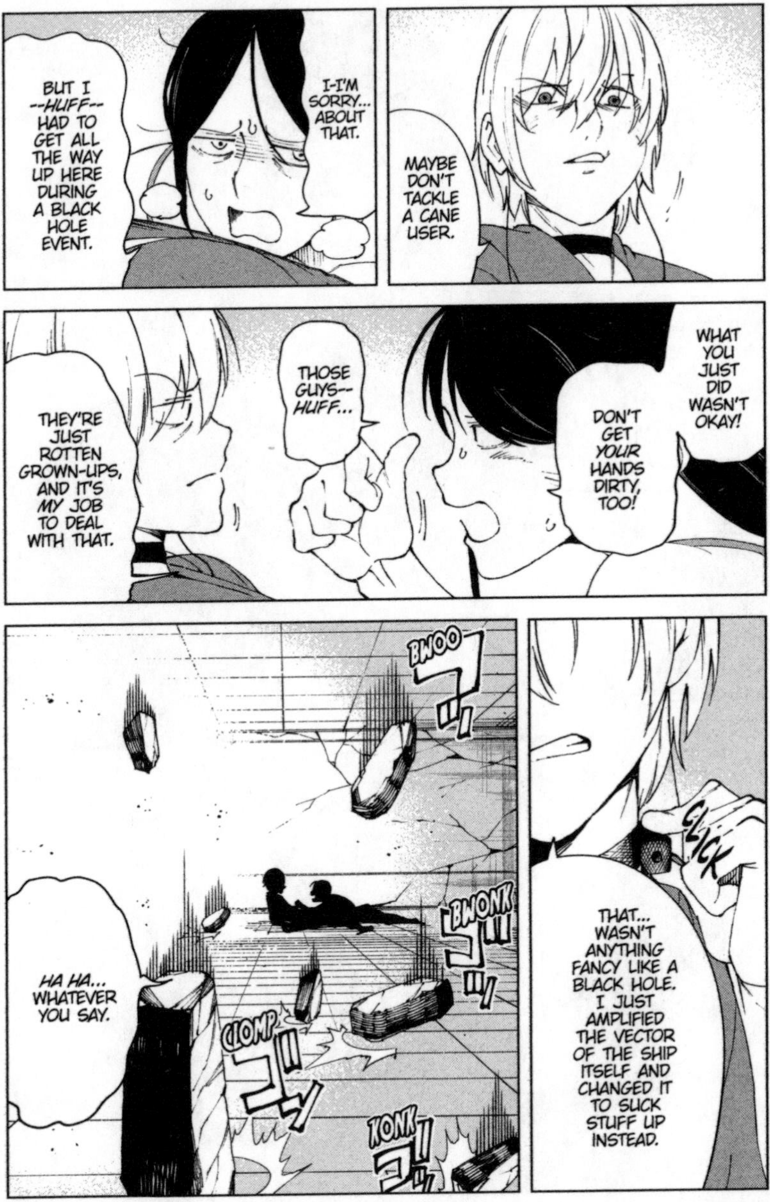
MAYBE DON'T TACKLE A CANE USER.
I-I'M SORRY... ABOUT THAT.
BUT I --*HUFF*-- HAD TO GET ALL THE WAY UP HERE DURING A BLACK HOLE EVENT.
WHAT YOU JUST DID WASN'T OKAY!
DON'T GET *YOUR* HANDS DIRTY, TOO!
THOSE GUYS-- *HUFF*...
THEY'RE JUST ROTTEN GROWN-UPS, AND IT'S *MY* JOB TO DEAL WITH THAT.
CLICK
THAT... WASN'T ANYTHING FANCY LIKE A BLACK HOLE. I JUST AMPLIFIED THE VECTOR OF THE SHIP ITSELF AND CHANGED IT TO SUCK STUFF UP INSTEAD.
BWOO
BWONK
CLOMP
KONK
HA HA... WHATEVER YOU SAY.

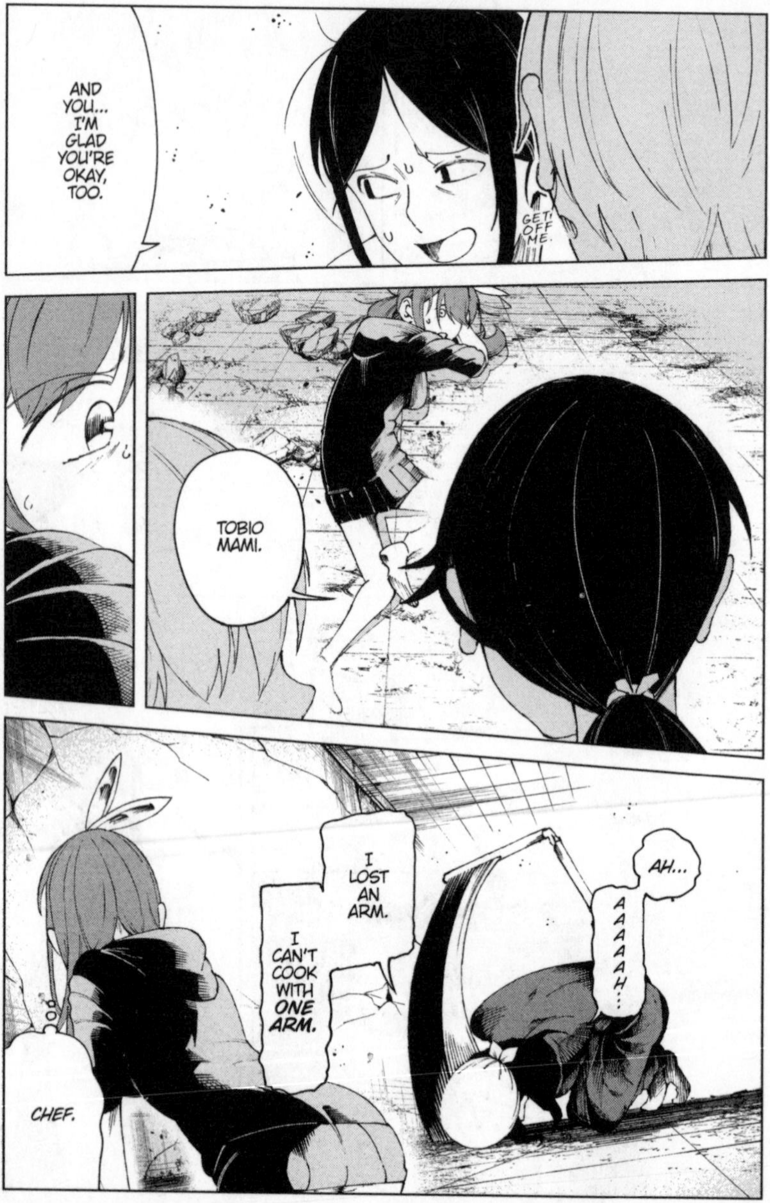
AND YOU... I'M GLAD YOU'RE OKAY, TOO.
GET OFF ME.
TOBIO MAMI.
AH...
AAAAAH...
I LOST AN ARM.
I CAN'T COOK WITH *ONE ARM.*
CHEF.

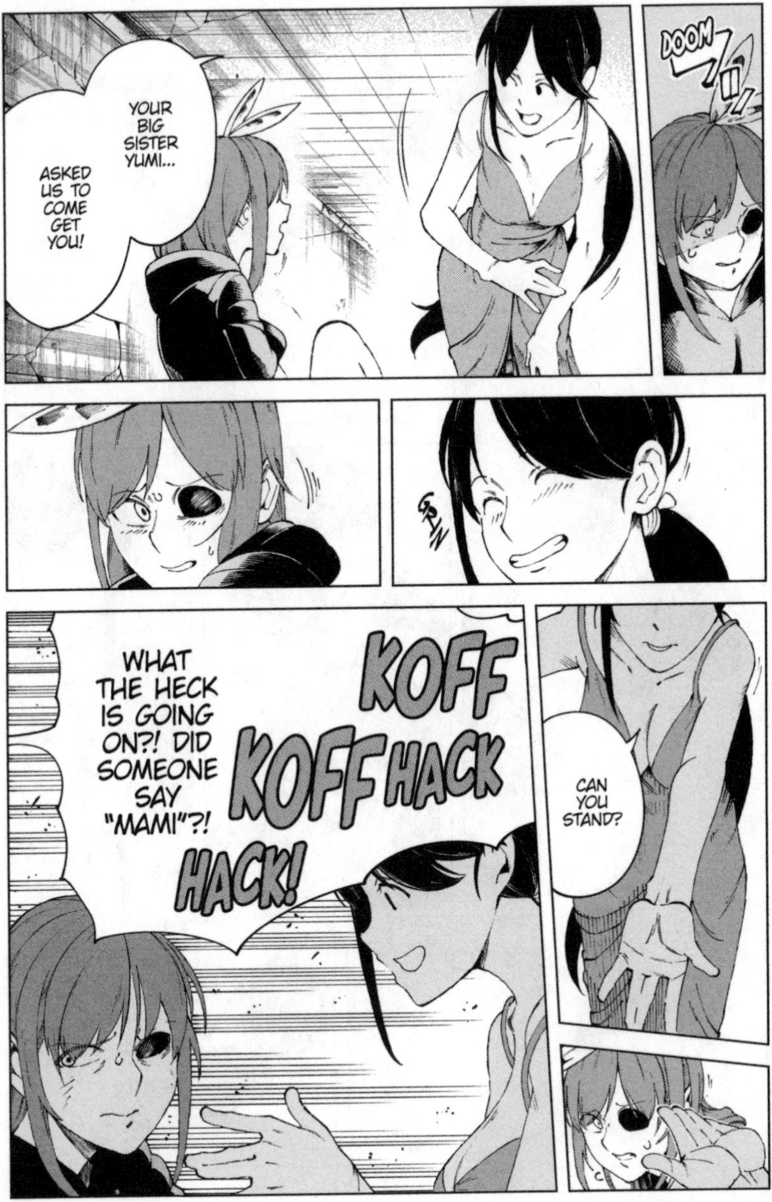
DOOM
YOUR BIG SISTER YUMI...
ASKED US TO COME GET YOU!
GRIN
CAN YOU STAND?
KOFF
KOFF HACK
HACK!
WHAT THE HECK IS GOING ON?! DID SOMEONE SAY "MAMI"?!

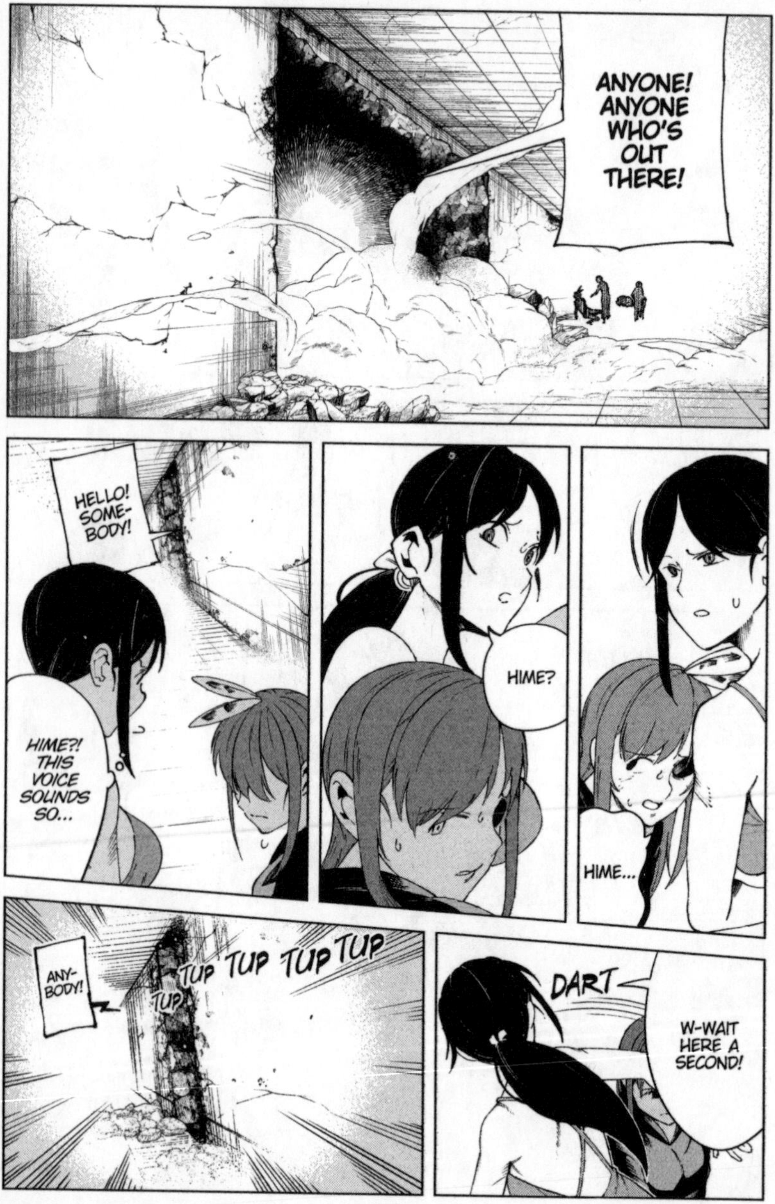
ANYONE! ANYONE WHO'S OUT THERE!
HIME...
HIME?
HELLO! SOME-BODY!
HIME?! THIS VOICE SOUNDS SO...
DART
W-WAIT HERE A SECOND!
ANY-BODY!
TUP TUP TUP TUP TUP

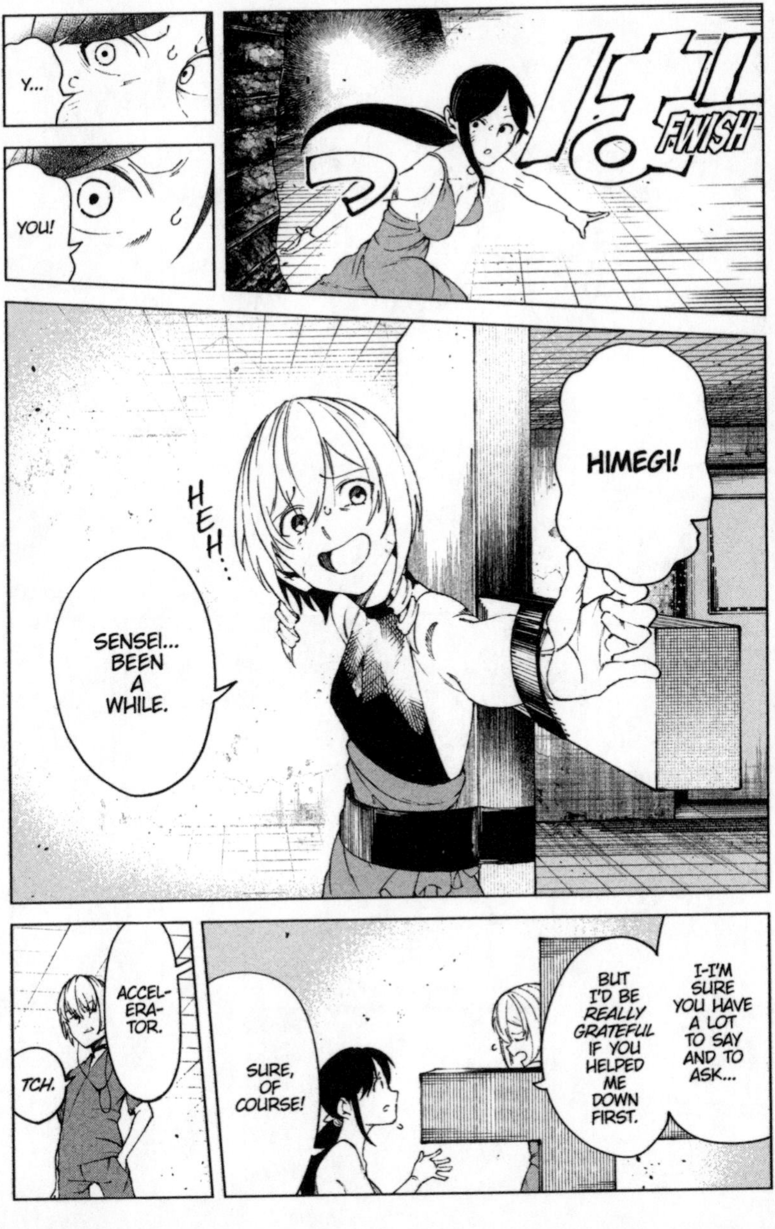
FWISH
Y...
YOU!
HIMEGI!
HEH...
SENSEI... BEEN A WHILE.
I-I'M SURE YOU HAVE A LOT TO SAY AND TO ASK...
BUT I'D BE *REALLY GRATEFUL* IF YOU HELPED ME DOWN FIRST.
SURE, OF COURSE!
ACCEL-ERA-TOR.
TCH.

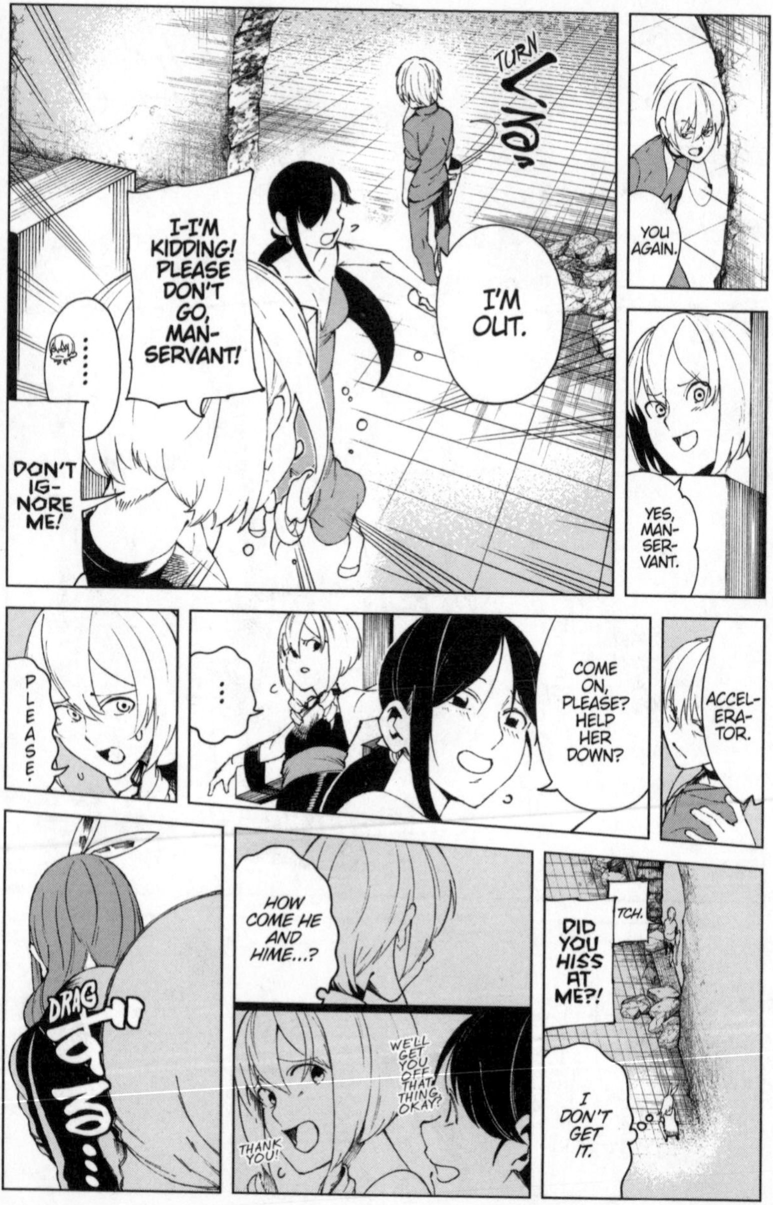
YOU AGAIN.
YES, MAN-SERVANT.
TURN
I'M OUT.
I-I'M KIDDING! PLEASE DON'T GO, MAN-SERVANT!
......
DON'T IG-NORE ME!
ACCEL-ERATOR.
COME ON, PLEASE? HELP HER DOWN?
...
PLEASE.
TCH.
DID YOU HISS AT ME?!
I DON'T GET IT.
HOW COME HE AND HIME...?
WE'LL GET YOU OFF THAT THING, OKAY?
THANK YOU!
DRAG

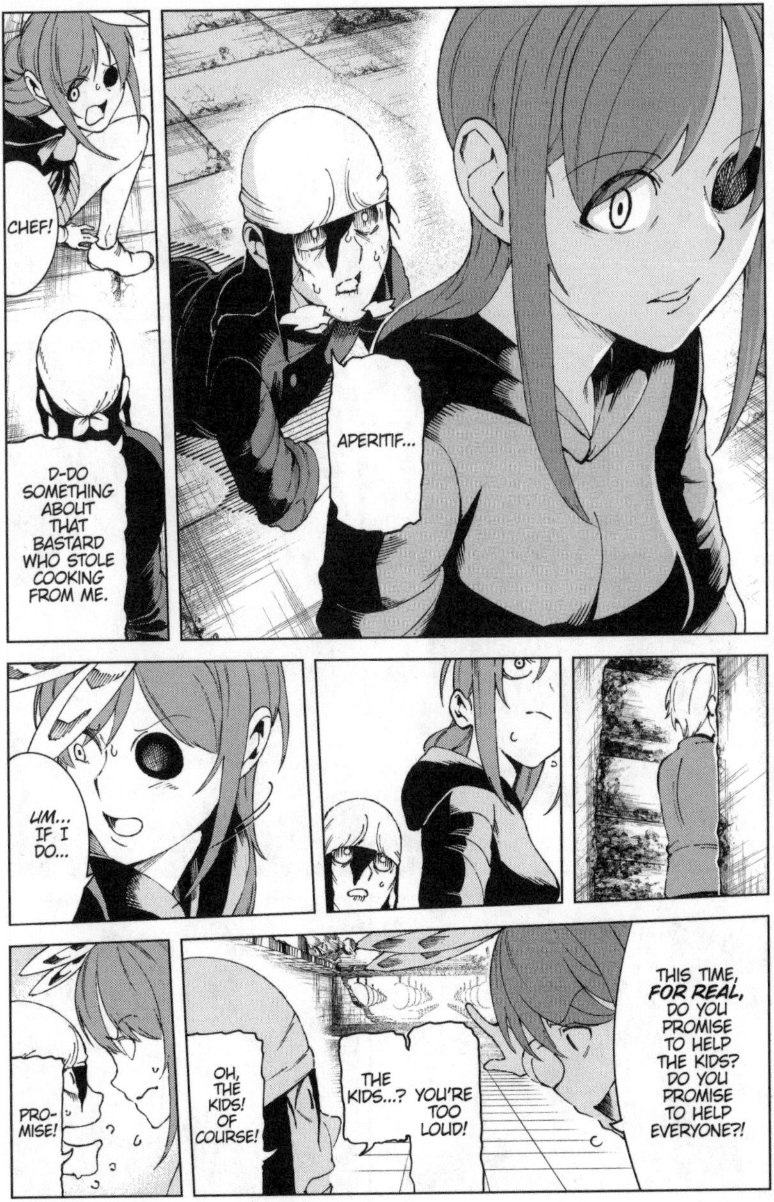
APERITIF...
CHEF!
D-DO SOMETHING ABOUT THAT BASTARD WHO STOLE COOKING FROM ME.
UM... IF I DO...
THIS TIME, **FOR REAL,** DO YOU PROMISE TO HELP THE KIDS? DO YOU PROMISE TO HELP EVERYONE?!
YOU'RE TOO LOUD!
THE KIDS...?
OH, THE KIDS! OF COURSE!
PRO-MISE!

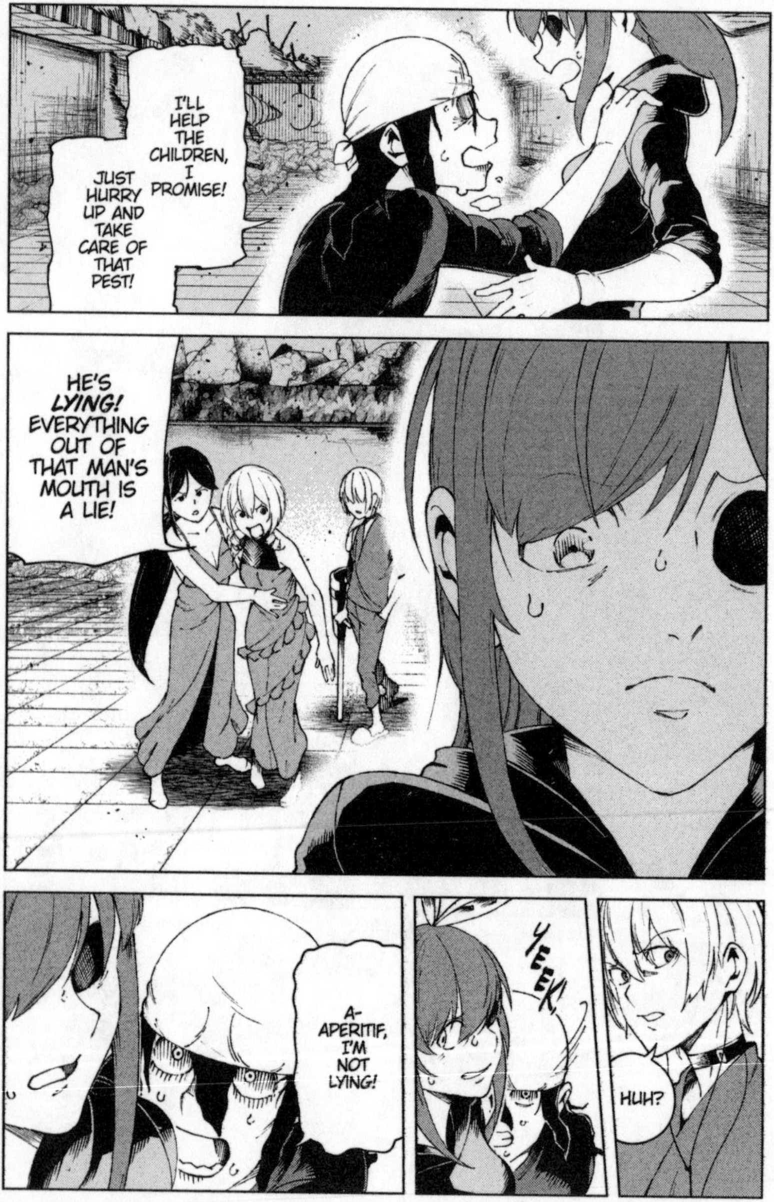
I'LL HELP THE CHILDREN, I PROMISE!
JUST HURRY UP AND TAKE CARE OF THAT PEST!
HE'S *LYING!* EVERYTHING OUT OF THAT MAN'S MOUTH IS A LIE!
HUH?
YEEK!
A- APERITIF, I'M NOT LYING!

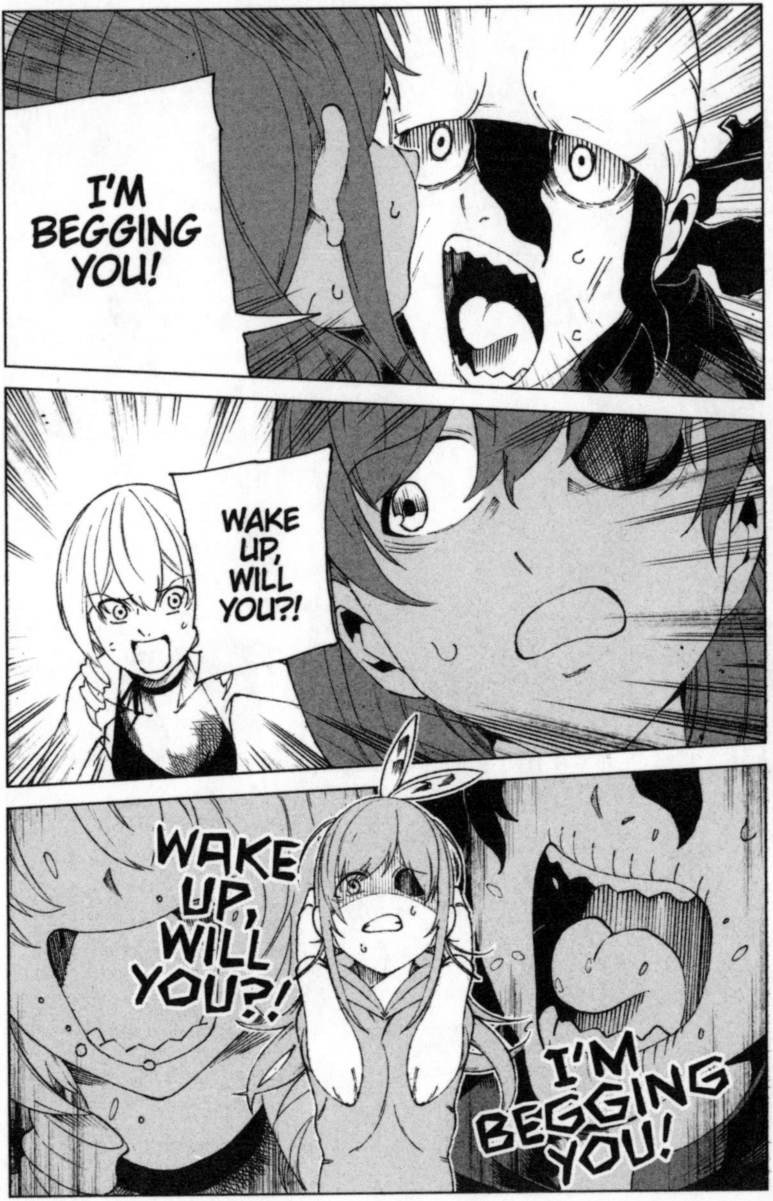
I'M BEGGING YOU!
WAKE UP, WILL YOU?!
I'M BEGGING YOU!
WAKE UP, WILL YOU?!

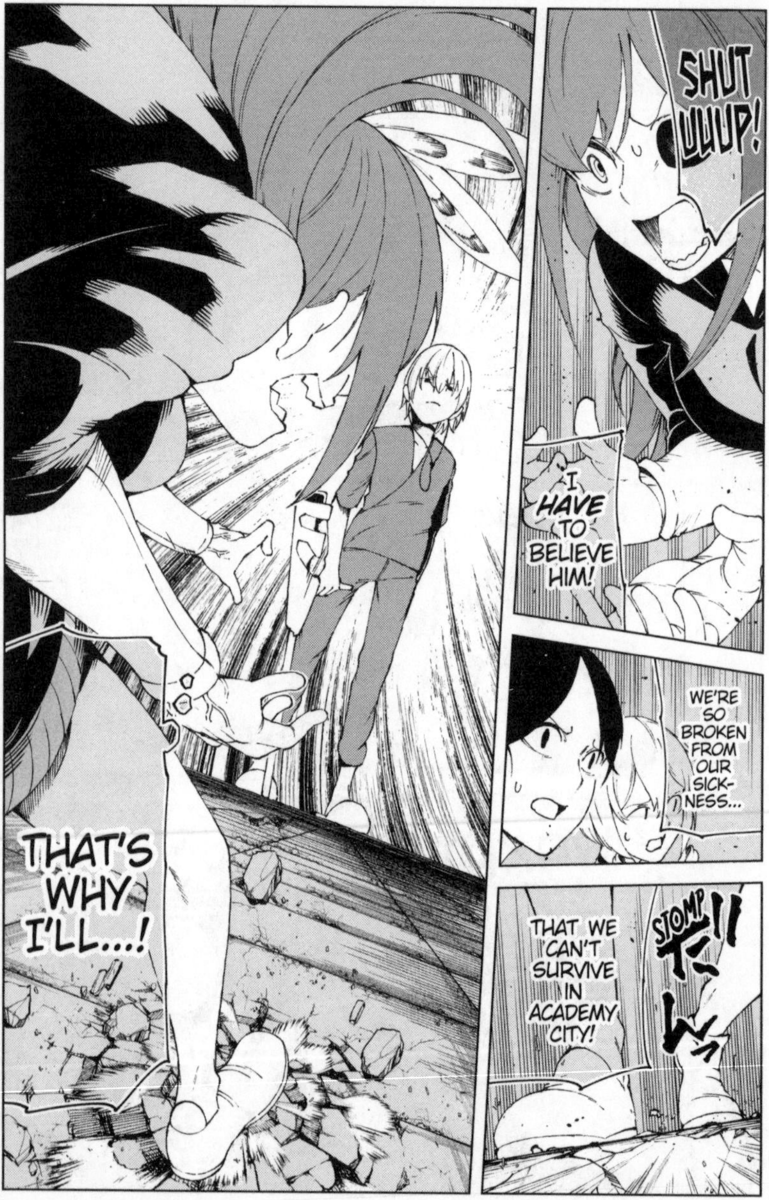
SHUT UUUP!
I HAVE TO BELIEVE HIM!
WE'RE SO BROKEN FROM OUR SICK-NESS...
THAT WE CAN'T SURVIVE IN ACADEMY CITY!
STOMP
THAT'S WHY I'LL...!

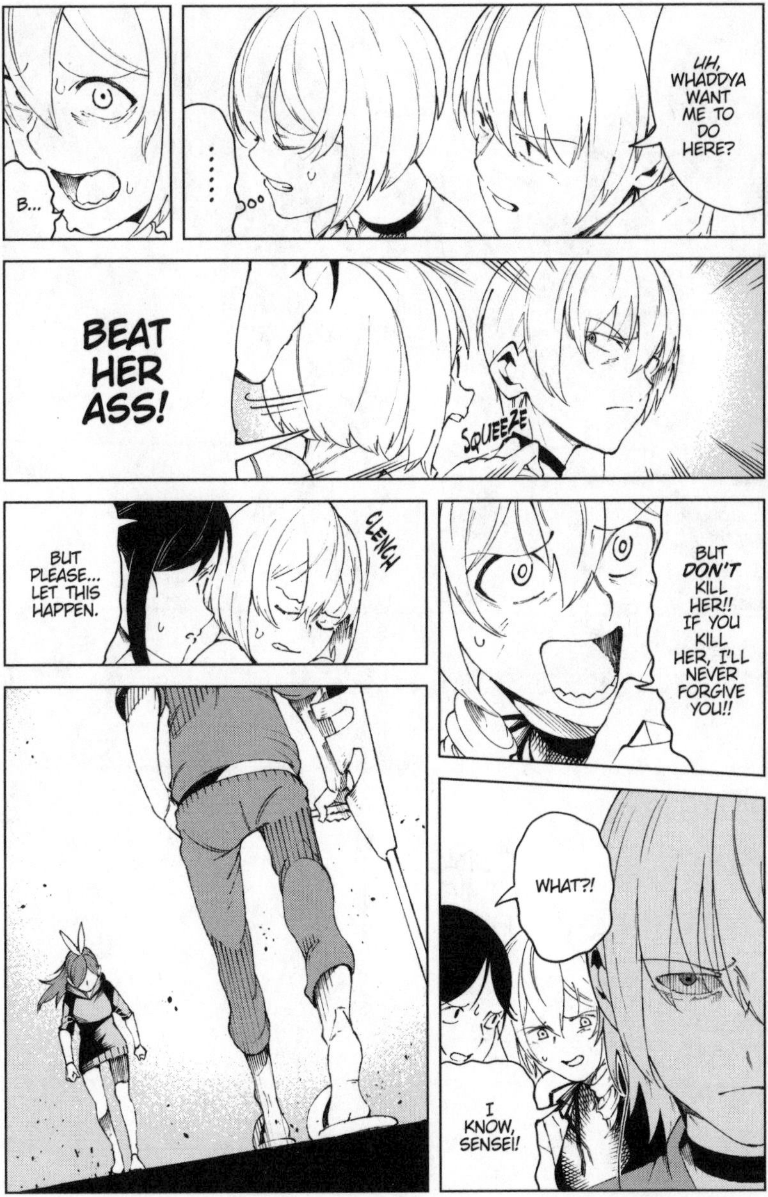
UH, WHADDYA WANT ME TO DO HERE?
......
B...
BEAT HER ASS!
SQUEEZE
BUT *DON'T* KILL HER!! IF YOU KILL HER, I'LL NEVER FORGIVE YOU!!
CLENCH
BUT PLEASE... LET THIS HAPPEN.
WHAT?!
I KNOW, SENSEI!

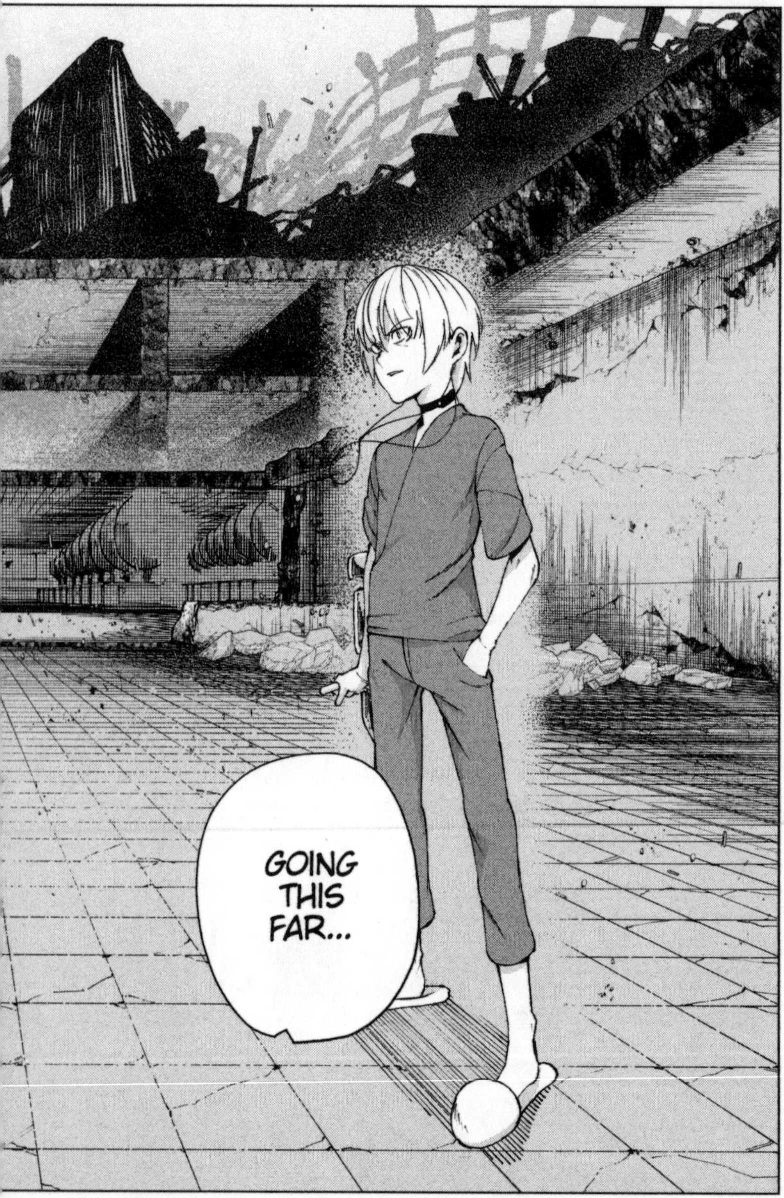
GOING THIS FAR...

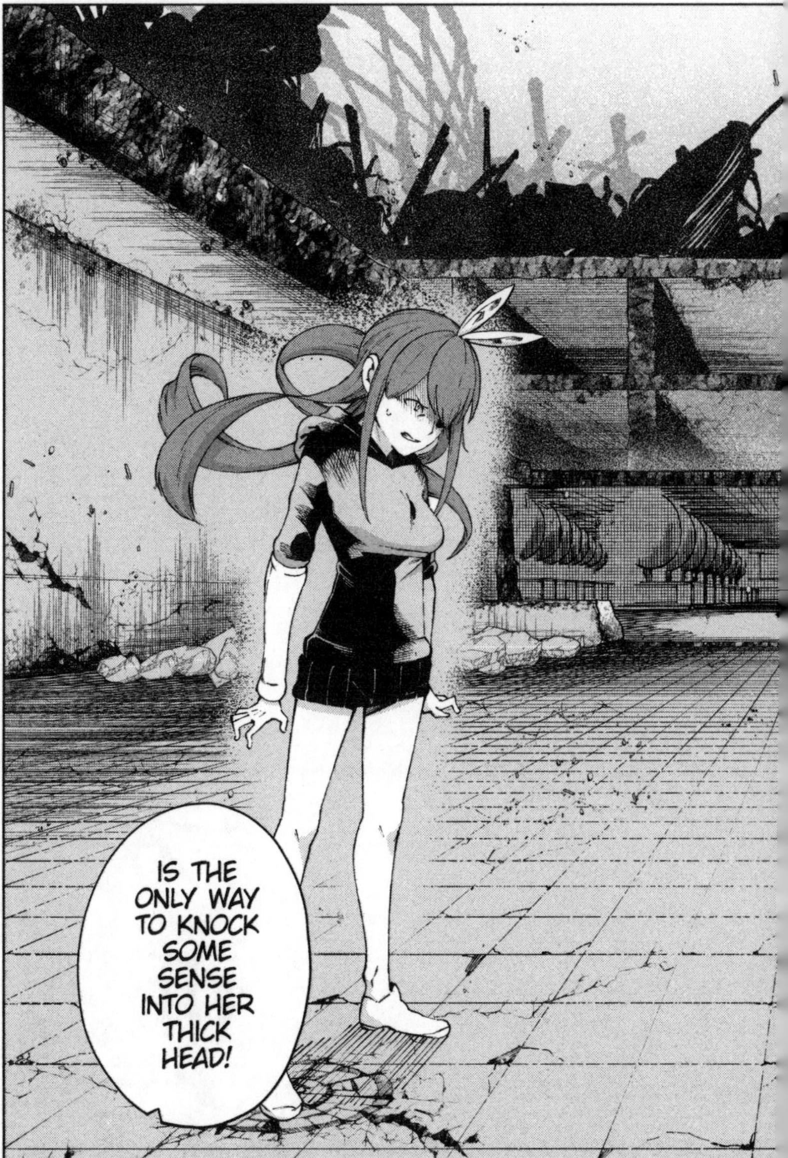
IS THE ONLY WAY TO KNOCK SOME SENSE INTO HER THICK HEAD!

とある科学の一方通行
アクセラレータ
とある魔術の禁書目録外伝

CHAPTER 61

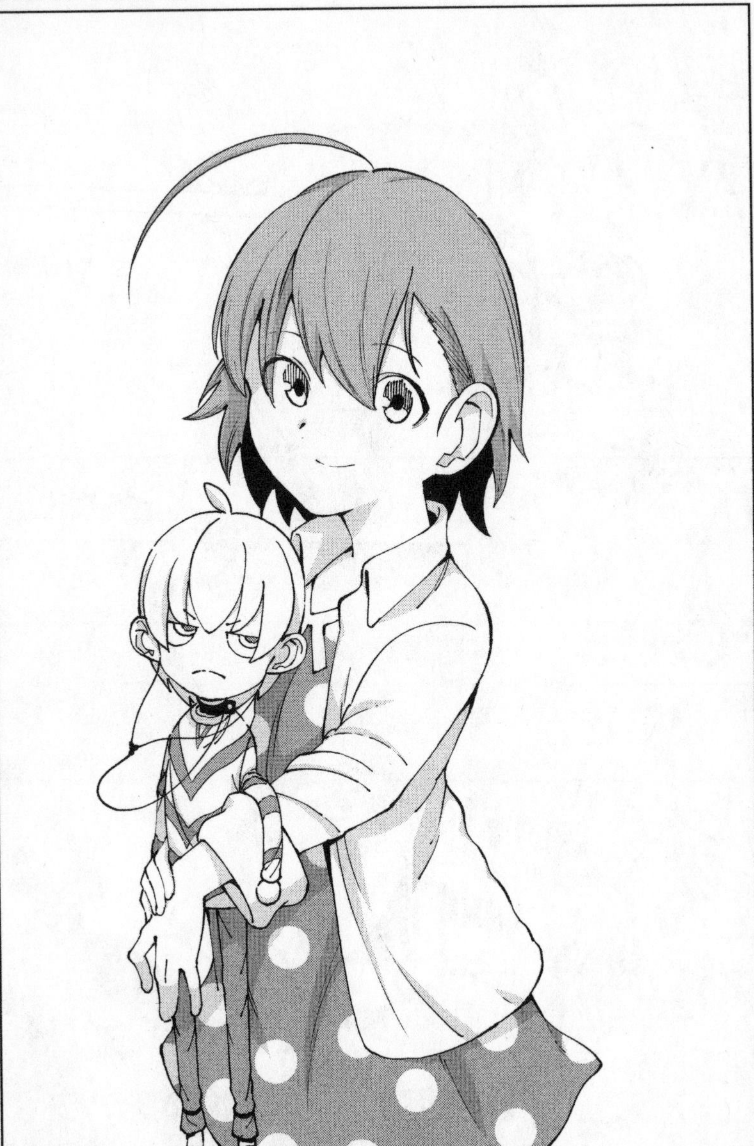

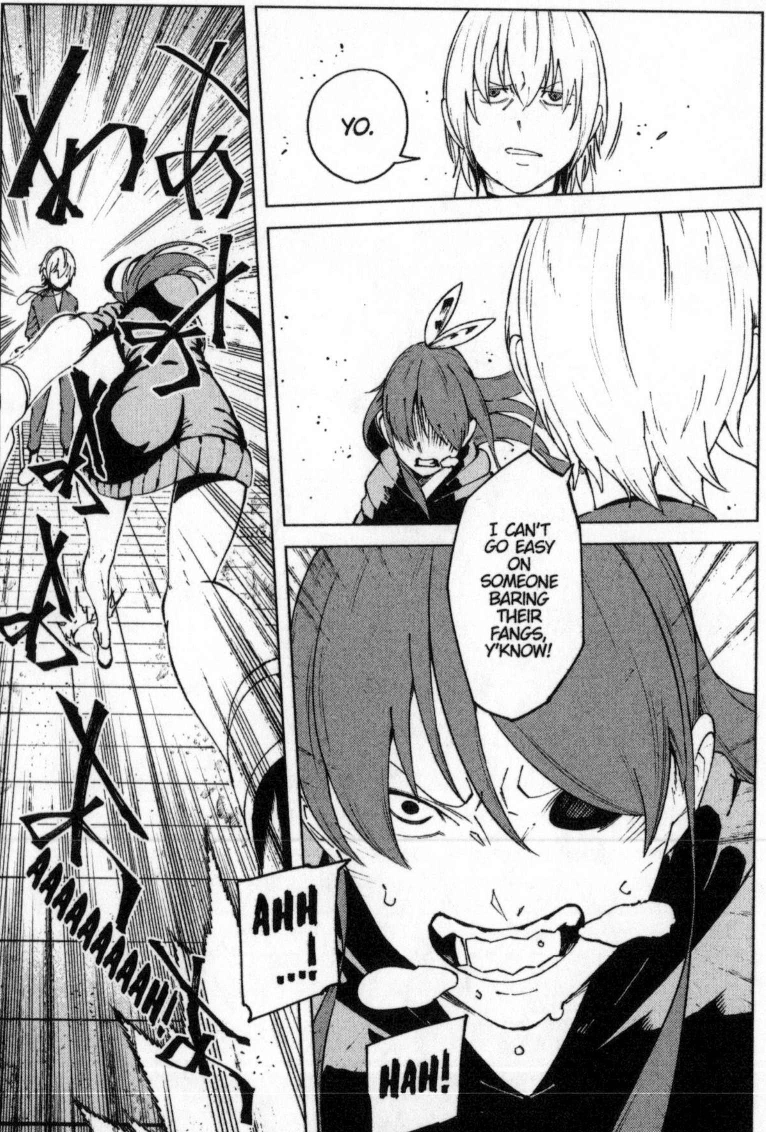
YO.
I CAN'T GO EASY ON SOMEONE BARING THEIR FANGS, Y'KNOW!
AHH ...!
HAH!
AAAAAAAAAH!!

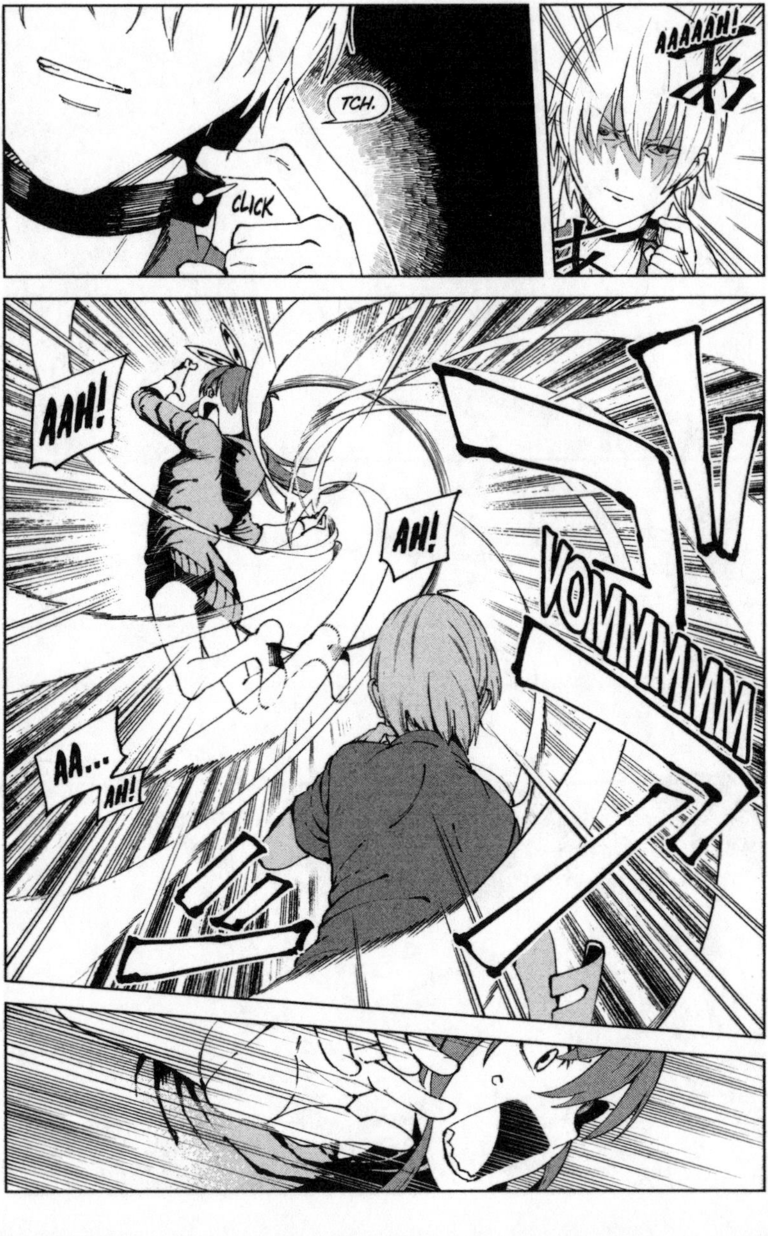
AAAAAH!
TCH.
CLICK
VOMMMMMM
AH!
AAH!
AA... AH!

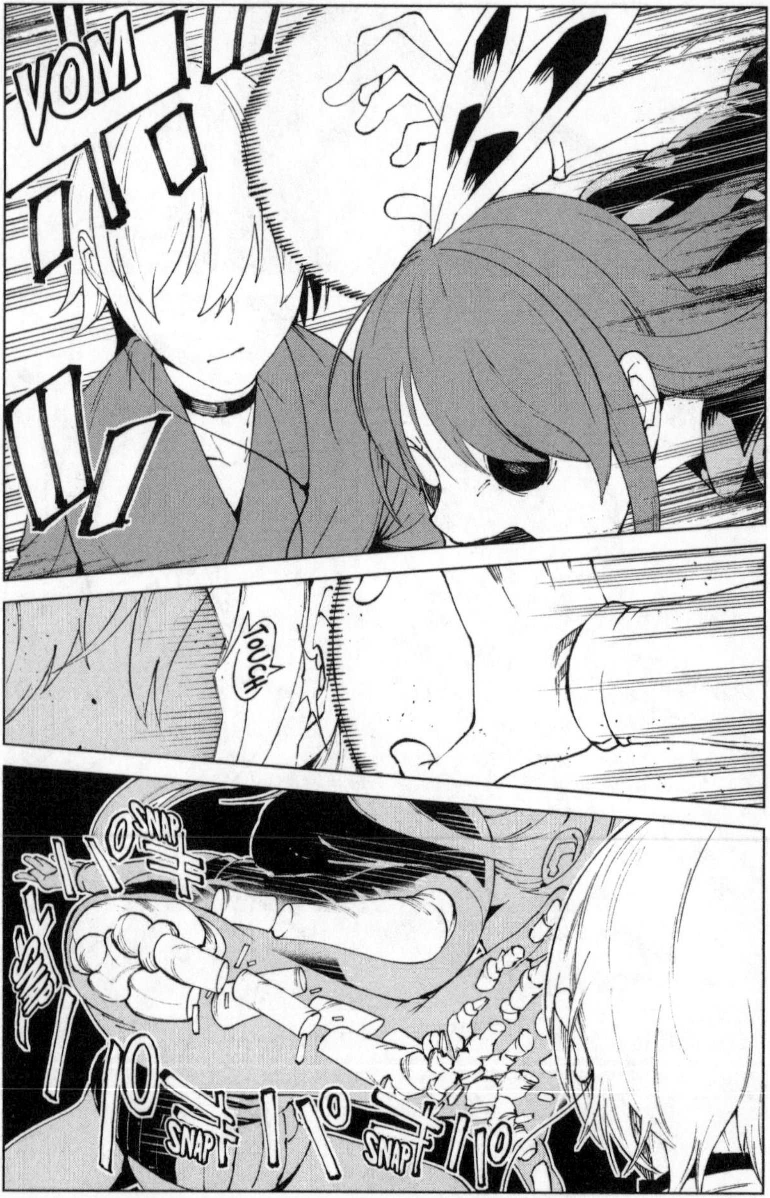
VOM
TOUCH
SNAP
SNAP
SNAP
SNAP

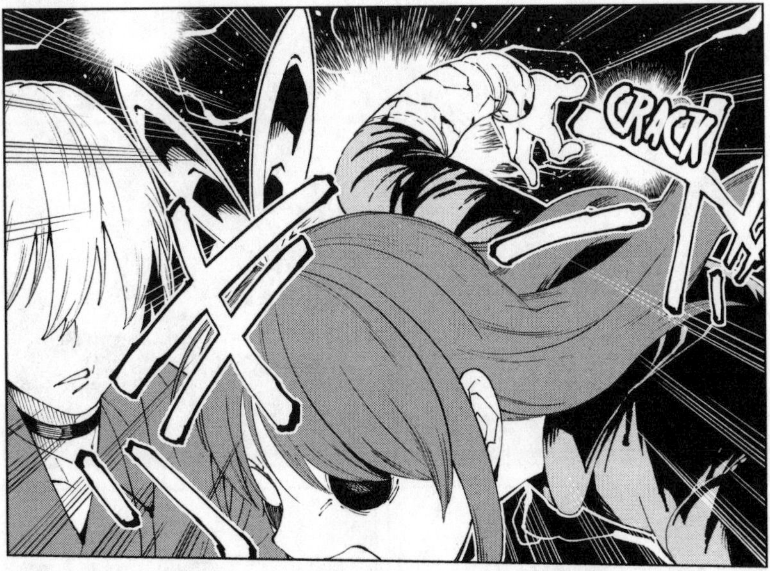
CRACK
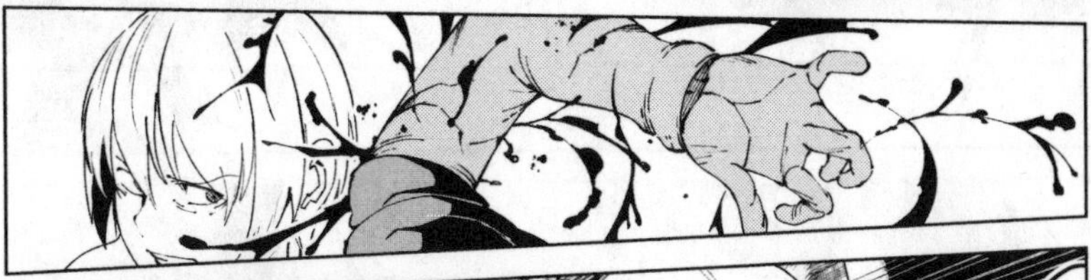
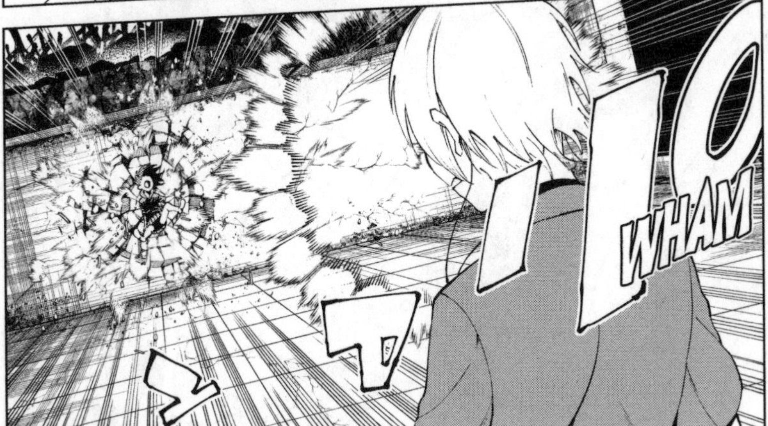
WHAM

CLUNK

CLUNK

STAGGER

CRICK

CRACK

FLOP

SOME-THING LIKE THIS...

S...

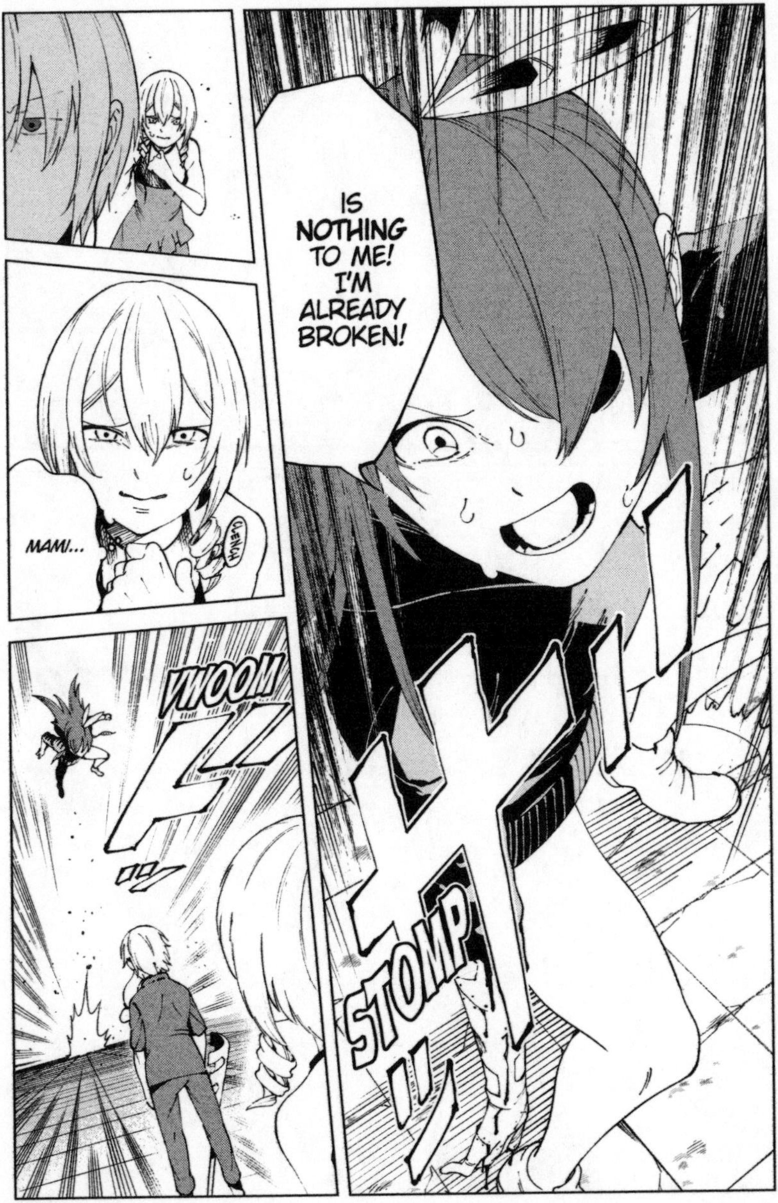
IS NOTHING TO ME! I'M ALREADY BROKEN!
STOMP
MAMI...
CLENCH
VWOOM

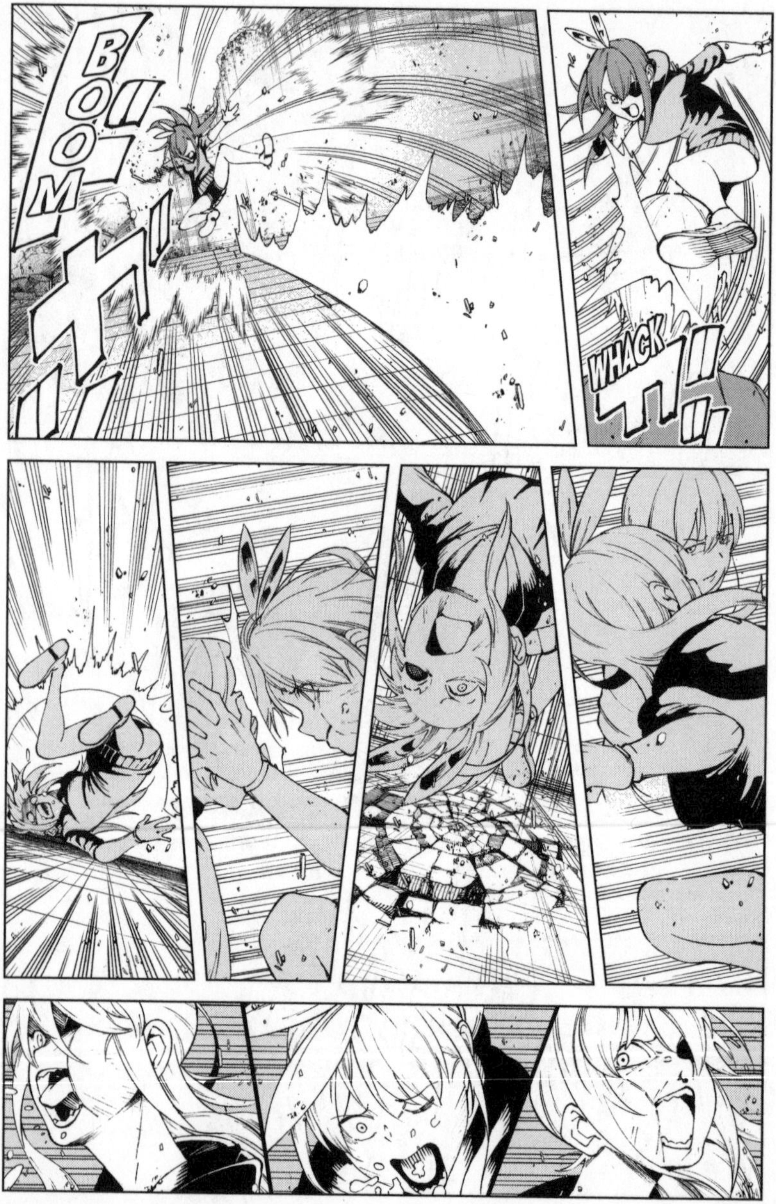
WHACK
BOOM

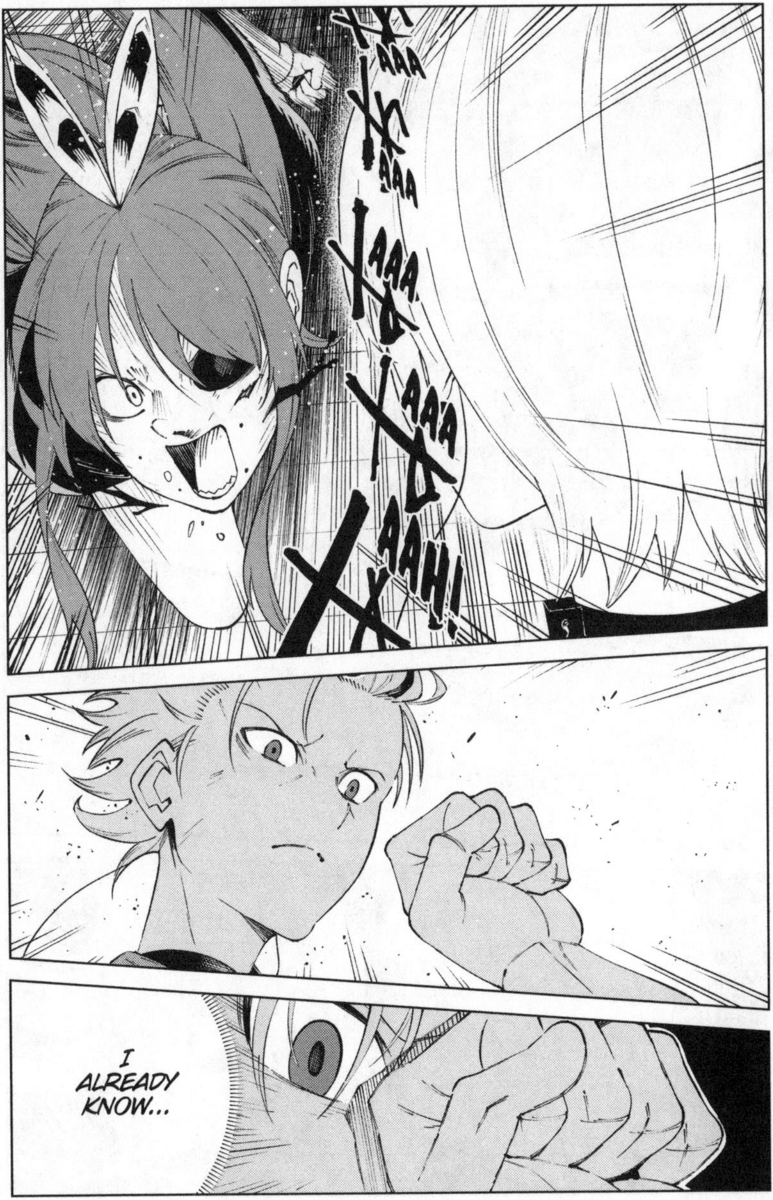
AAAAAAAAAAAAAAH!
I ALREADY KNOW...

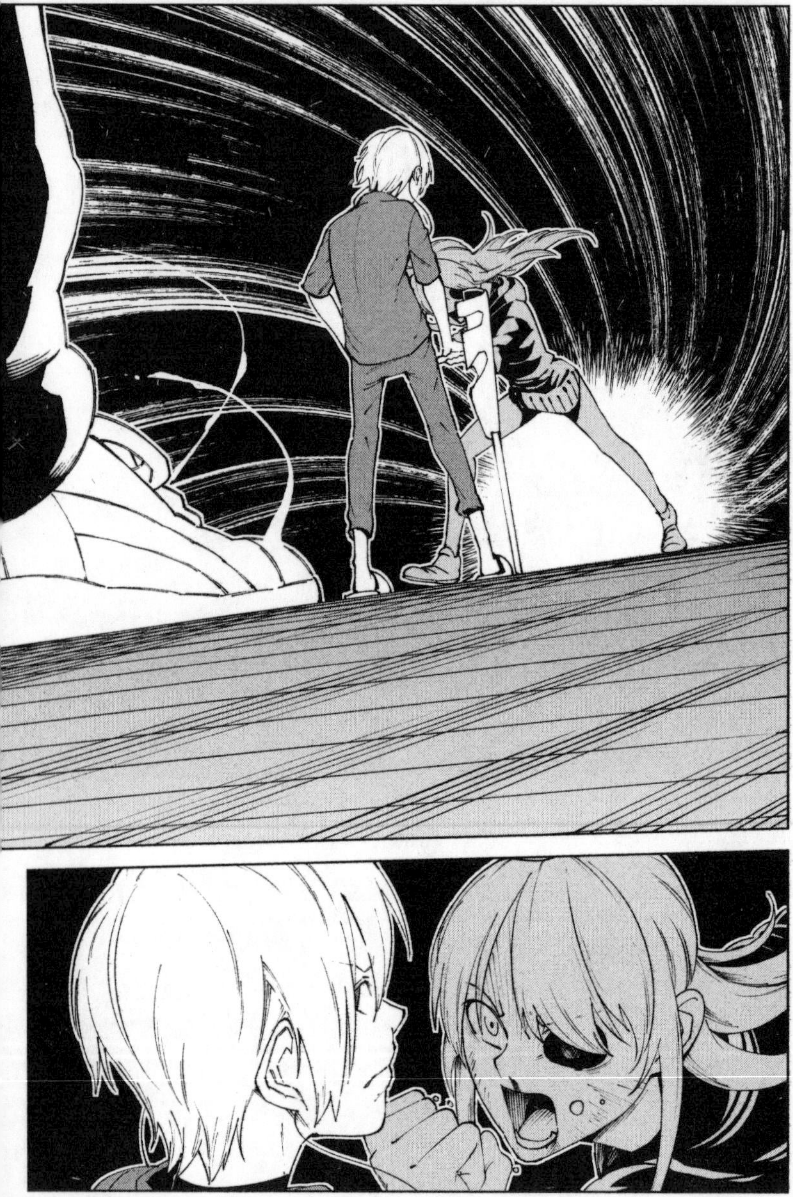

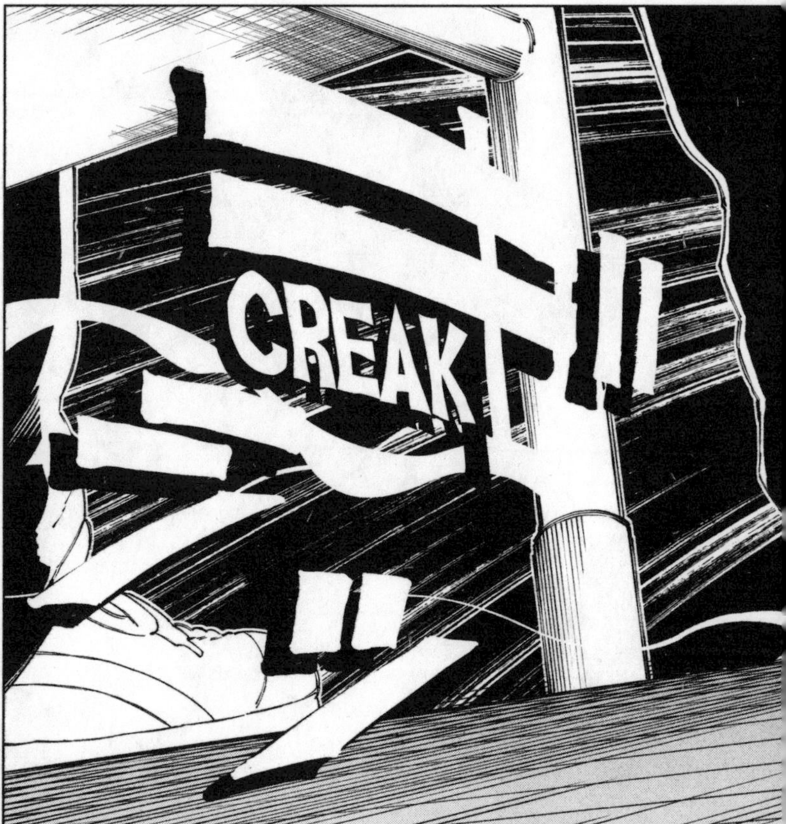
CREAK
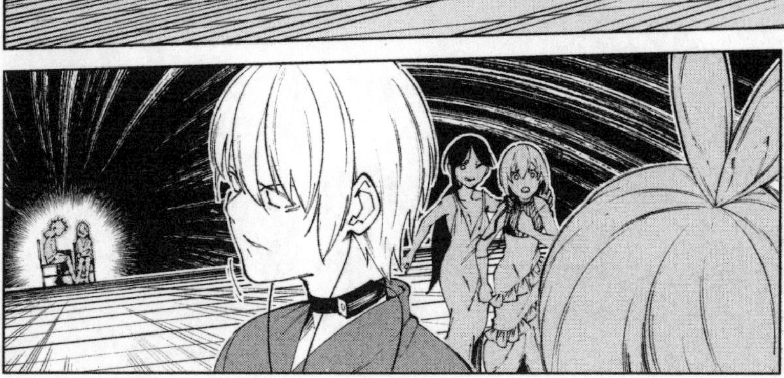

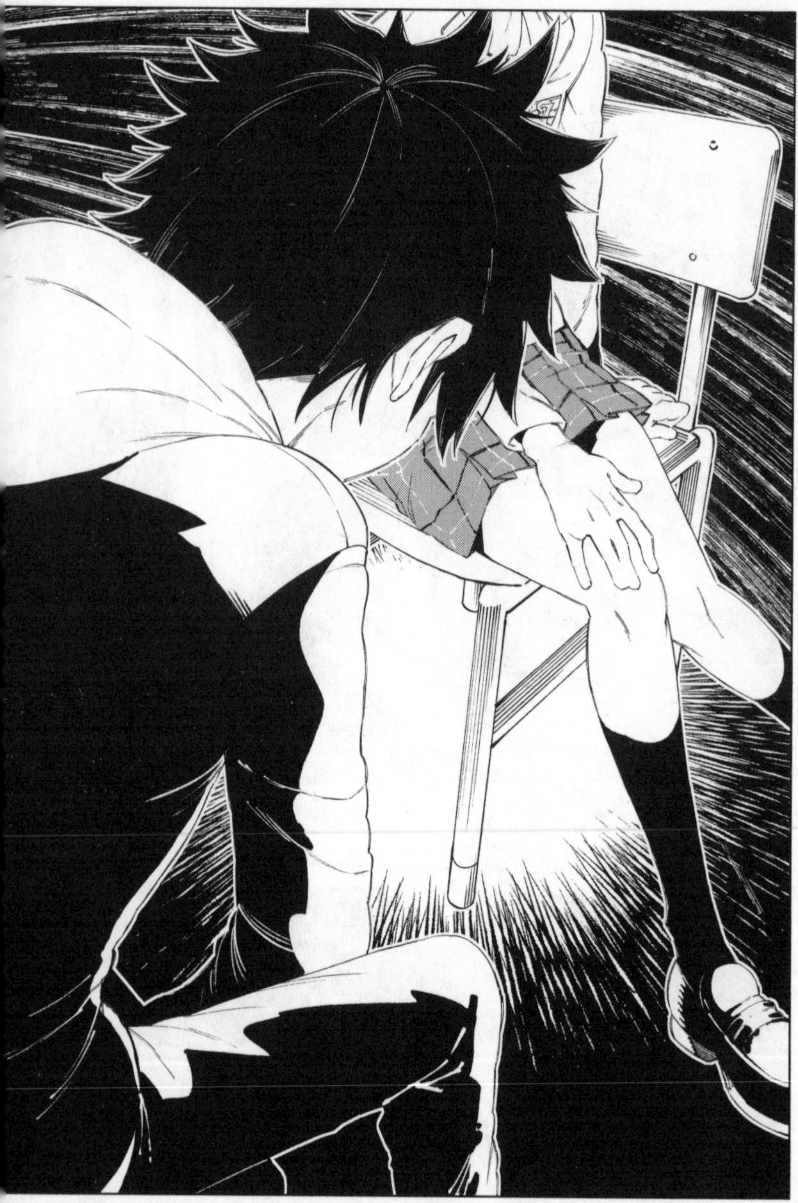

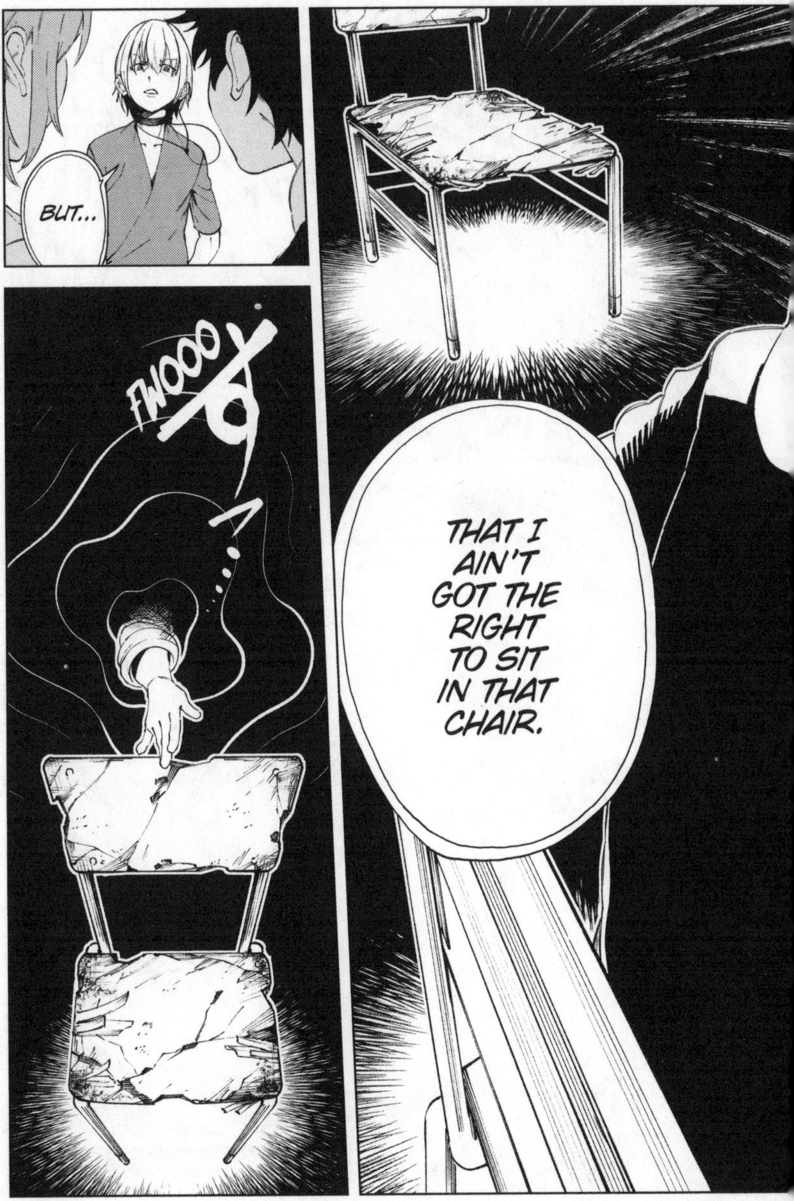
THAT I AIN'T GOT THE RIGHT TO SIT IN THAT CHAIR.
BUT...
FWOOO
...

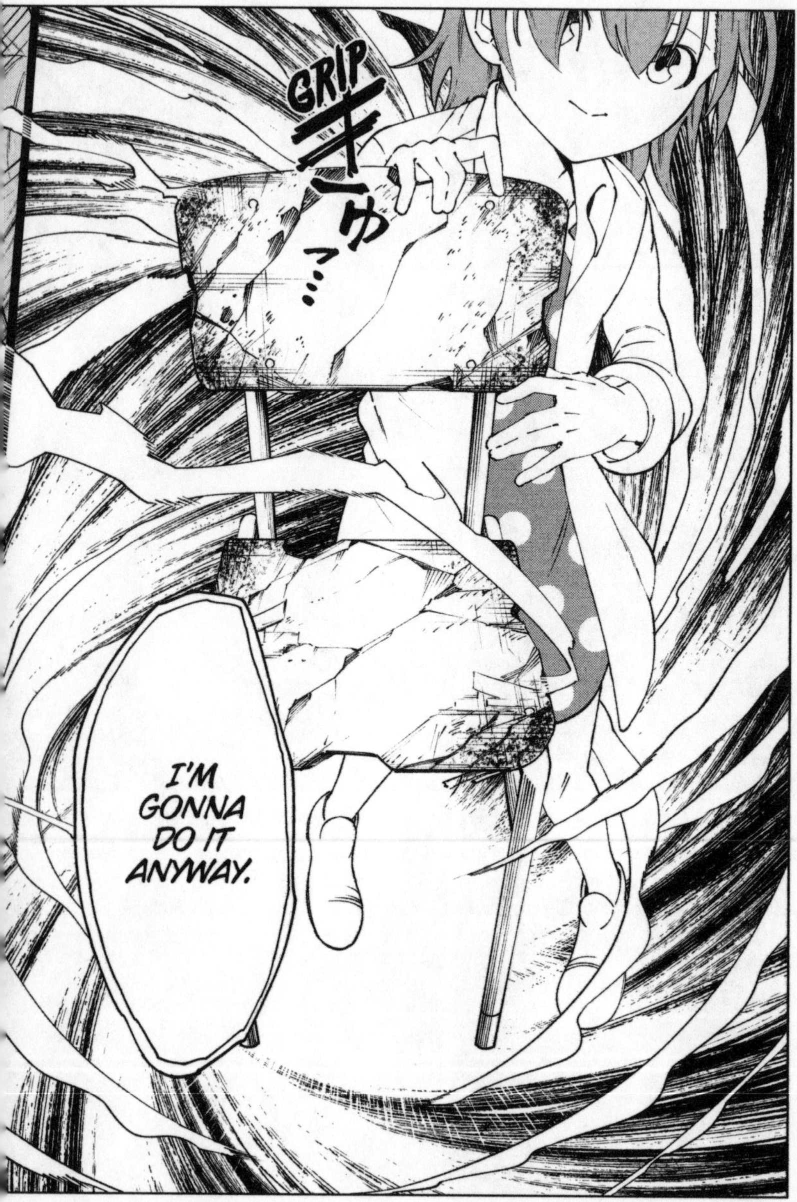
GRIP
I'M GONNA DO IT ANYWAY.

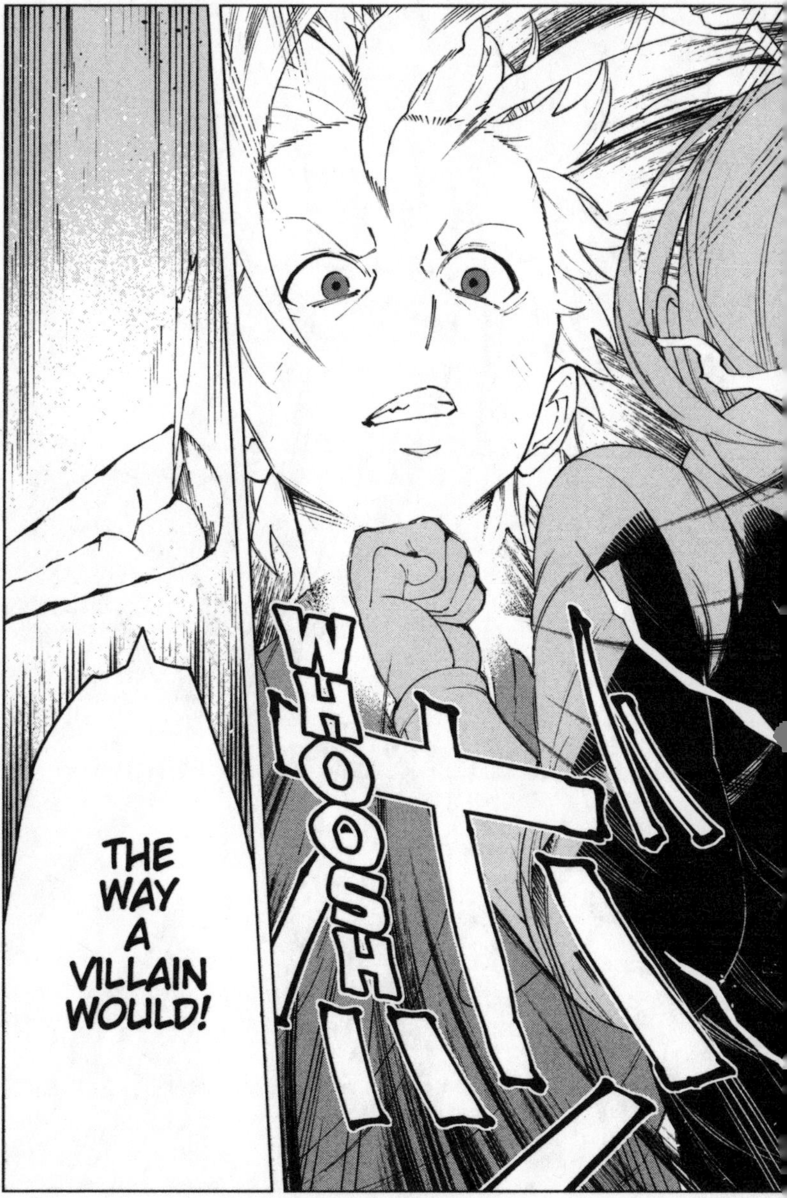
WHOOSH
THE WAY A VILLAIN WOULD!

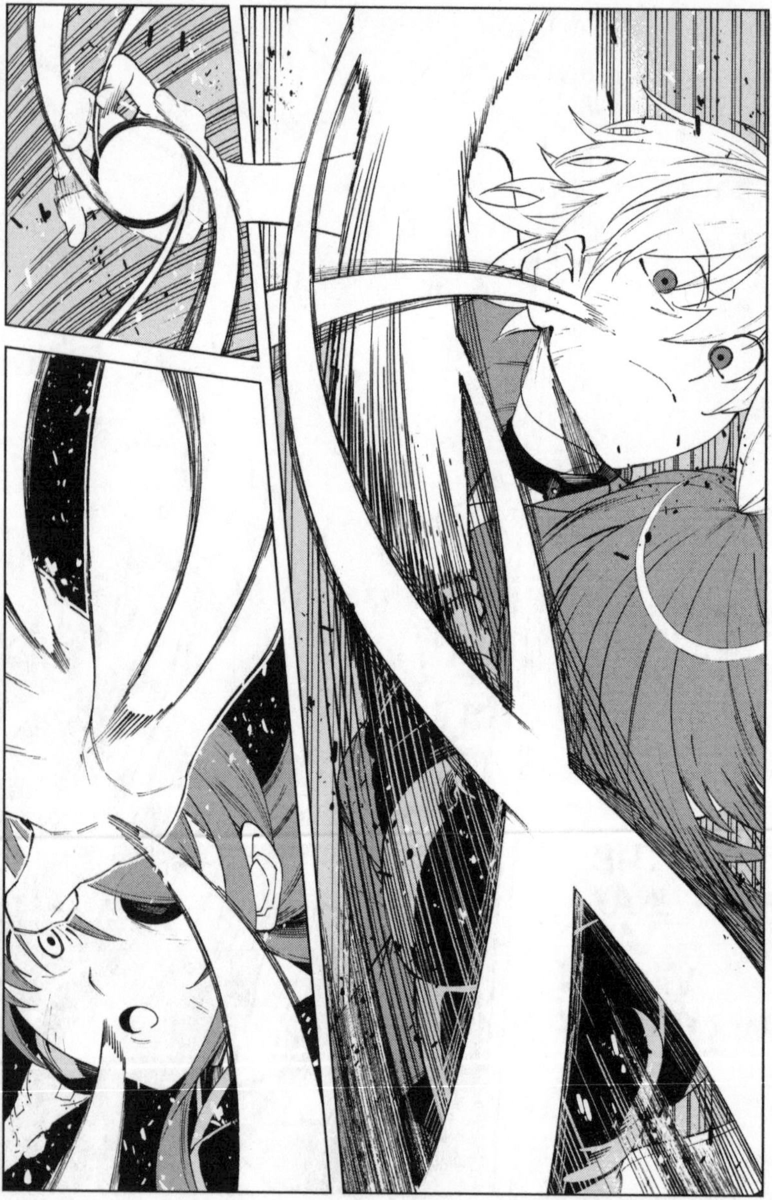

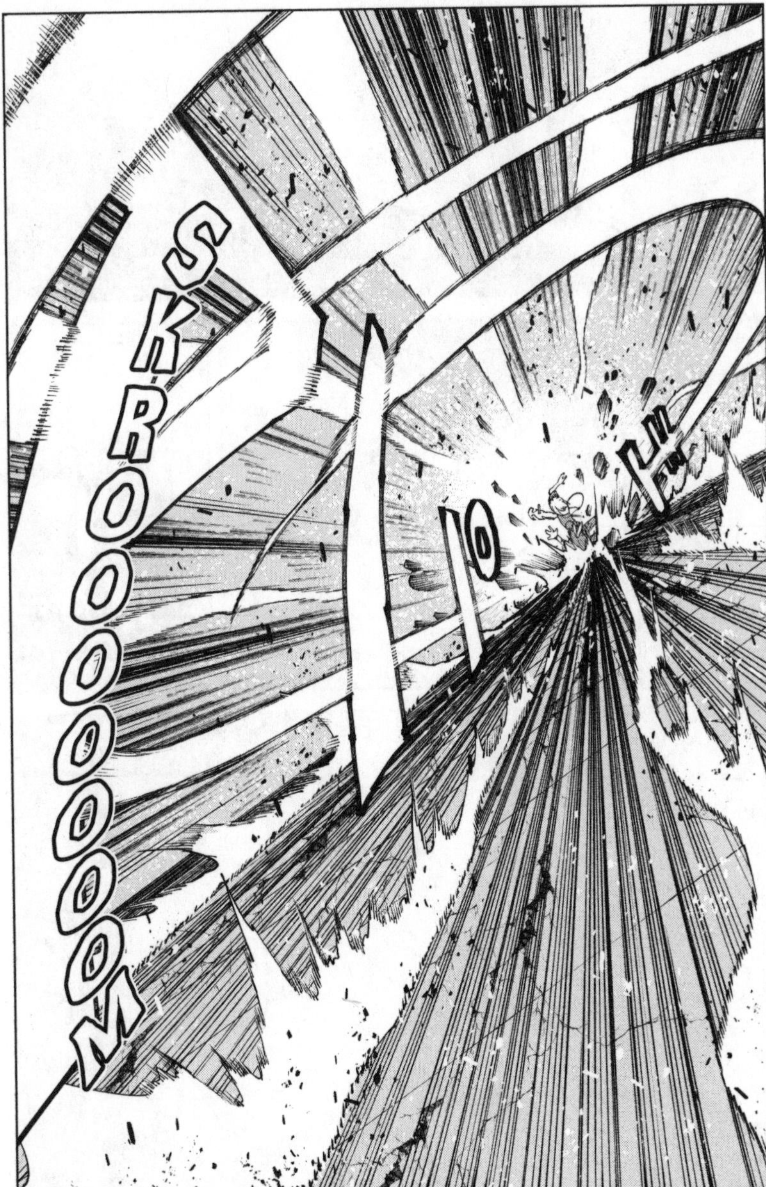
SKROOOOOOOM

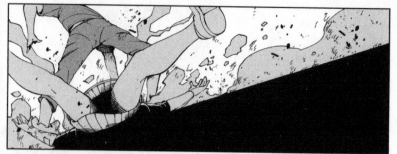

ACCELER-ATOR, YOU...!

W-WAIT...

PA... THUMP

WOULD YOU TWO CHILL? DAMN.

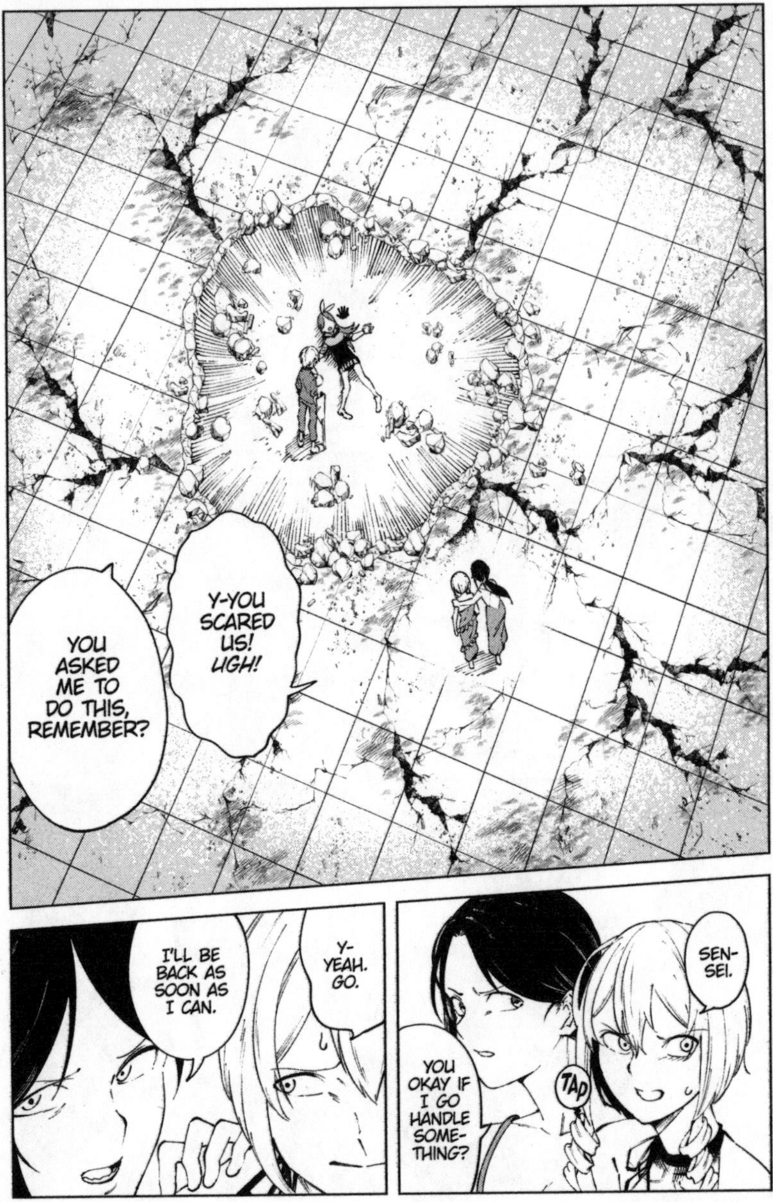
Y-YOU SCARED US! UGH!
YOU ASKED ME TO DO THIS, REMEMBER?
SEN-SEI.
TAP
YOU OKAY IF I GO HANDLE SOME-THING?
Y-YEAH. GO.
I'LL BE BACK AS SOON AS I CAN.

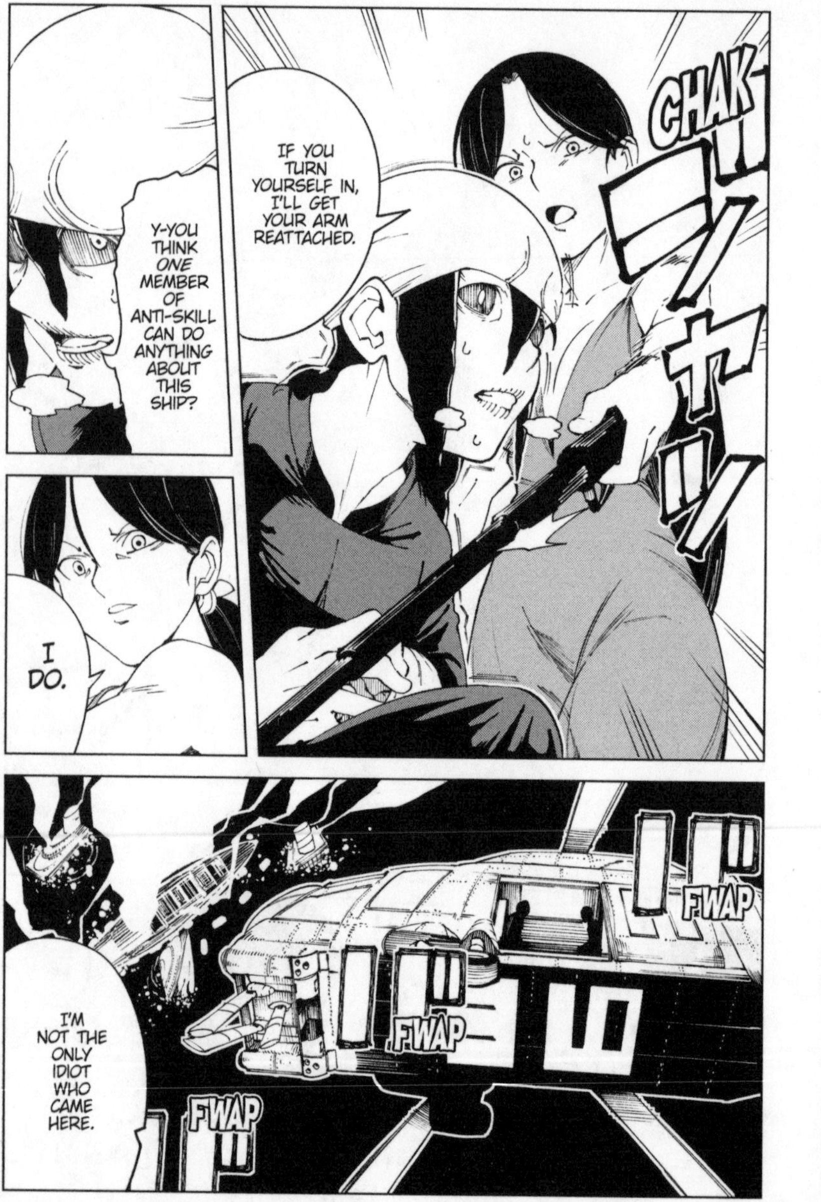
CHAK
IF YOU TURN YOURSELF IN, I'LL GET YOUR ARM REATTACHED.
Y-YOU THINK *ONE* MEMBER OF ANTI-SKILL CAN DO ANYTHING ABOUT THIS SHIP?
I DO.
FWAP
FWAP
FWAP
I'M NOT THE ONLY IDIOT WHO CAME HERE.

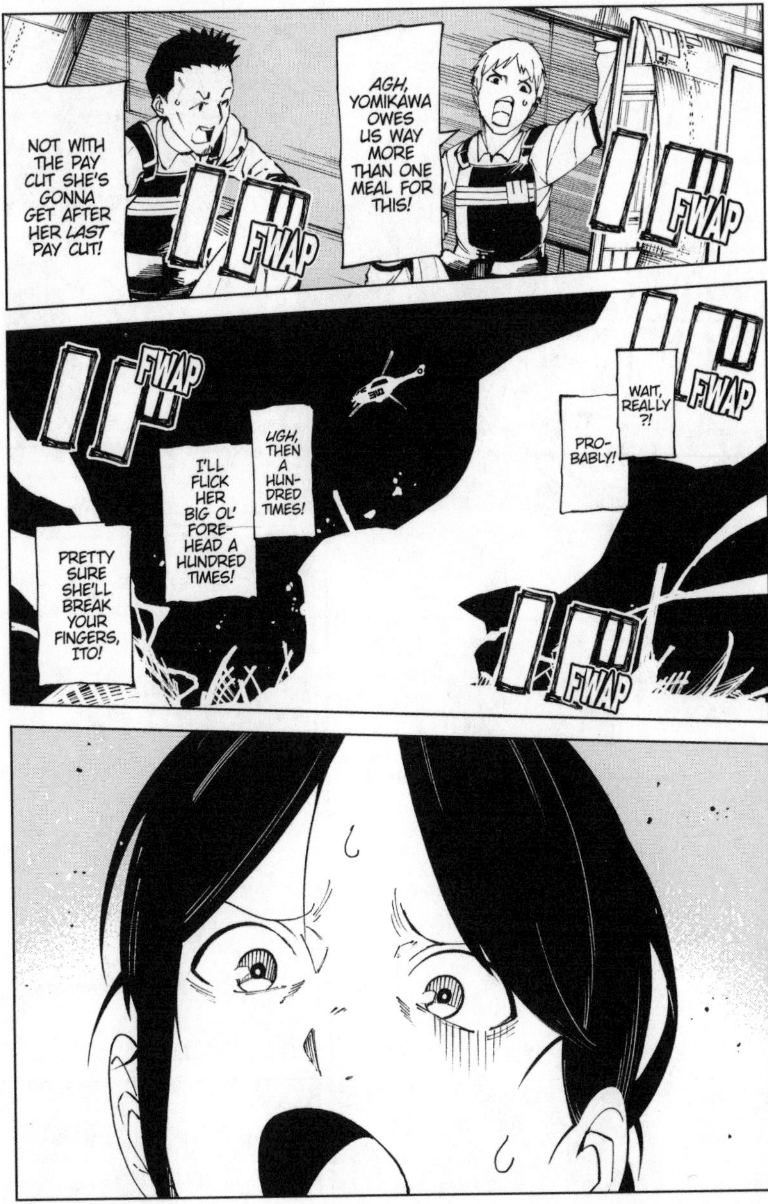
AGH, YOMIKAWA OWES US WAY MORE THAN ONE MEAL FOR THIS!
FWAP
NOT WITH THE PAY CUT SHE'S GONNA GET AFTER HER *LAST* PAY CUT!
FWAP
FWAP
WAIT, REALLY?!
PROBABLY!
UGH, THEN A HUNDRED TIMES!
I'LL FLICK HER BIG OL' FOREHEAD A HUNDRED TIMES!
FWAP
PRETTY SURE SHE'LL BREAK YOUR FINGERS, ITO!
FWAP

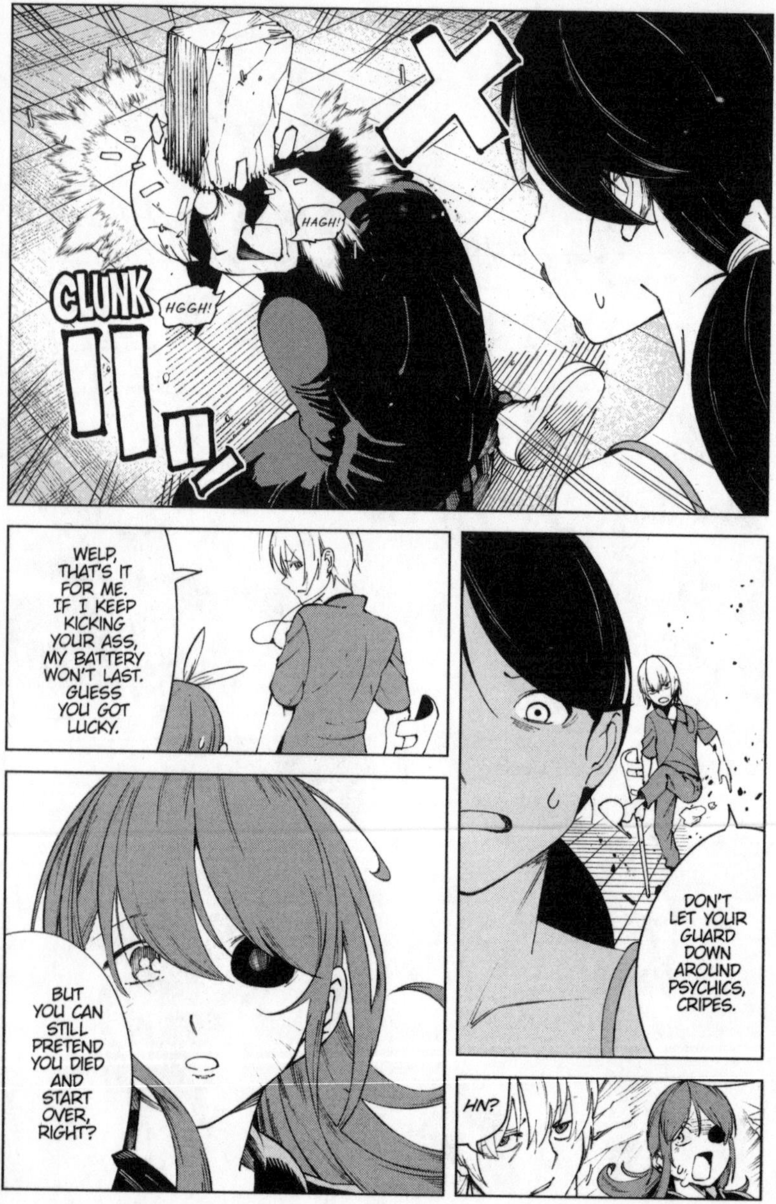
HAGH!
HGGH!
CLUNK
DON'T LET YOUR GUARD DOWN AROUND PSYCHICS, CRIPES.
WELP, THAT'S IT FOR ME. IF I KEEP KICKING YOUR ASS, MY BATTERY WON'T LAST. GUESS YOU GOT LUCKY.
BUT YOU CAN STILL PRETEND YOU DIED AND START OVER, RIGHT?
HN?

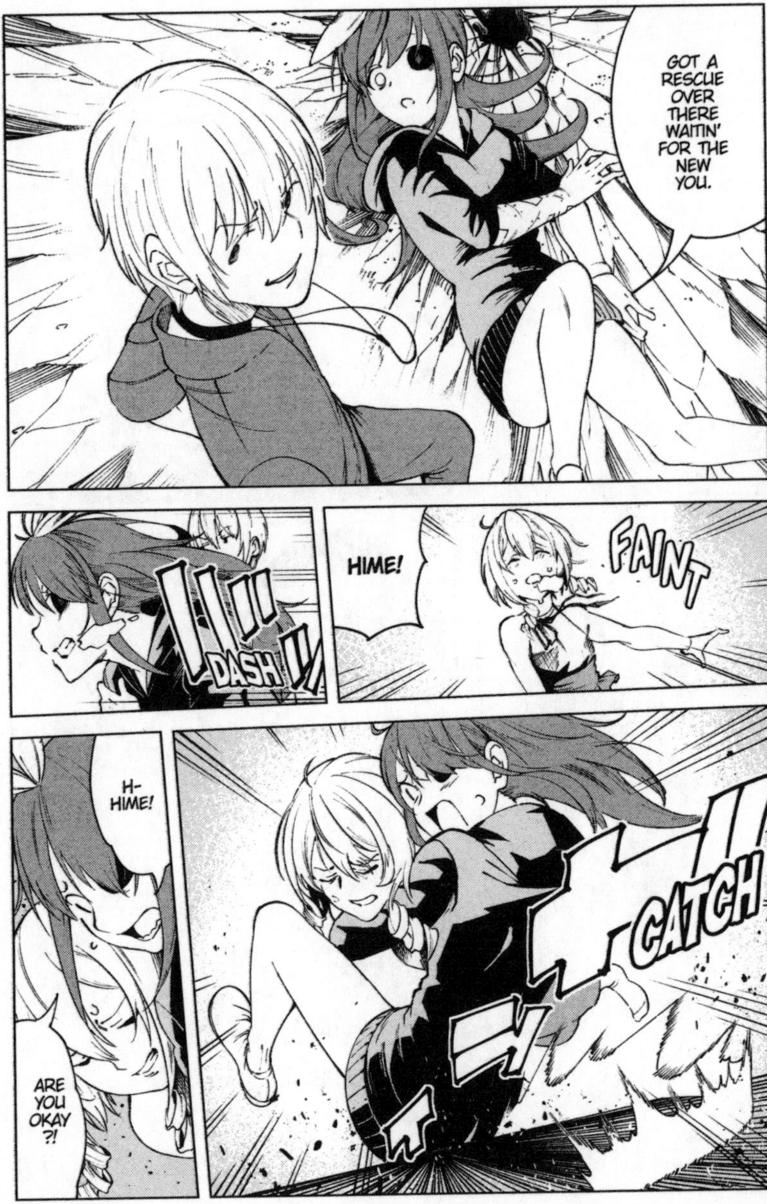
GOT A RESCUE OVER THERE WAITIN' FOR THE NEW YOU.
HIME!
FAINT
DASH
CATCH
H- HIME!
ARE YOU OKAY ?!

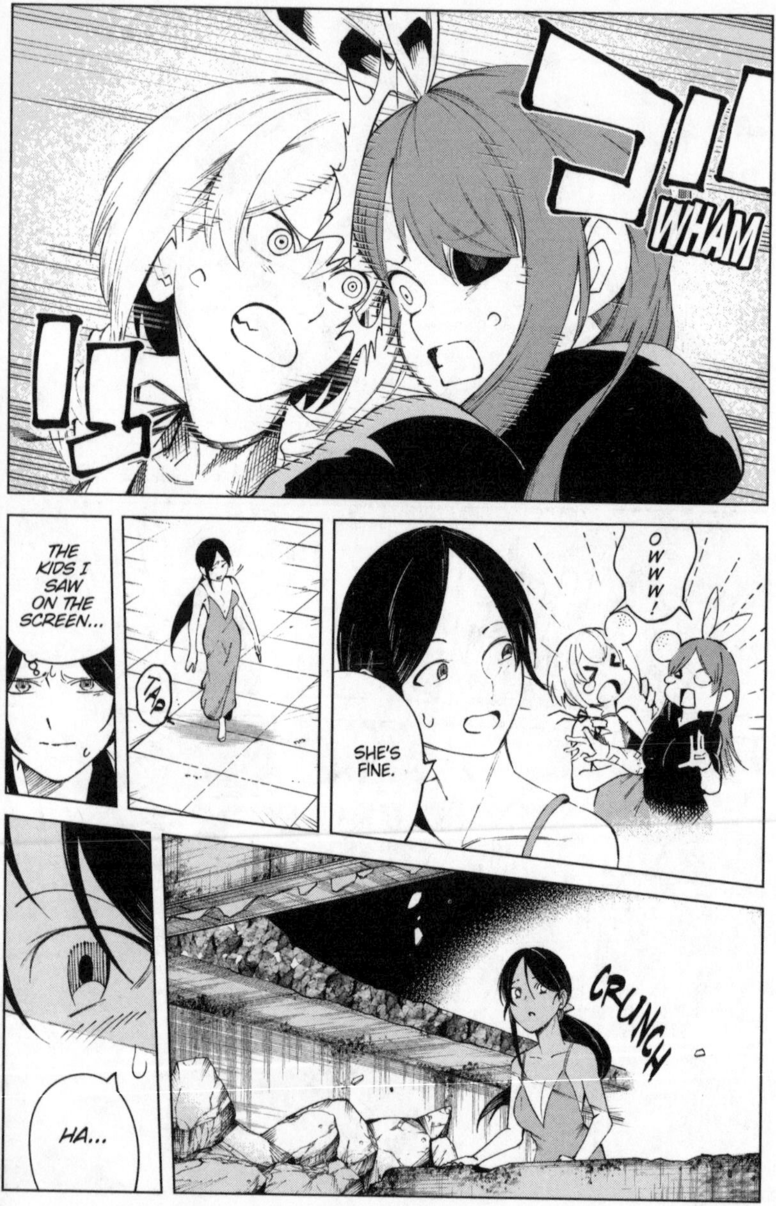
WHAM
OWWW!
SHE'S FINE.
TAP
THE KIDS I SAW ON THE SCREEN...
CRUNCH
HA...

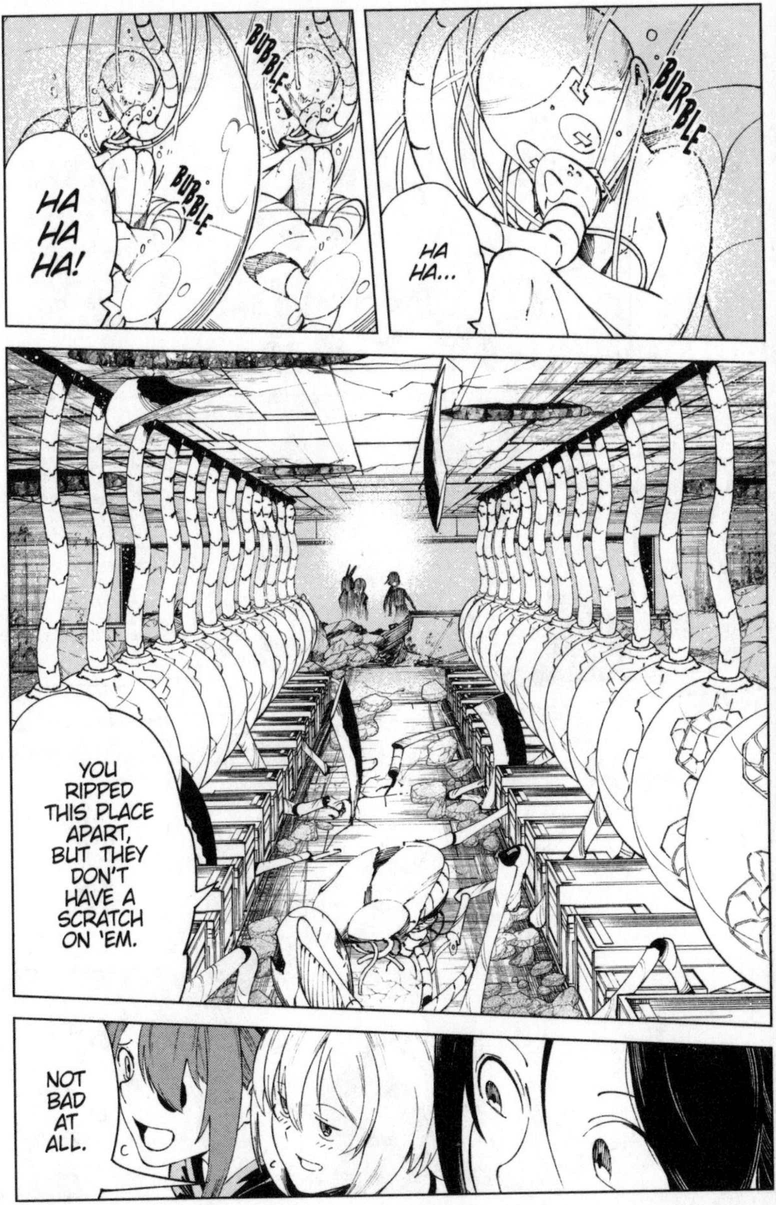
BURBLE
HA HA...
BUBBLE
BUBBLE
HA HA HA!
YOU RIPPED THIS PLACE APART, BUT THEY DON'T HAVE A SCRATCH ON 'EM.
NOT BAD AT ALL.

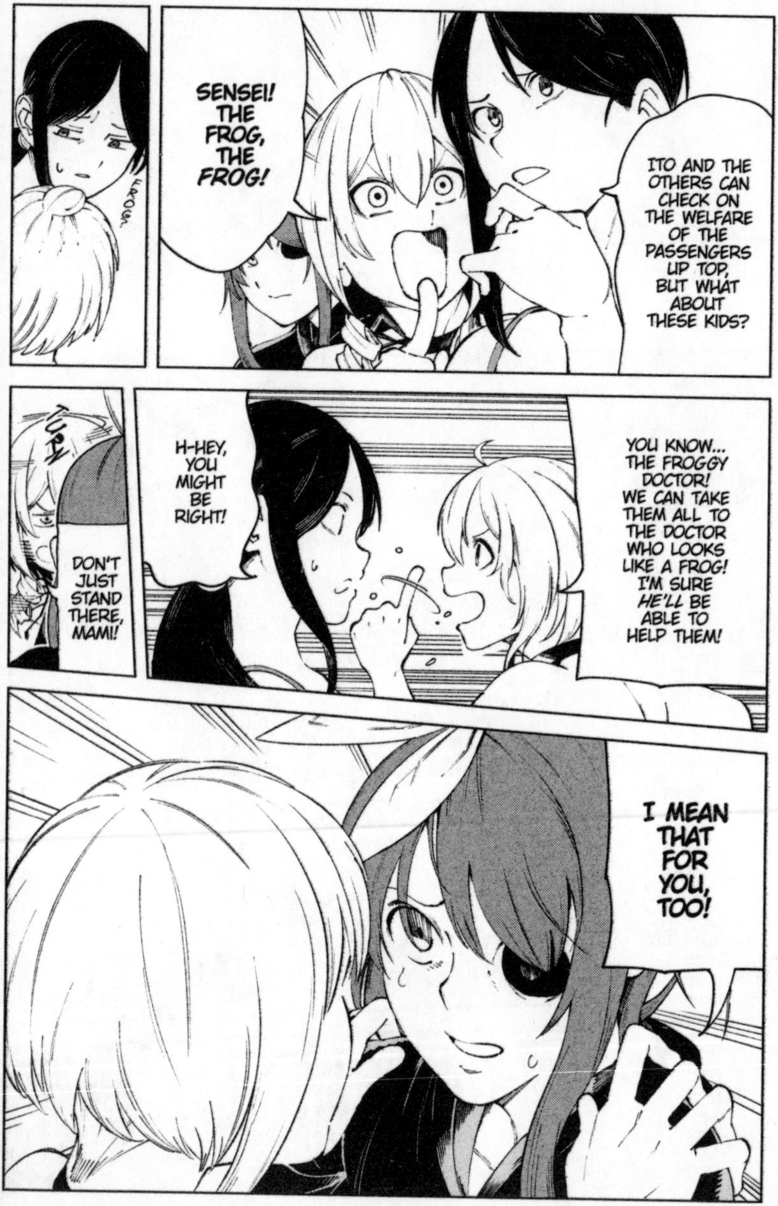
ITO AND THE OTHERS CAN CHECK ON THE WELFARE OF THE PASSENGERS UP TOP, BUT WHAT ABOUT THESE KIDS?
SENSEI! THE FROG, THE FROG!
FROG.
YOU KNOW... THE FROGGY DOCTOR! WE CAN TAKE THEM ALL TO THE DOCTOR WHO LOOKS LIKE A FROG! I'M SURE *HE'LL* BE ABLE TO HELP THEM!
H-HEY, YOU MIGHT BE RIGHT!
TURN
DON'T JUST STAND THERE, MAMI!
I MEAN THAT FOR YOU, TOO!

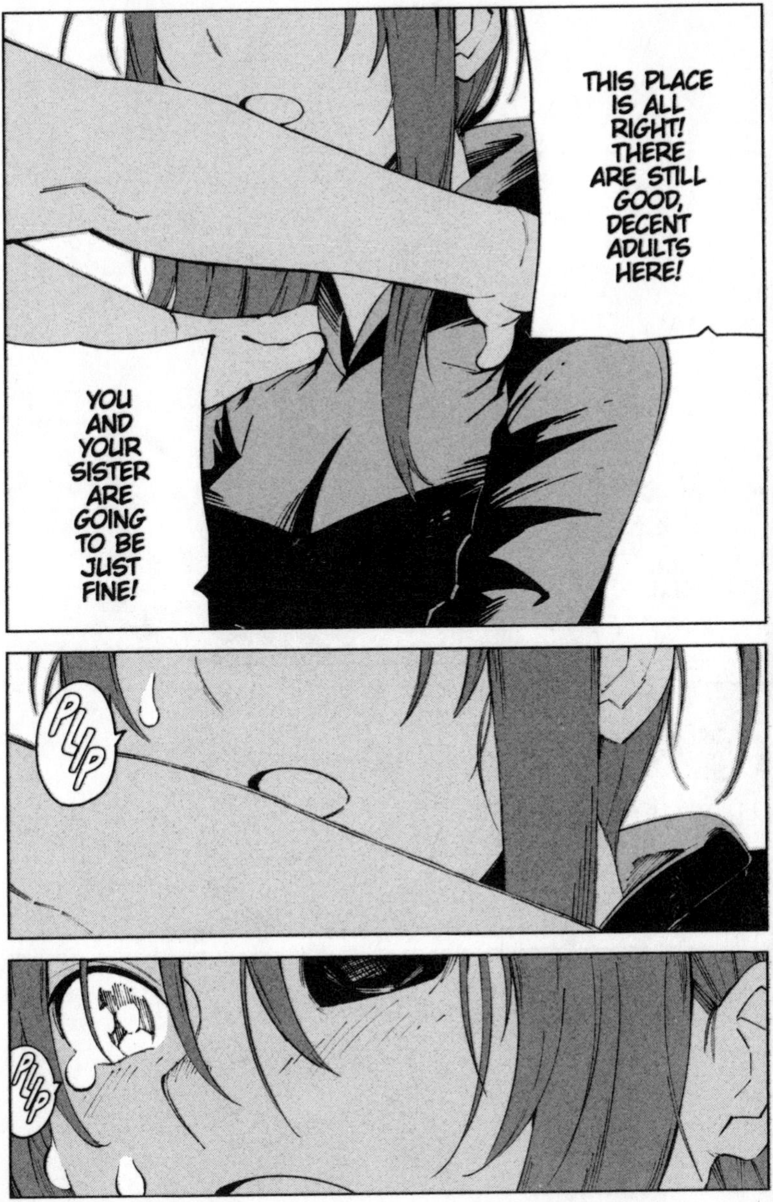
THIS PLACE IS ALL RIGHT! THERE ARE STILL GOOD, DECENT ADULTS HERE!
YOU AND YOUR SISTER ARE GOING TO BE JUST FINE!
PLIP
PLIP

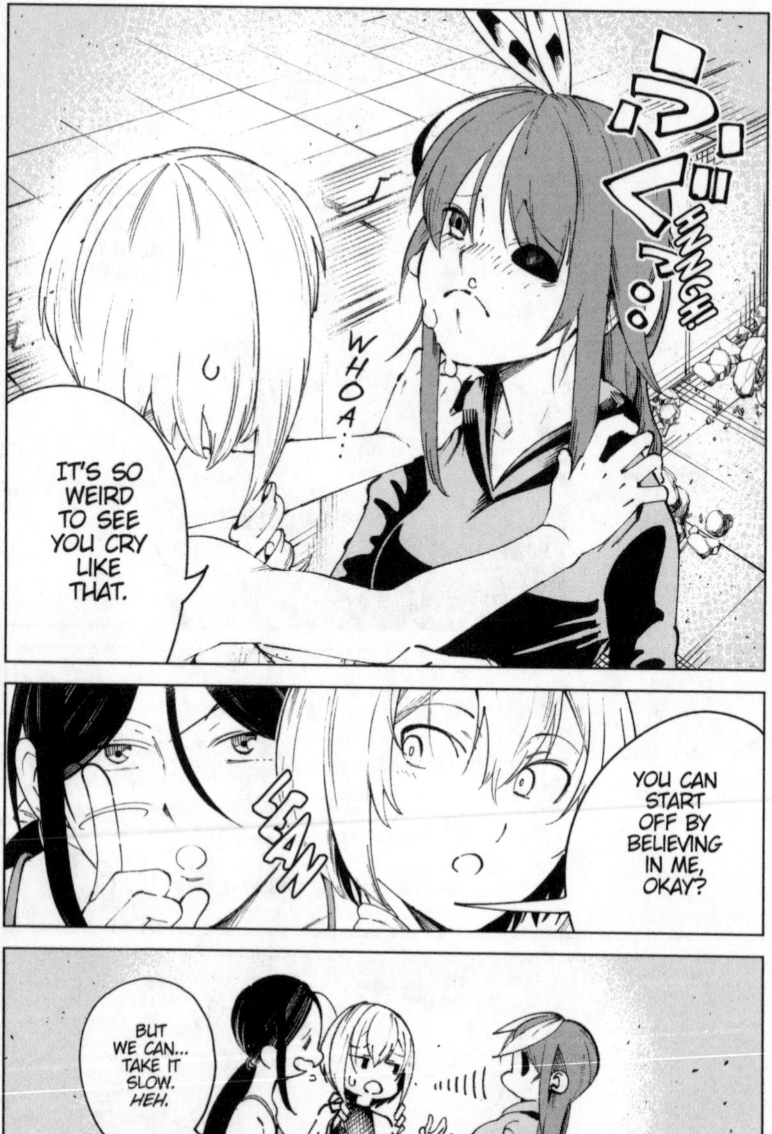
うぐぅ…
HNNGH!
WHOA...
IT'S SO WEIRD TO SEE YOU CRY LIKE THAT.
YOU CAN START OFF BY BELIEVING IN ME, OKAY?
LEAN
BUT WE CAN... TAKE IT SLOW. HEH.

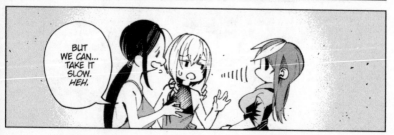

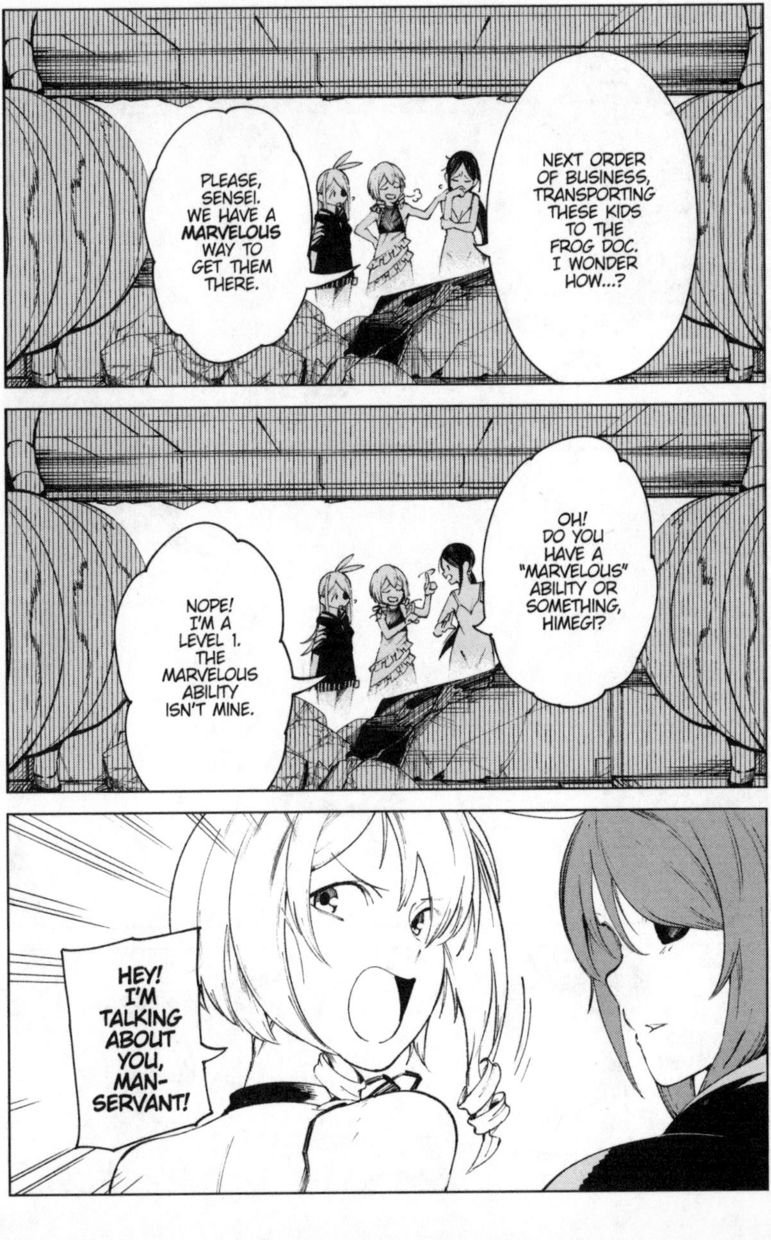
NEXT ORDER OF BUSINESS, TRANSPORTING THESE KIDS TO THE FROG DOC. I WONDER HOW...?
PLEASE, SENSEI. WE HAVE A **MARVELOUS** WAY TO GET THEM THERE.
OH! DO YOU HAVE A "MARVELOUS" ABILITY OR SOMETHING, HIMEGI?
NOPE! I'M A LEVEL 1. THE MARVELOUS ABILITY ISN'T MINE.
HEY! I'M TALKING ABOUT YOU, MAN-SERVANT!

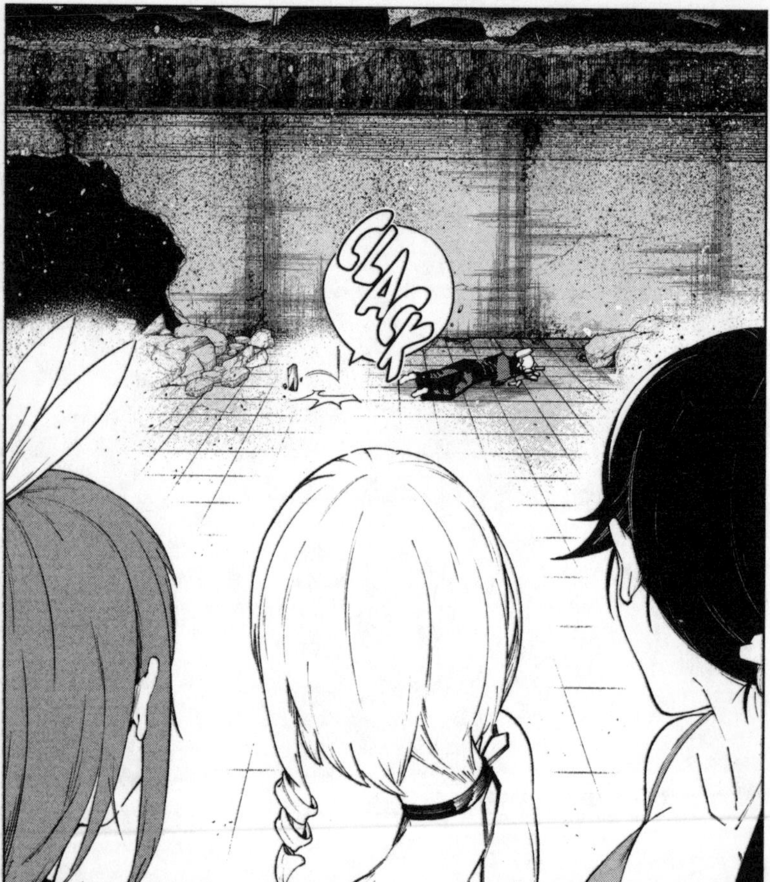
CLACK
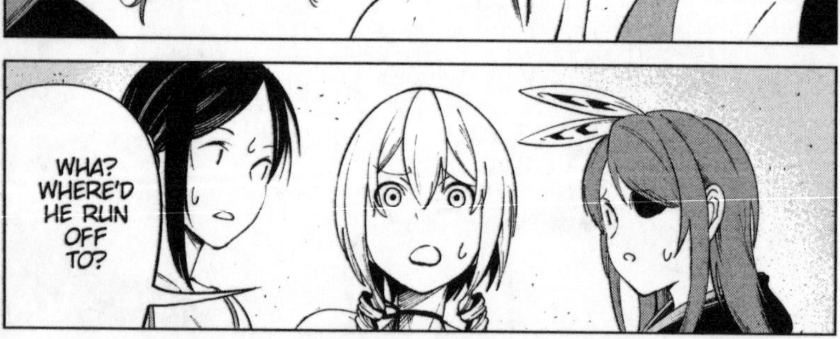
WHA? WHERE'D HE RUN OFF TO?

a certain
SCIENTIFIC
ACCELERATOR

とある科学の一方通行
アクセラレータ
とある魔術の禁書目録外伝

CHAPTER 62

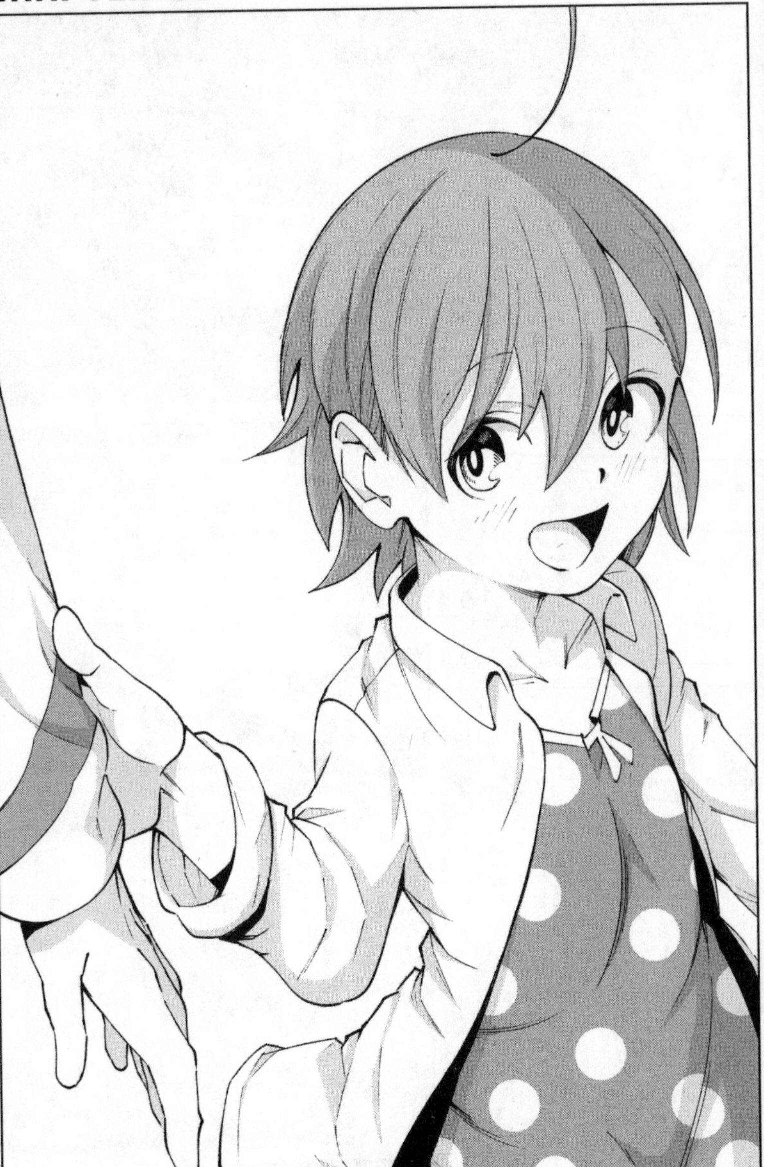

SPLSH
SPLSH
SPLSH

YOU'LL PAY DEARLY FOR THIS, ACCELERATOR.

CLOSE

CREAK

WE'RE DEPARTING NOW. ALL CARS, PLEASE ESCORT.

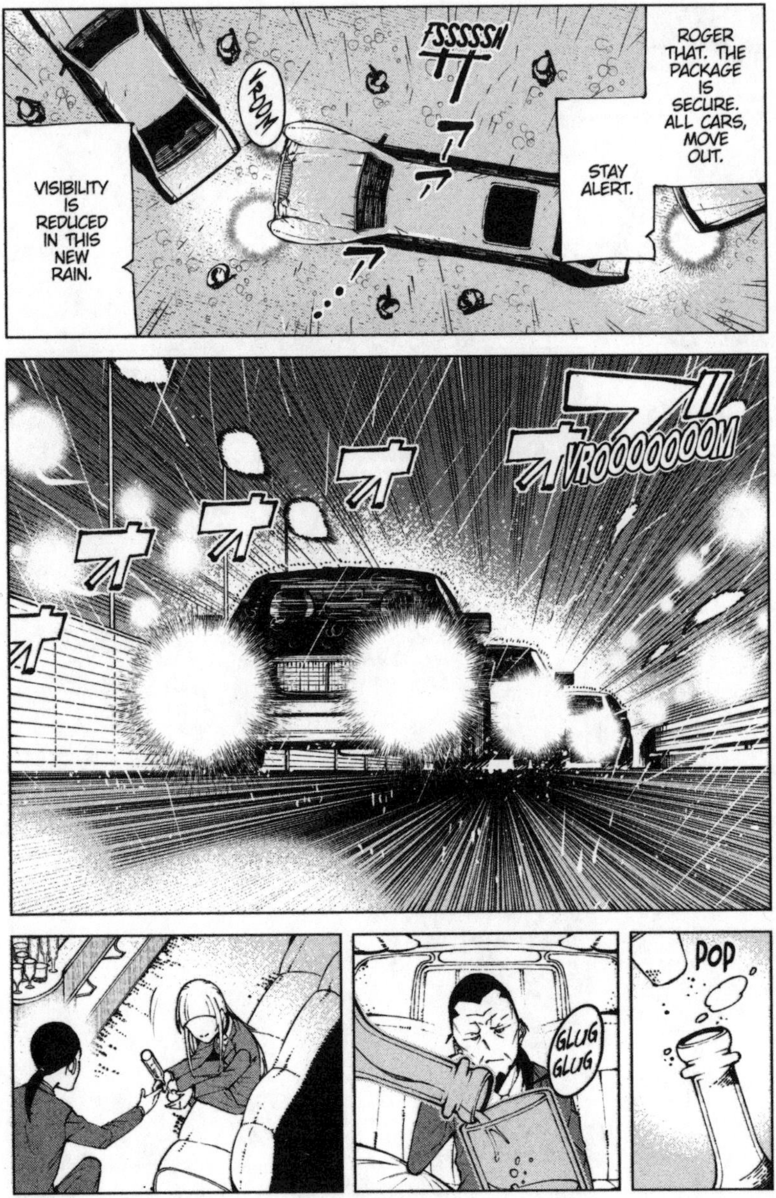
ROGER THAT. THE PACKAGE IS SECURE. ALL CARS, MOVE OUT.
STAY ALERT.
FSSSSSH
VROOM
VISIBILITY IS REDUCED IN THIS NEW RAIN.
VROOOOOOOOM
POP
GLUG GLUG

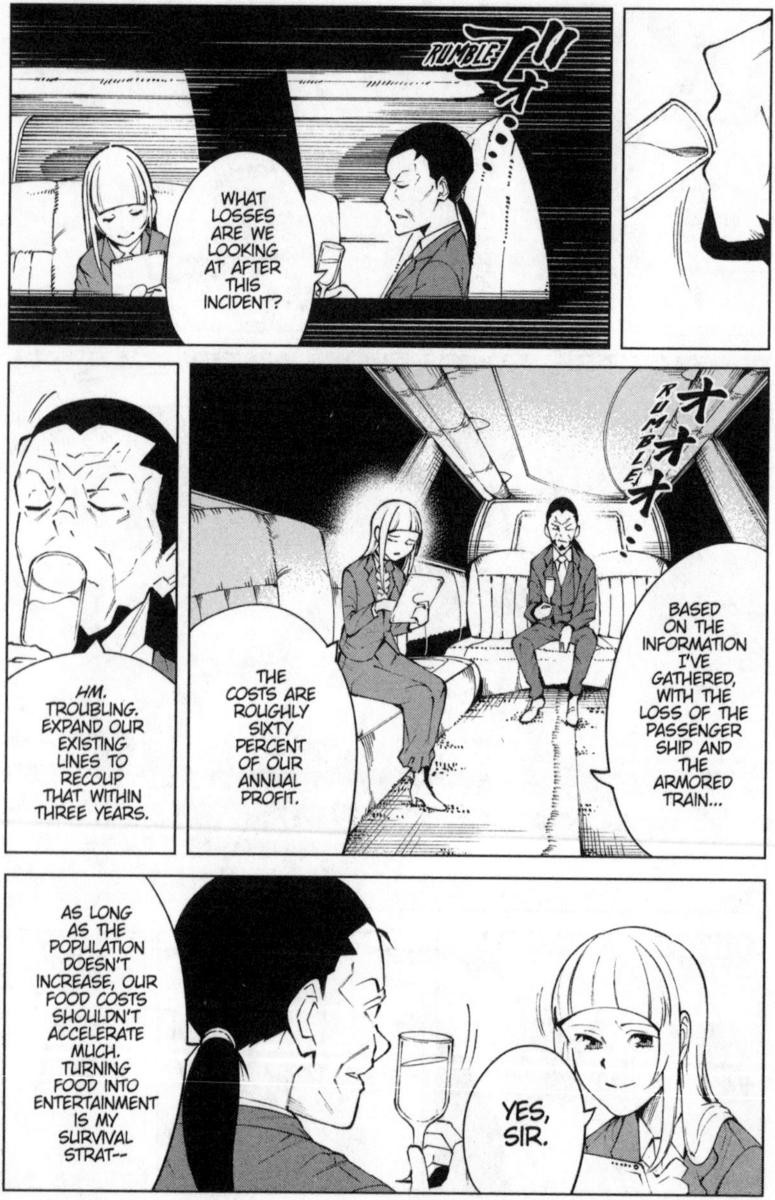
RUMBLE
WHAT LOSSES ARE WE LOOKING AT AFTER THIS INCIDENT?
RUMBLE
BASED ON THE INFORMATION I'VE GATHERED, WITH THE LOSS OF THE PASSENGER SHIP AND THE ARMORED TRAIN...
THE COSTS ARE ROUGHLY SIXTY PERCENT OF OUR ANNUAL PROFIT.
HM. TROUBLING. EXPAND OUR EXISTING LINES TO RECOUP THAT WITHIN THREE YEARS.
YES, SIR.
AS LONG AS THE POPULATION DOESN'T INCREASE, OUR FOOD COSTS SHOULDN'T ACCELERATE MUCH. TURNING FOOD INTO ENTERTAINMENT IS MY SURVIVAL STRAT--

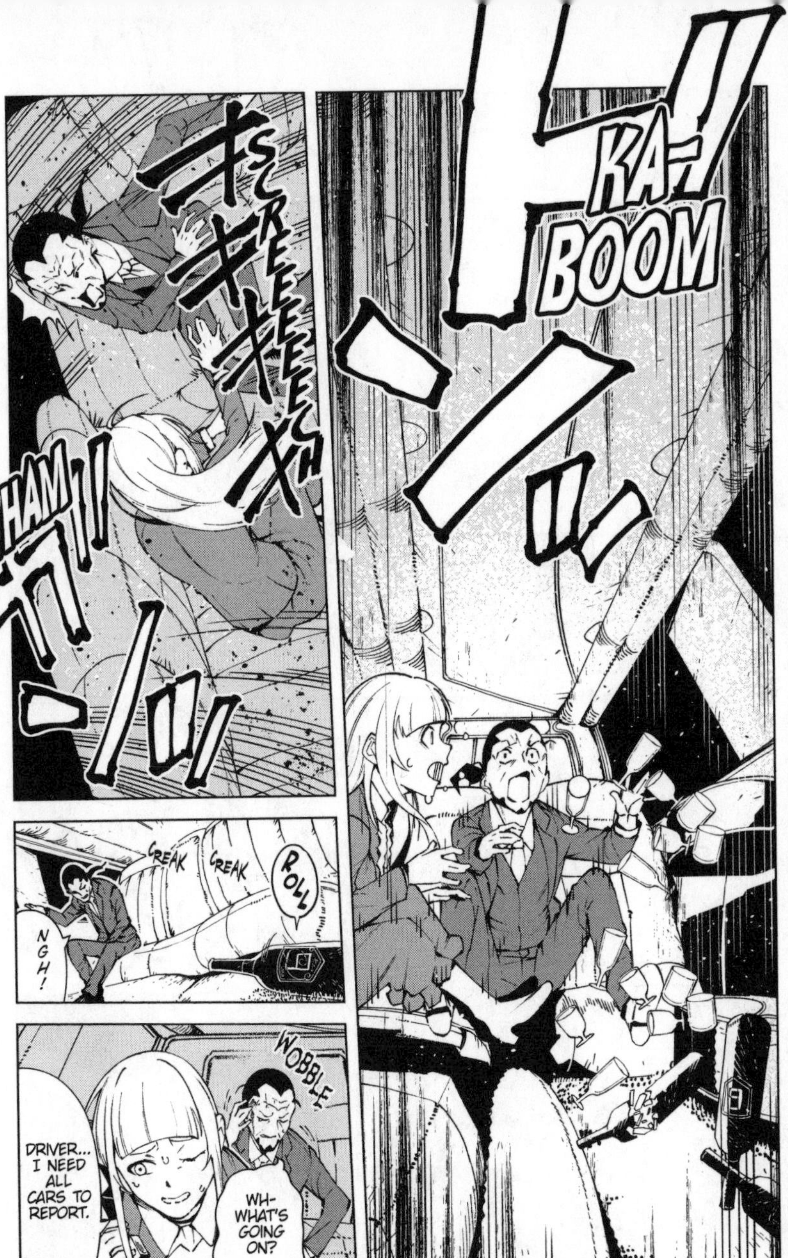
KA-BOOM
SCREEEEECH
WHAM
CREAK CREAK
ROLL
NGH!
WOBBLE
WH-WHAT'S GOING ON?
DRIVER... I NEED ALL CARS TO REPORT.

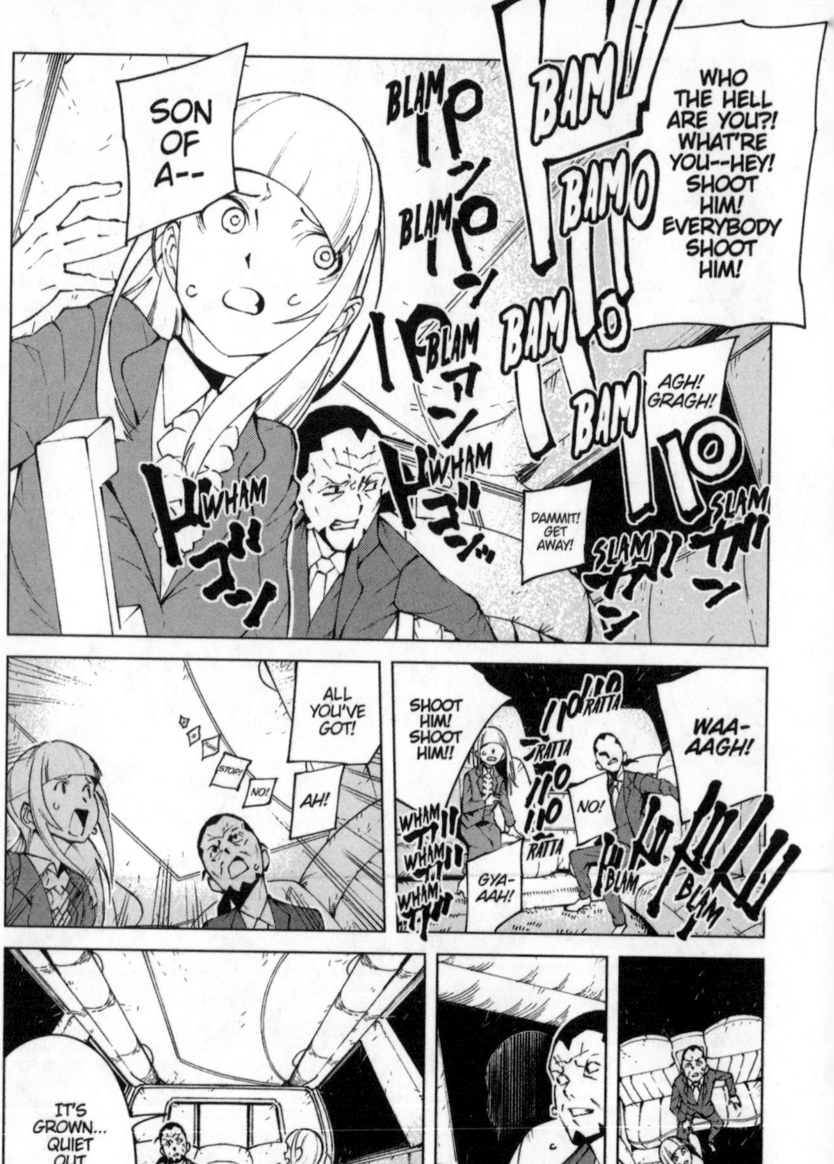
WHO THE HELL ARE YOU?! WHAT'RE YOU--HEY! SHOOT HIM! EVERYBODY SHOOT HIM!
BAM
BAM
BAM
BAM
BLAM
BLAM
BLAM
SON OF A--
AGH! GRAGH!
SLAM
SLAM
DAMMIT! GET AWAY!
WHAM
WHAM
WAA-AAGH!
RATTA
RATTA
RATTA
SHOOT HIM! SHOOT HIM!!
NO!
BLAM
BLAM
GYA-AAH!
WHAM
WHAM
WHAM
ALL YOU'VE GOT!
AH!
STOP!
NO!
IT'S GROWN... QUIET OUT THERE.

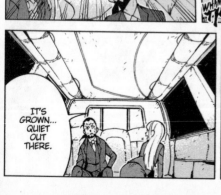

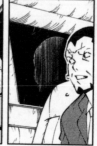

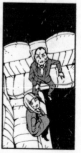

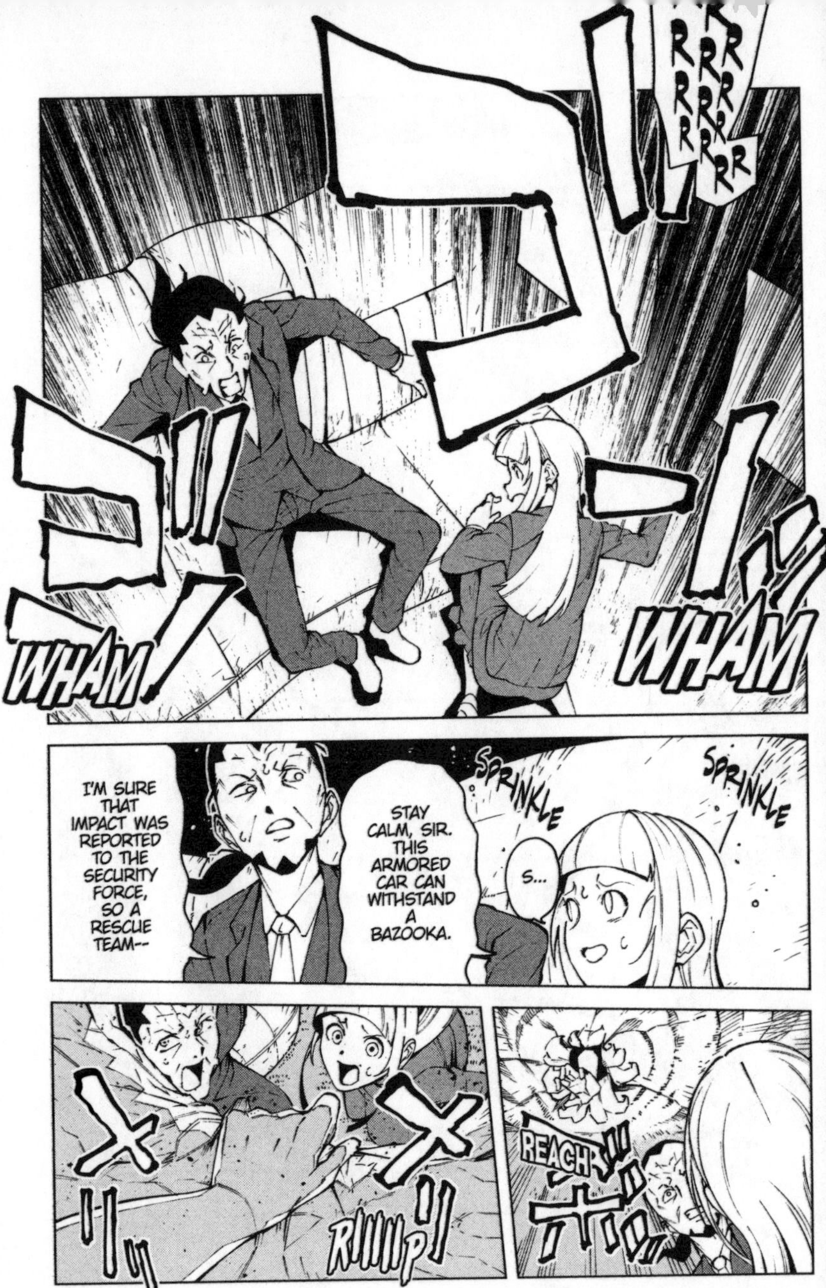
RRRRRRRRRRRRR
WHAM
WHAM
SPRINKLE
SPRINKLE
S...
STAY CALM, SIR. THIS ARMORED CAR CAN WITHSTAND A BAZOOKA.
I'M SURE THAT IMPACT WAS REPORTED TO THE SECURITY FORCE, SO A RESCUE TEAM--
REACH
RIIIIP

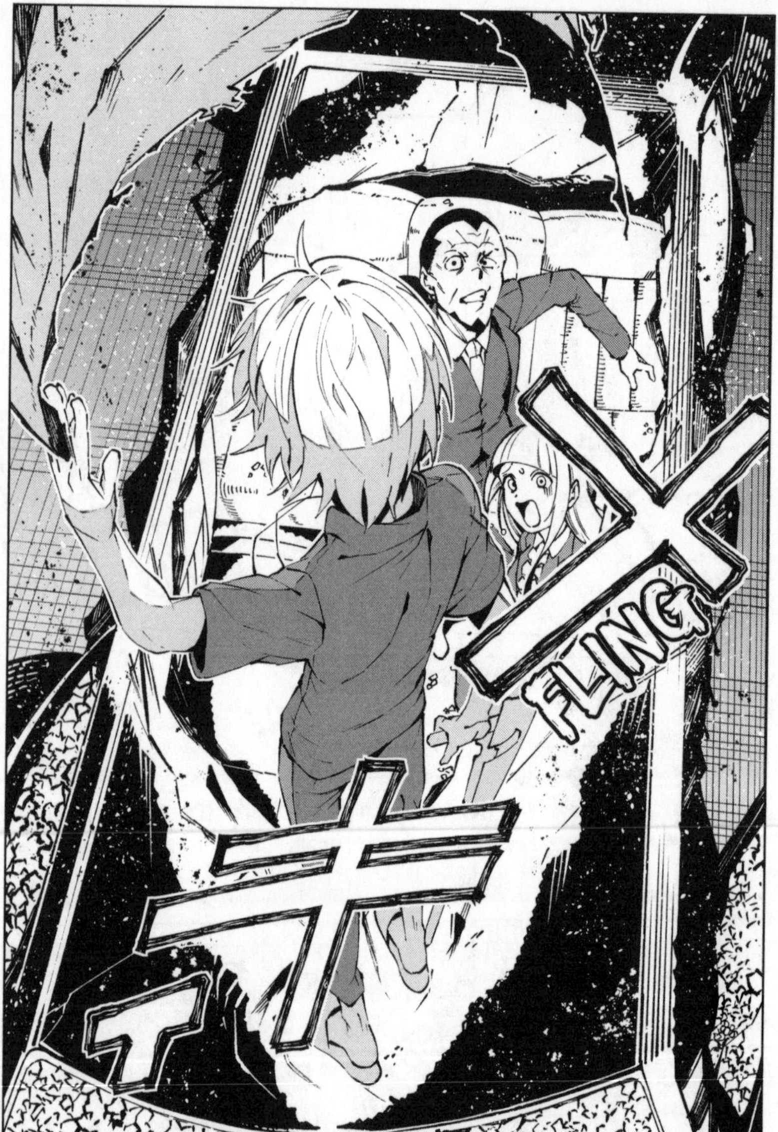
FLING

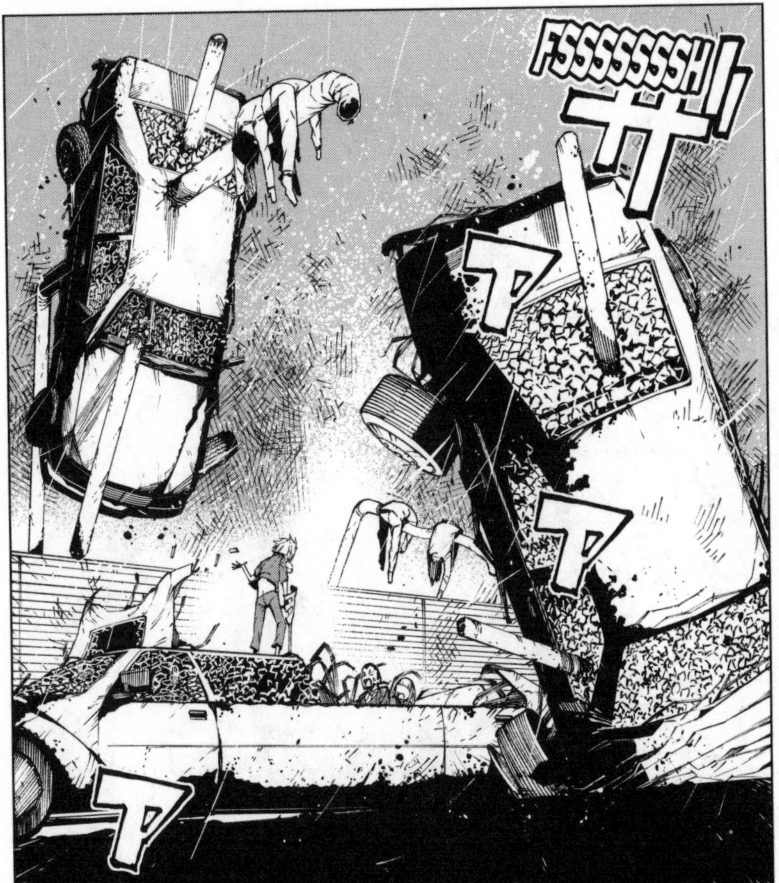
FSSSSSSSSH
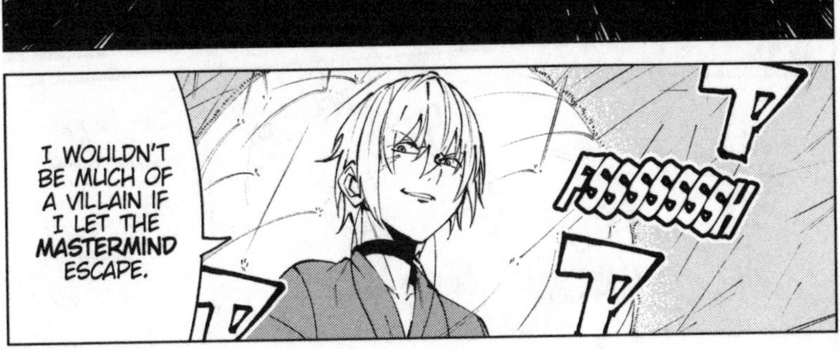
I WOULDN'T BE MUCH OF A VILLAIN IF I LET THE MASTERMIND ESCAPE.
FSSSSSSSSH

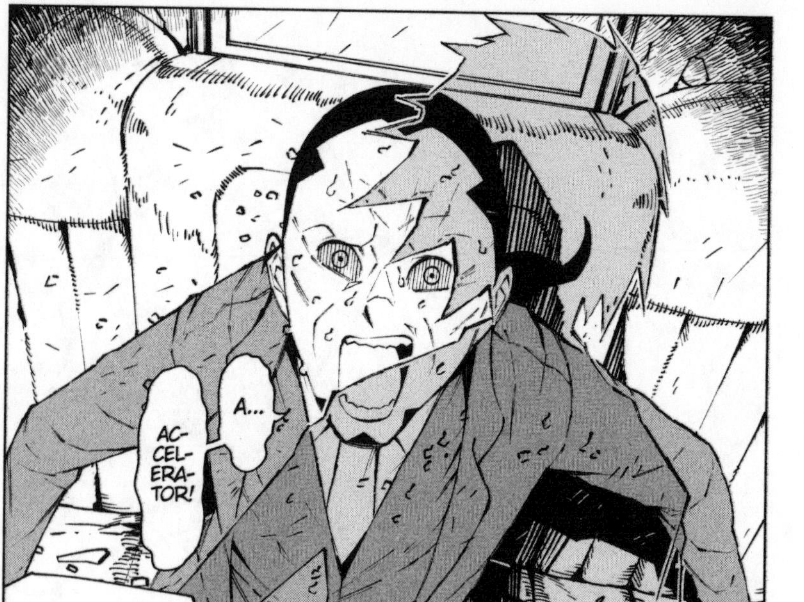
A...
ACCELERATOR!
THE WAY I SEE IT, YOU'VE GOT TWO OPTIONS HERE.
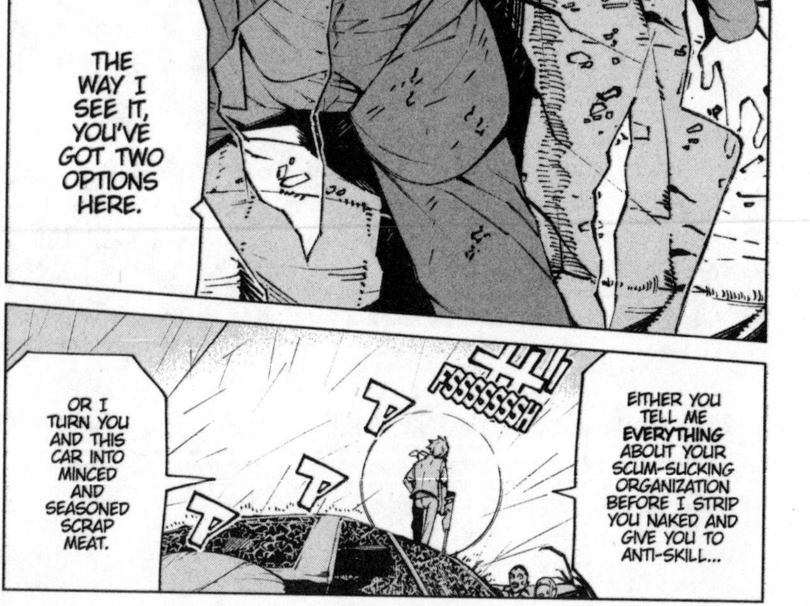
EITHER YOU TELL ME **EVERYTHING** ABOUT YOUR SCUM-SUCKING ORGANIZATION BEFORE I STRIP YOU NAKED AND GIVE YOU TO ANTI-SKILL...
FSSSSSSSH
OR I TURN YOU AND THIS CAR INTO MINCED AND SEASONED SCRAP MEAT.

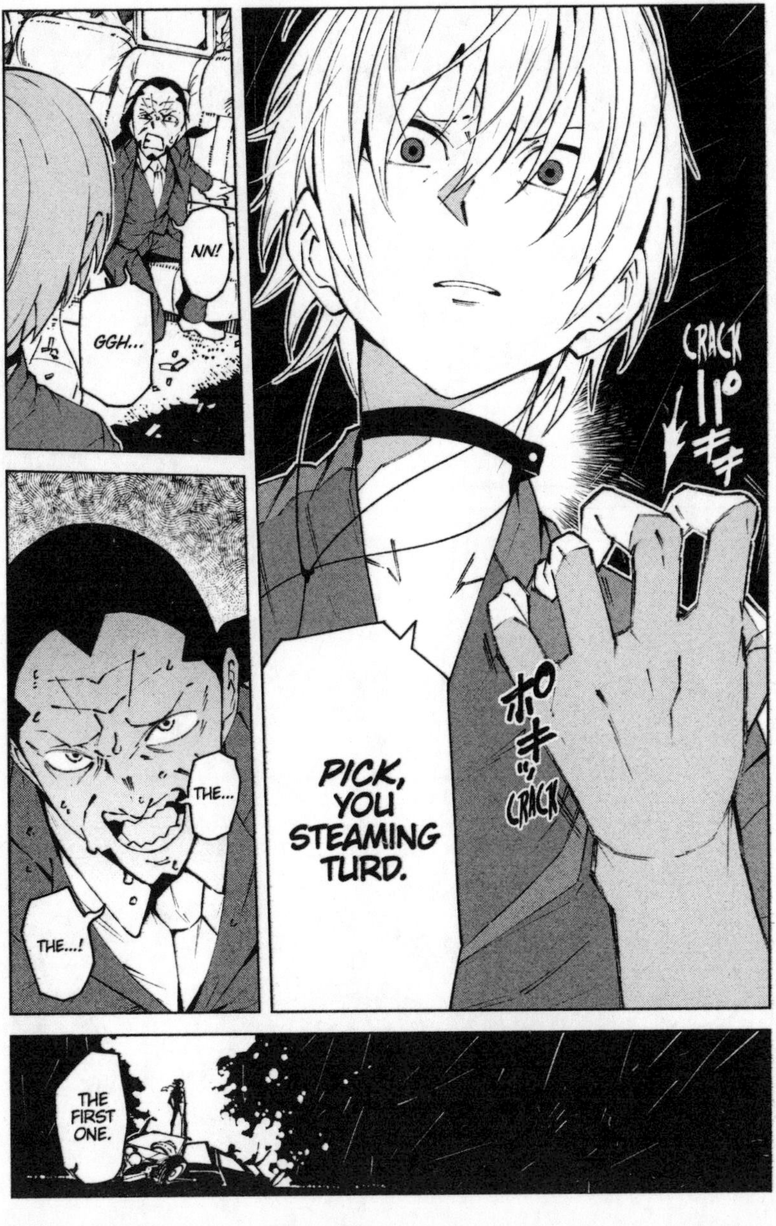
CRACK
パキキ
PICK, YOU STEAMING TURD.
ポキッ
CRACK
NN!
GGH...
THE...
THE...!
THE FIRST ONE.

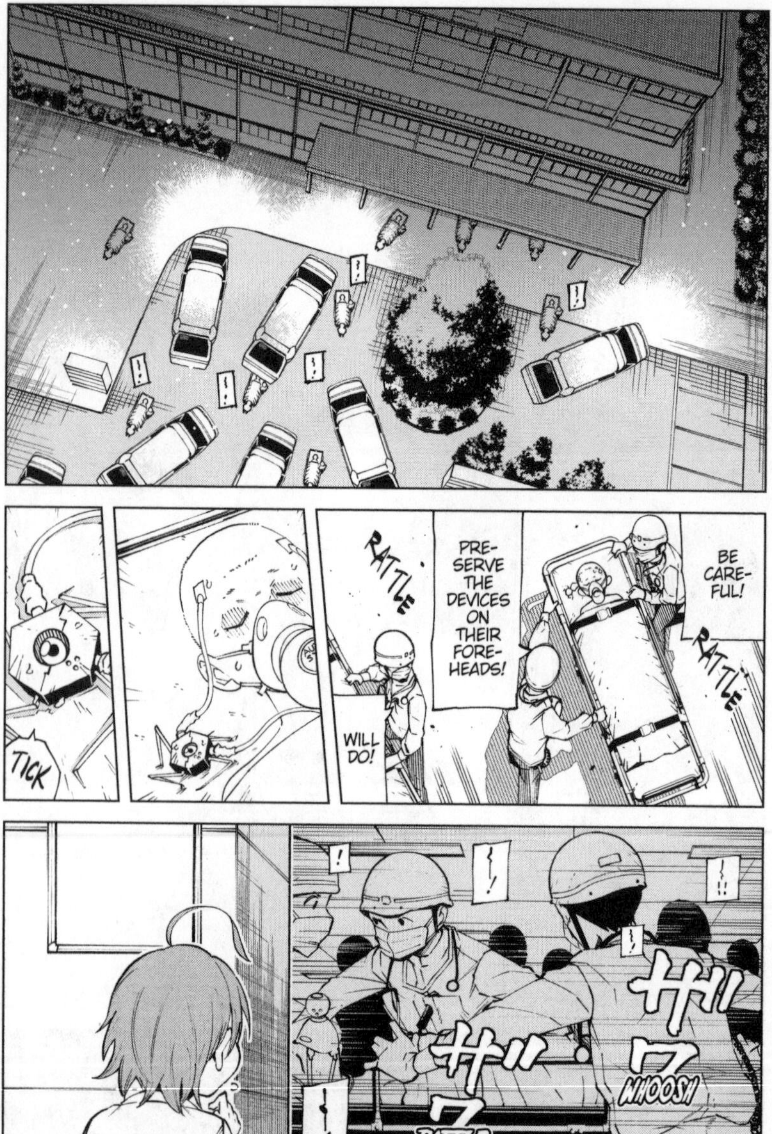
BE CAREFUL!
RATTLE
PRESERVE THE DEVICES ON THEIR FOREHEADS!
RATTLE
WILL DO!
TICK
ザワ
WHOOSH
ザワ
RATTLE

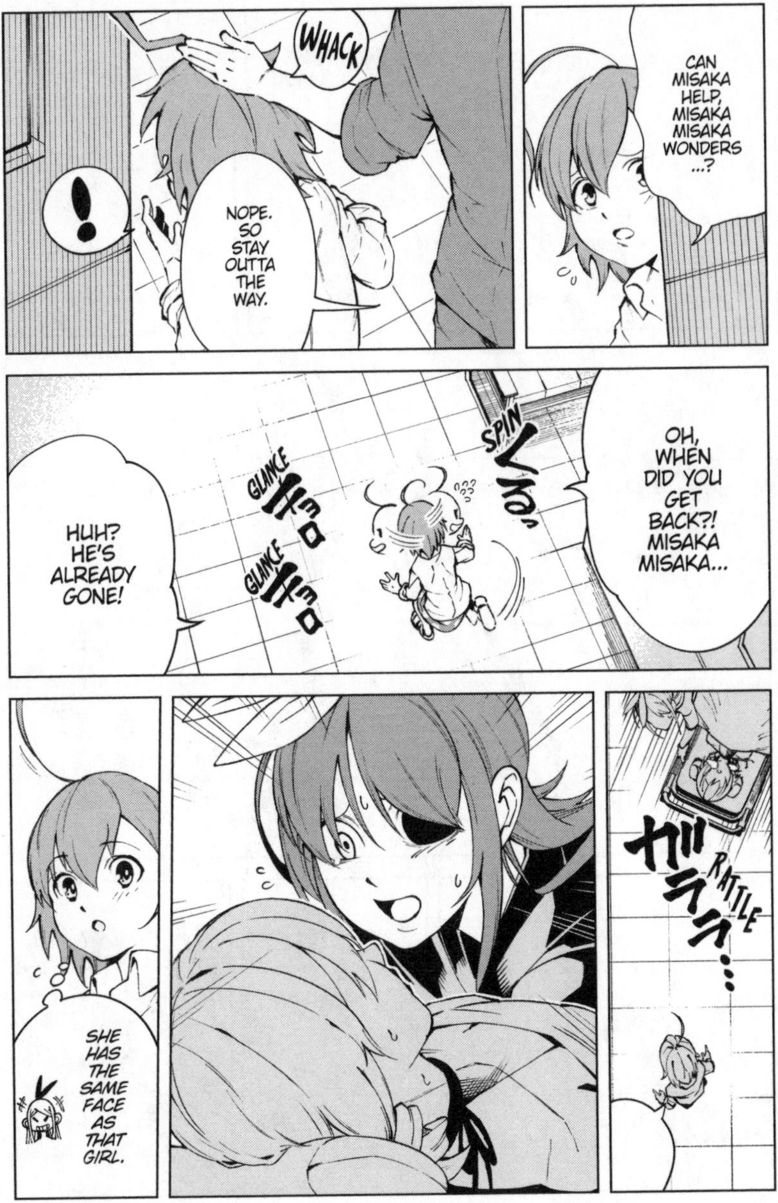
CAN MISAKA HELP, MISAKA MISAKA WONDERS ...?
WHACK
NOPE. SO STAY OUTTA THE WAY.
!
OH, WHEN DID YOU GET BACK?! MISAKA MISAKA...
SPIN
GLANCE
GLANCE
HUH? HE'S ALREADY GONE!
RATTLE
SHE HAS THE SAME FACE AS THAT GIRL.

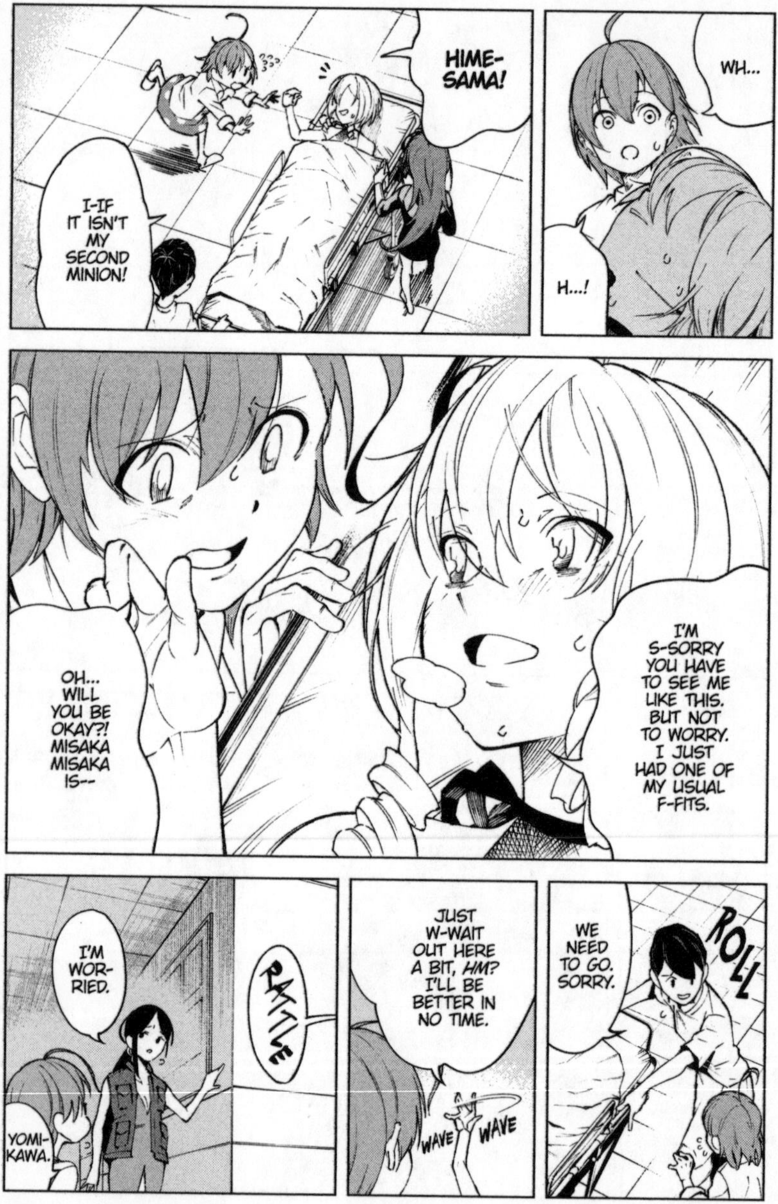
WH...
H...!
HIME-SAMA!
I-IF IT ISN'T MY SECOND MINION!
I'M S-SORRY YOU HAVE TO SEE ME LIKE THIS. BUT NOT TO WORRY. I JUST HAD ONE OF MY USUAL F-FITS.
OH... WILL YOU BE OKAY?! MISAKA MISAKA IS--
ROLL
WE NEED TO GO. SORRY.
JUST W-WAIT OUT HERE A BIT, HM? I'LL BE BETTER IN NO TIME.
WAVE WAVE
RATTLE
I'M WOR-RIED.
YOMI-KAWA.

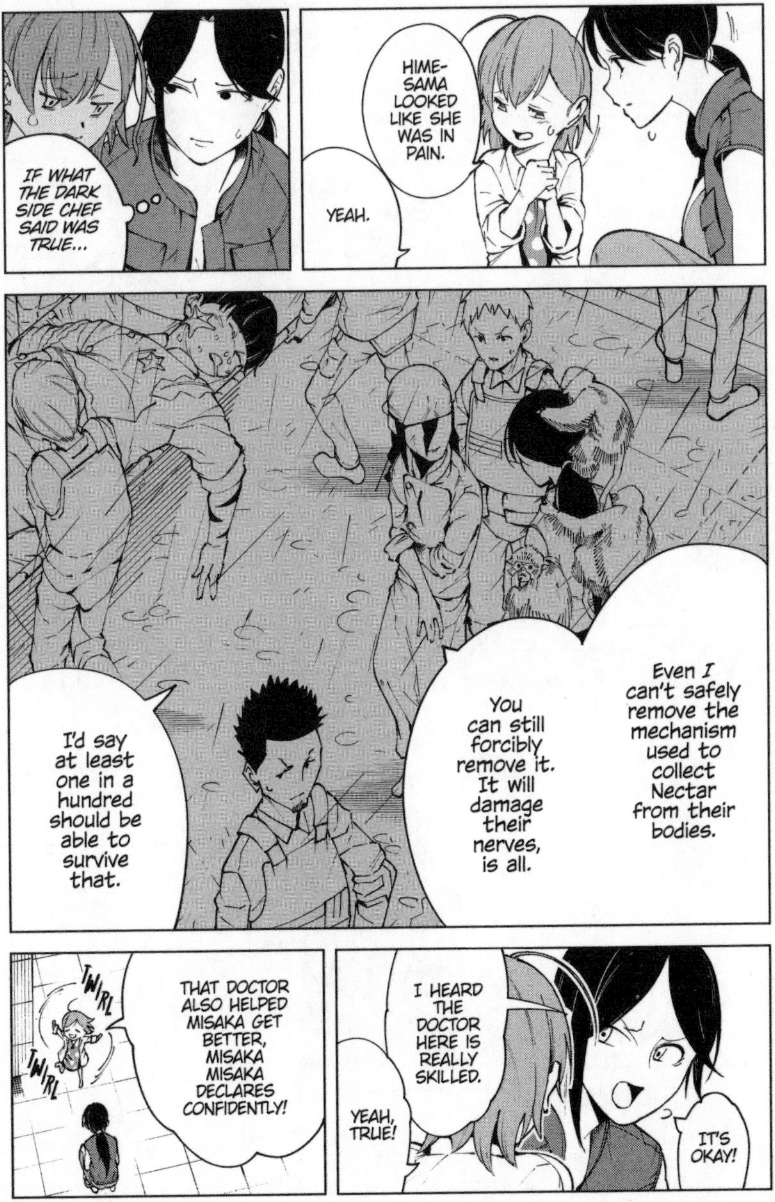
HIME-SAMA LOOKED LIKE SHE WAS IN PAIN.
YEAH.
IF WHAT THE DARK SIDE CHEF SAID WAS TRUE...
Even *I* can't safely remove the mechanism used to collect Nectar from their bodies.
You can still forcibly remove it. It will damage their nerves, is all.
I'd say at least one in a hundred should be able to survive that.
I HEARD THE DOCTOR HERE IS REALLY SKILLED.
IT'S OKAY!
YEAH, TRUE!
TWIRL
TWIRL
THAT DOCTOR ALSO HELPED MISAKA GET BETTER, MISAKA MISAKA DECLARES CONFIDENTLY!

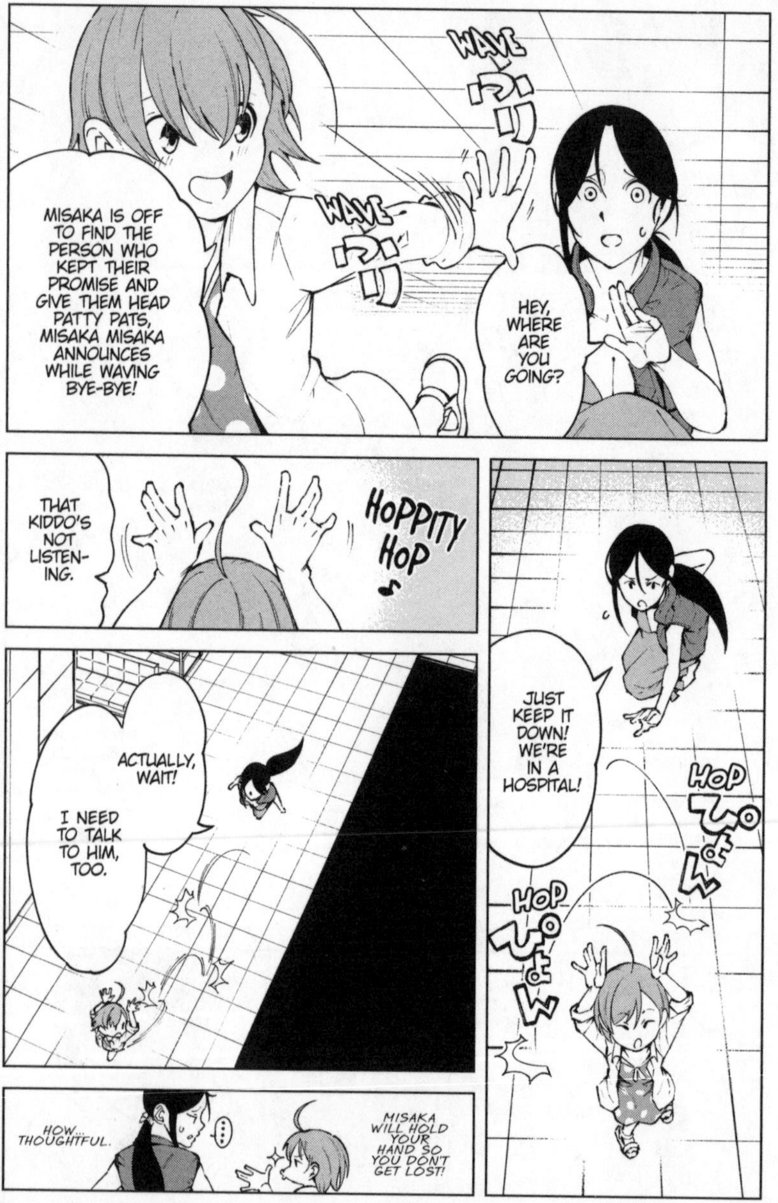
WAVE
WAVE
HEY, WHERE ARE YOU GOING?
MISAKA IS OFF TO FIND THE PERSON WHO KEPT THEIR PROMISE AND GIVE THEM HEAD PATTY PATS, MISAKA MISAKA ANNOUNCES WHILE WAVING BYE-BYE!
JUST KEEP IT DOWN! WE'RE IN A HOSPITAL!
HOP
HOP
HOPPITY HOP
THAT KIDDO'S NOT LISTEN-ING.
ACTUALLY, WAIT!
I NEED TO TALK TO HIM, TOO.
MISAKA WILL HOLD YOUR HAND SO YOU DON'T GET LOST!
...
HOW... THOUGHTFUL.

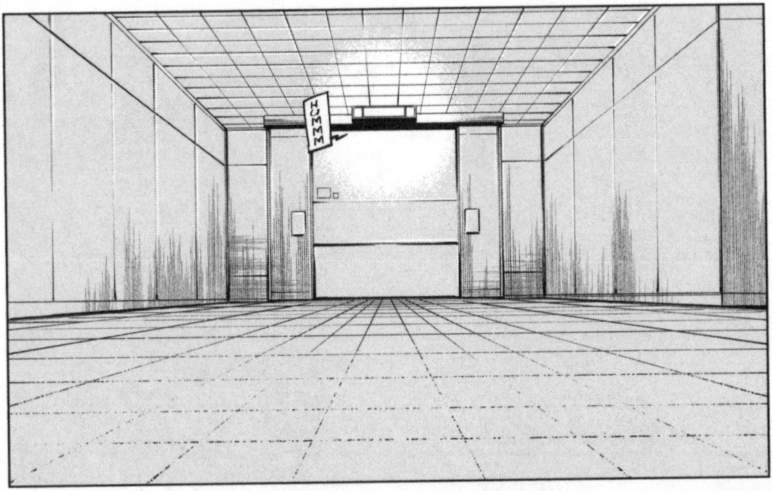
HUMMM
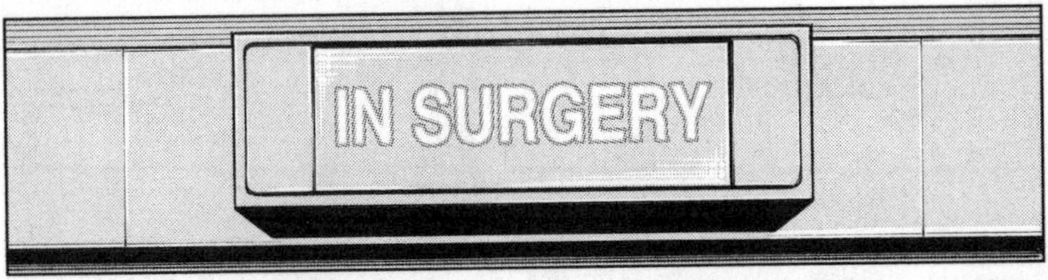
IN SURGERY
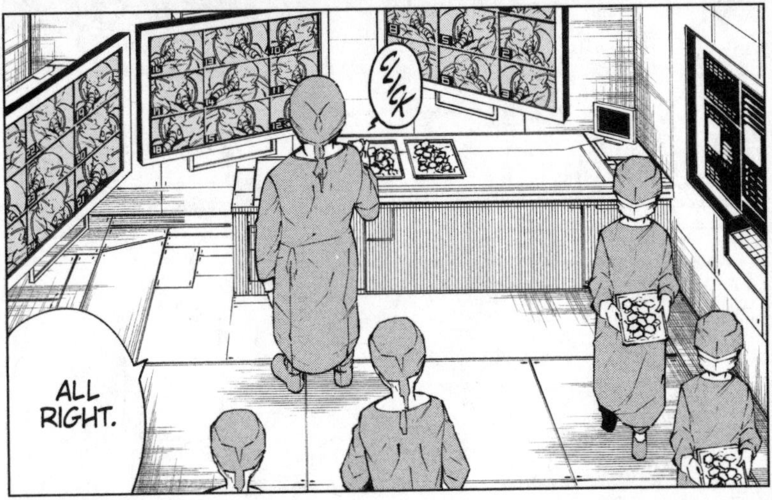
CLICK
ALL RIGHT.

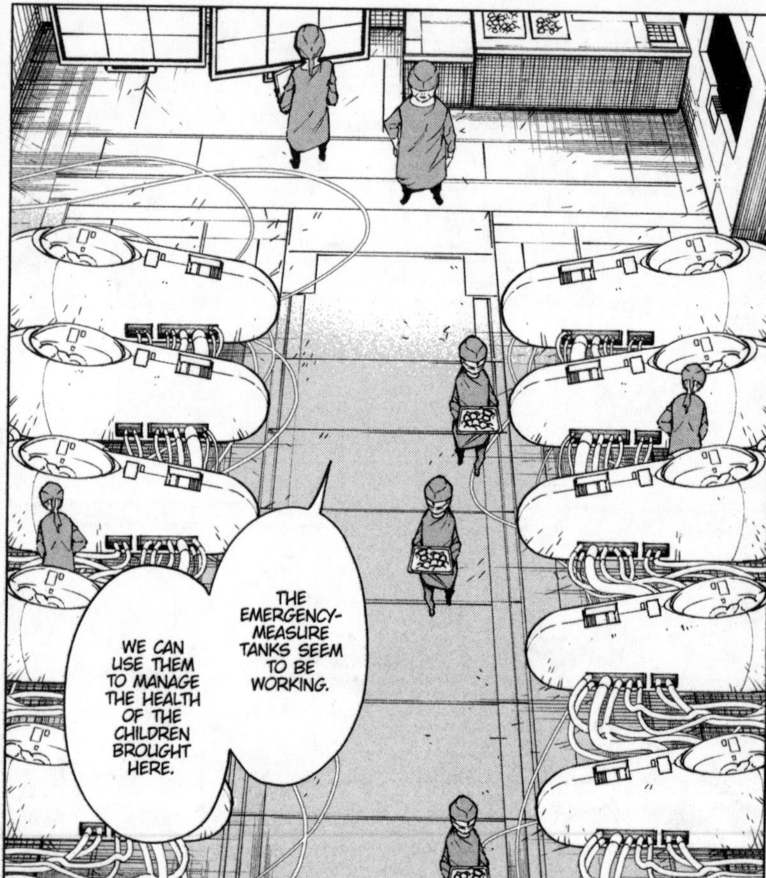
THE EMERGENCY-MEASURE TANKS SEEM TO BE WORKING.
WE CAN USE THEM TO MANAGE THE HEALTH OF THE CHILDREN BROUGHT HERE.
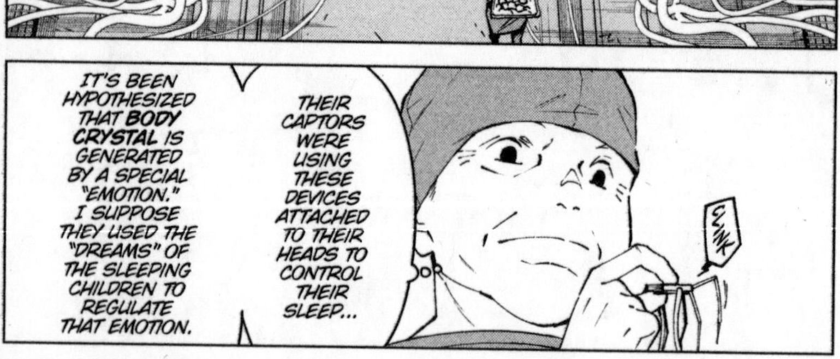
THEIR CAPTORS WERE USING THESE DEVICES ATTACHED TO THEIR HEADS TO CONTROL THEIR SLEEP...
IT'S BEEN HYPOTHESIZED THAT **BODY CRYSTAL** IS GENERATED BY A SPECIAL "EMOTION." I SUPPOSE THEY USED THE "DREAMS" OF THE SLEEPING CHILDREN TO REGULATE THAT EMOTION.
CLINK

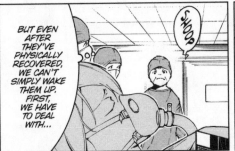

FWISH
BUT THE PROCESS IS DESTRUCTIVE.
KEEPING THE CHILDREN ASLEEP HELPED PRESERVE THEIR BODIES WHILE GENERATING BODY CRYSTAL ATE AWAY AT THEM.
SHOOP
BUT EVEN AFTER THEY'VE PHYSICALLY RECOVERED, WE CAN'T SIMPLY WAKE THEM UP. FIRST, WE HAVE TO DEAL WITH...
ROTATE
THE ARTIFICIAL HEART THAT DESTROYS THEIR BODIES AND ITS SPRAWLING METALLIC STRINGS WOUND TIGHTLY AROUND THEIR NERVES.
TUG
DOCTOR ...!
I'LL BE FINE. DO WHAT YOU HAVE TO.
PLEASE DON'T REMOVE THE MASK, OKAY?
IF IT'S YOU, DOCTOR... I KNOW YOU CAN DO IT.
I DON'T HAVE THE TIME TO BE AS CAREFUL AS I NEED TO BE.

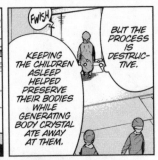

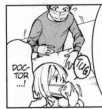

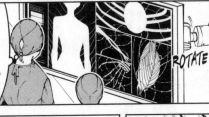

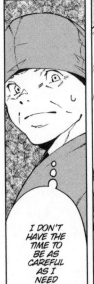

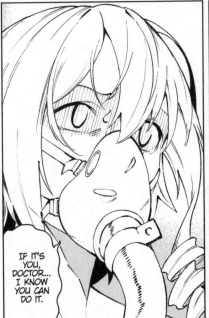

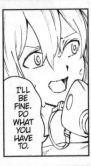

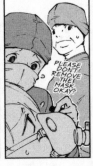

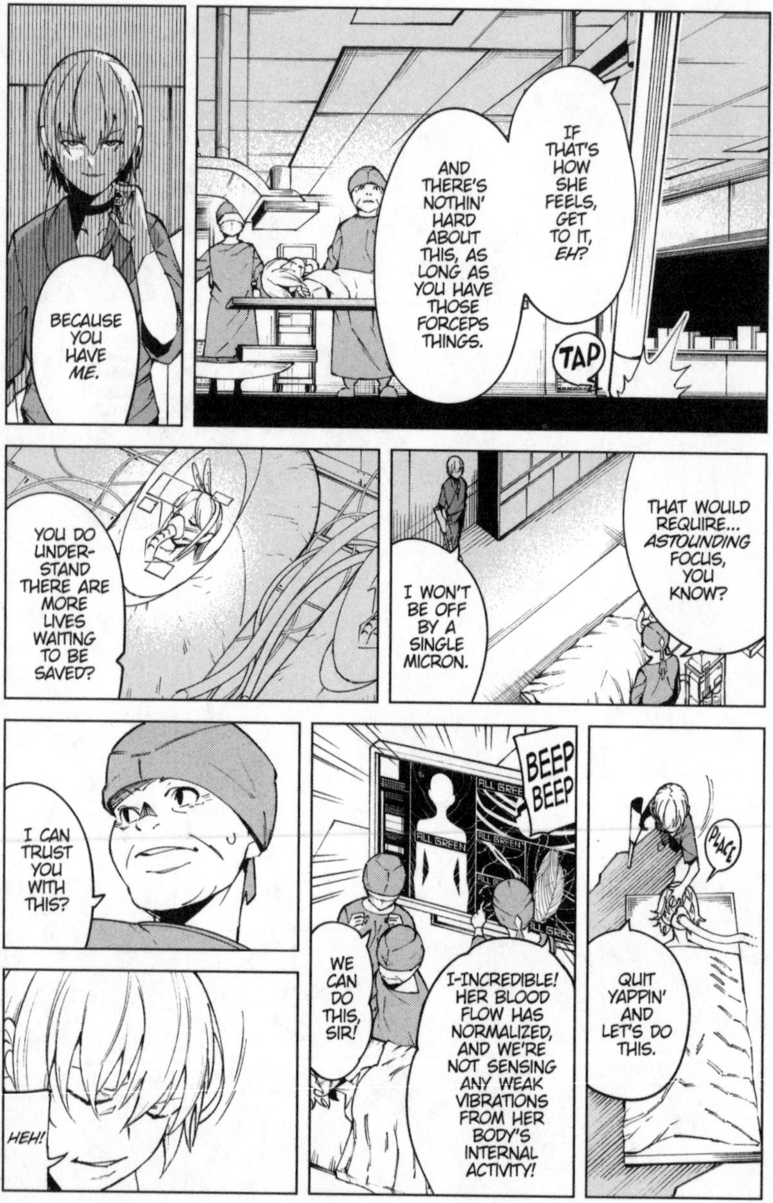

IF THAT'S HOW SHE FEELS, GET TO IT, *EH?*
AND THERE'S NOTHIN' HARD ABOUT THIS, AS LONG AS YOU HAVE THOSE FORCEPS THINGS.
TAP
BECAUSE YOU HAVE *ME.*
THAT WOULD REQUIRE... *ASTOUNDING* FOCUS, YOU KNOW?
I WON'T BE OFF BY A SINGLE MICRON.
YOU DO UNDER-STAND THERE ARE MORE LIVES WAITING TO BE SAVED?
PLACE
QUIT YAPPIN' AND LET'S DO THIS.
BEEP BEEP
ALL GREEN
ALL GREEN
ALL GREEN
I-INCREDIBLE! HER BLOOD FLOW HAS NORMALIZED, AND WE'RE NOT SENSING ANY WEAK VIBRATIONS FROM HER BODY'S INTERNAL ACTIVITY!
WE CAN DO THIS, SIR!
I CAN TRUST YOU WITH THIS?
HEH!

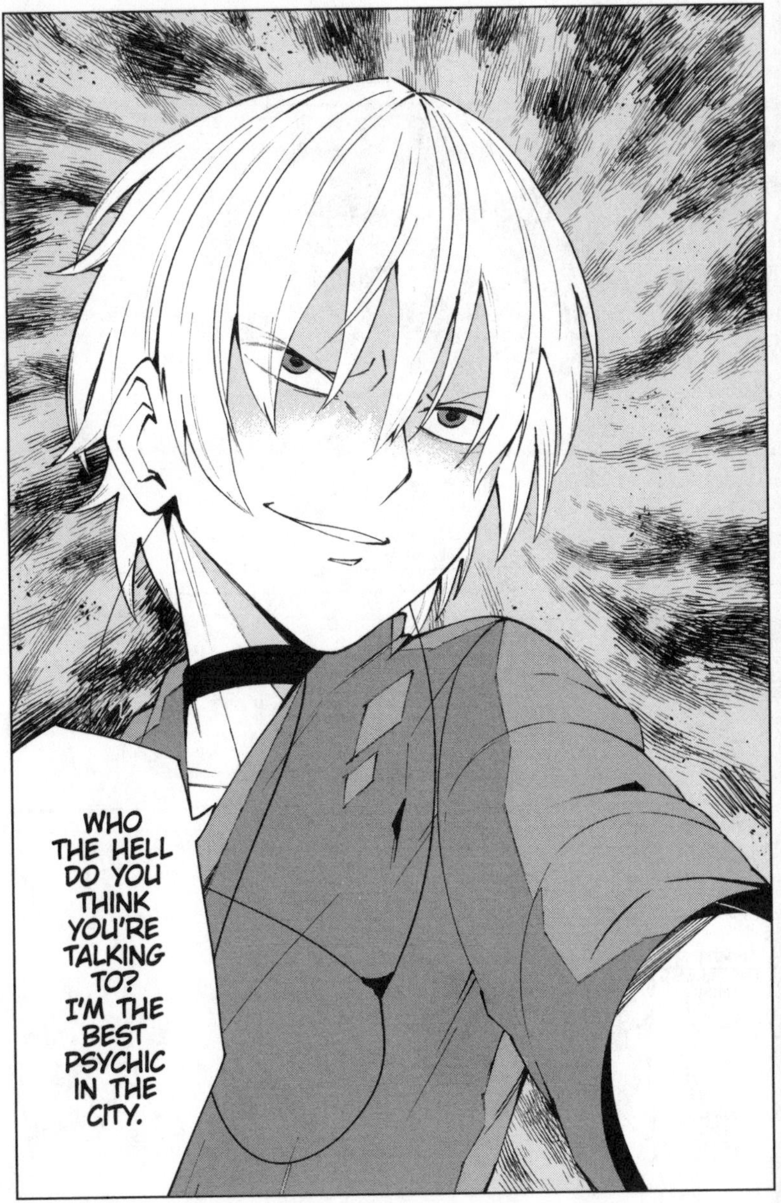
WHO THE HELL DO YOU THINK YOU'RE TALKING TO? I'M THE BEST PSYCHIC IN THE CITY.

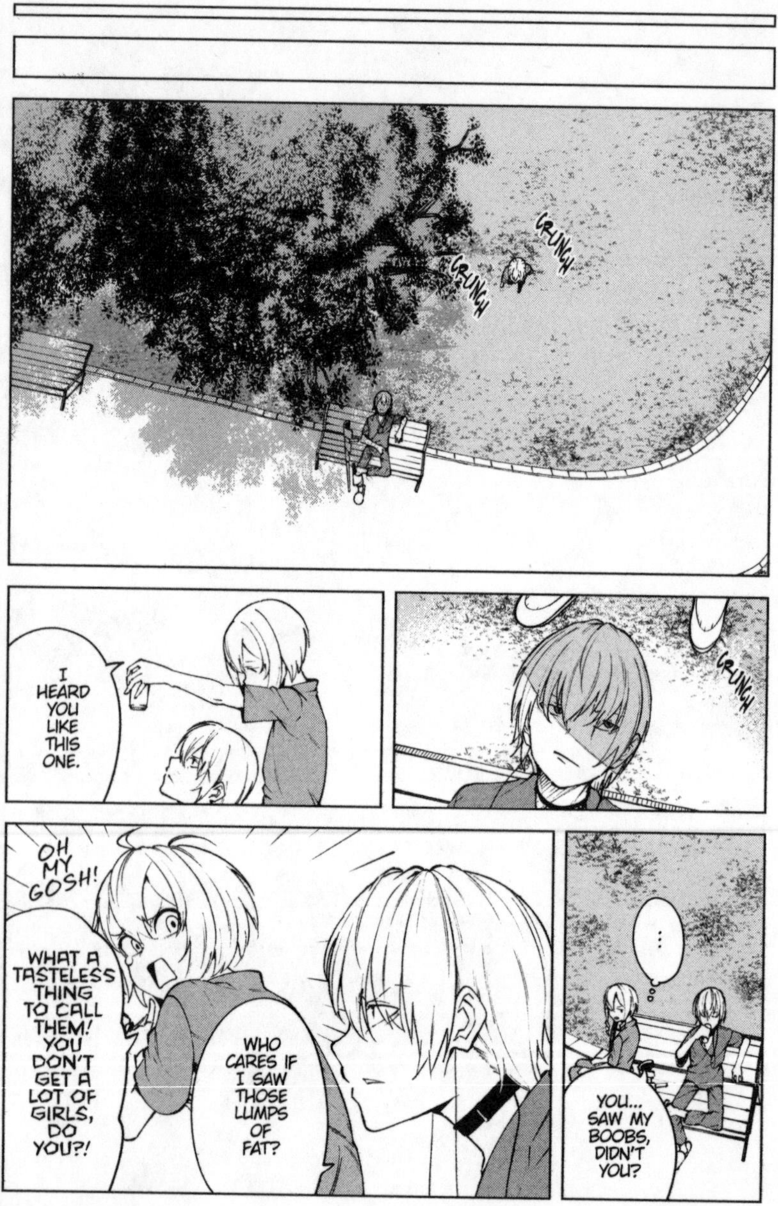
CRUNCH
CRUNCH
CRUNCH
I HEARD YOU LIKE THIS ONE.
...
YOU... SAW MY BOOBS, DIDN'T YOU?
WHO CARES IF I SAW THOSE LUMPS OF FAT?
OH MY GOSH!
WHAT A TASTELESS THING TO CALL THEM! YOU DON'T GET A LOT OF GIRLS, DO YOU?!

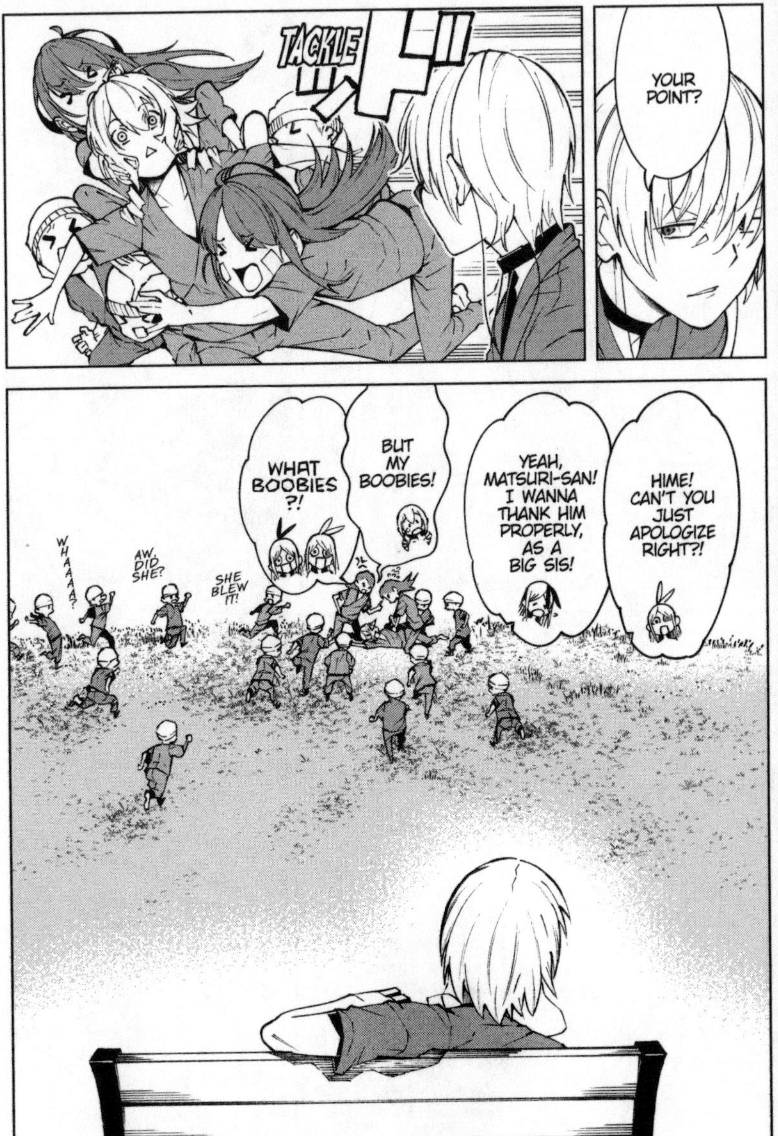
YOUR POINT?
TACKLE
HIME! CAN'T YOU JUST APOLOGIZE RIGHT?!
YEAH, MATSURI-SAN! I WANNA THANK HIM PROPERLY, AS A BIG SIS!
BUT MY BOOBIES!
WHAT BOOBIES?!
SHE BLEW IT!
AW, DID SHE?
WHAAAA?

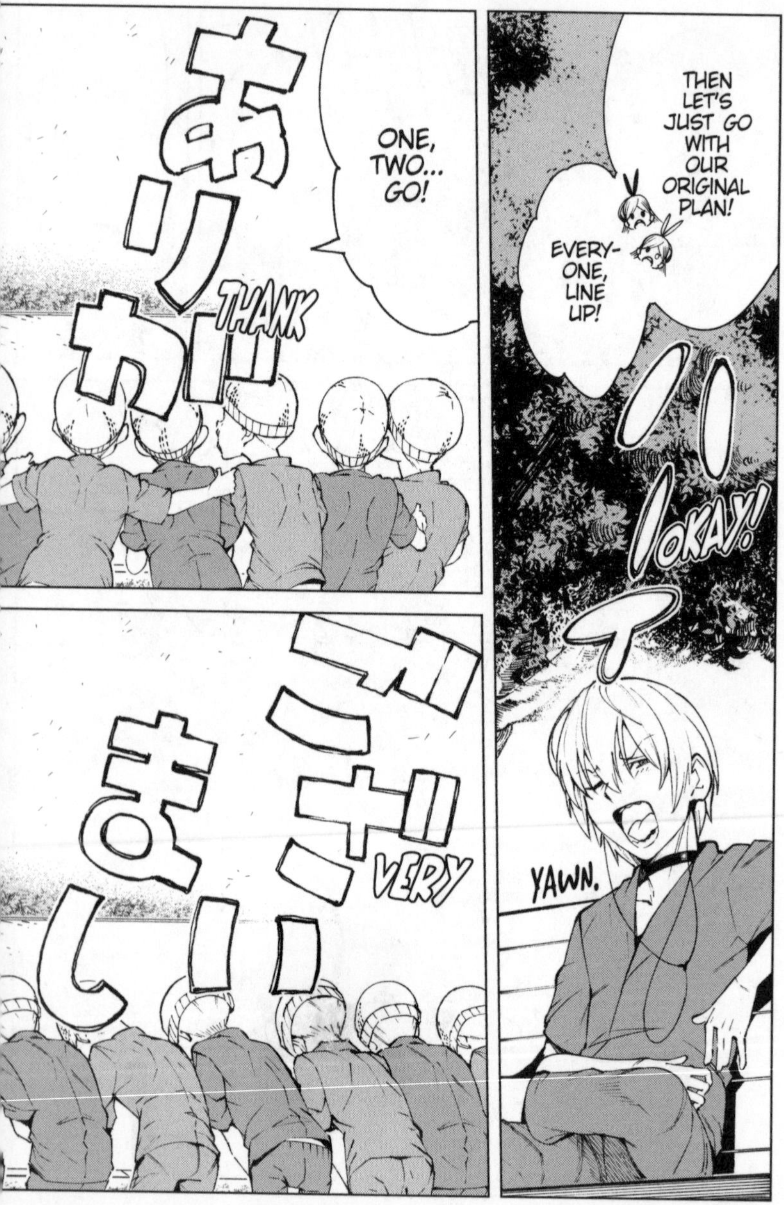
THEN LET'S JUST GO WITH OUR ORIGINAL PLAN!
EVERY-ONE, LINE UP!
OKAY!
YAWN.
ONE, TWO... GO!
ありが
THANK
ございまし
VERY

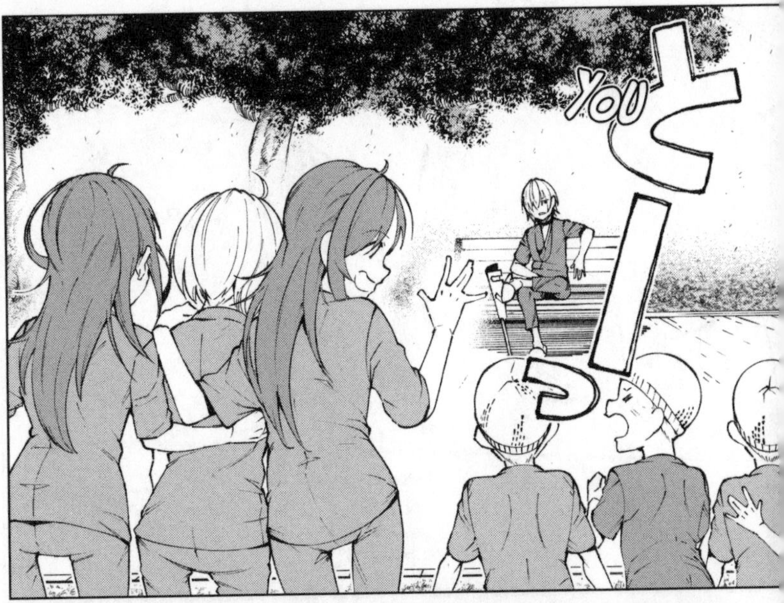
YOU
とーっ

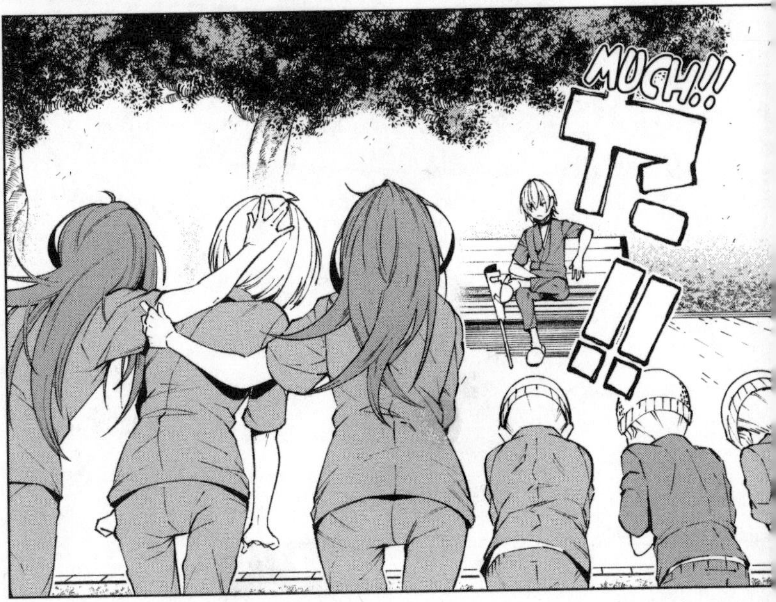
MUCH!!

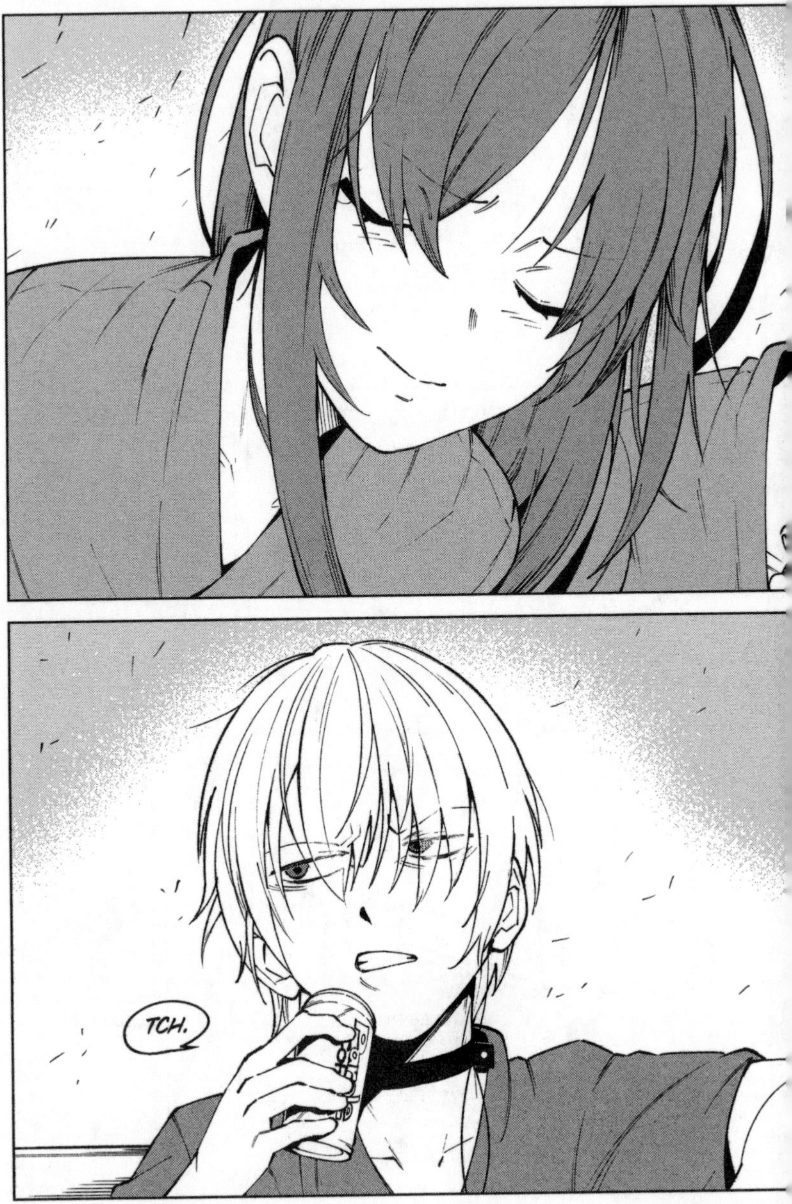
TCH.

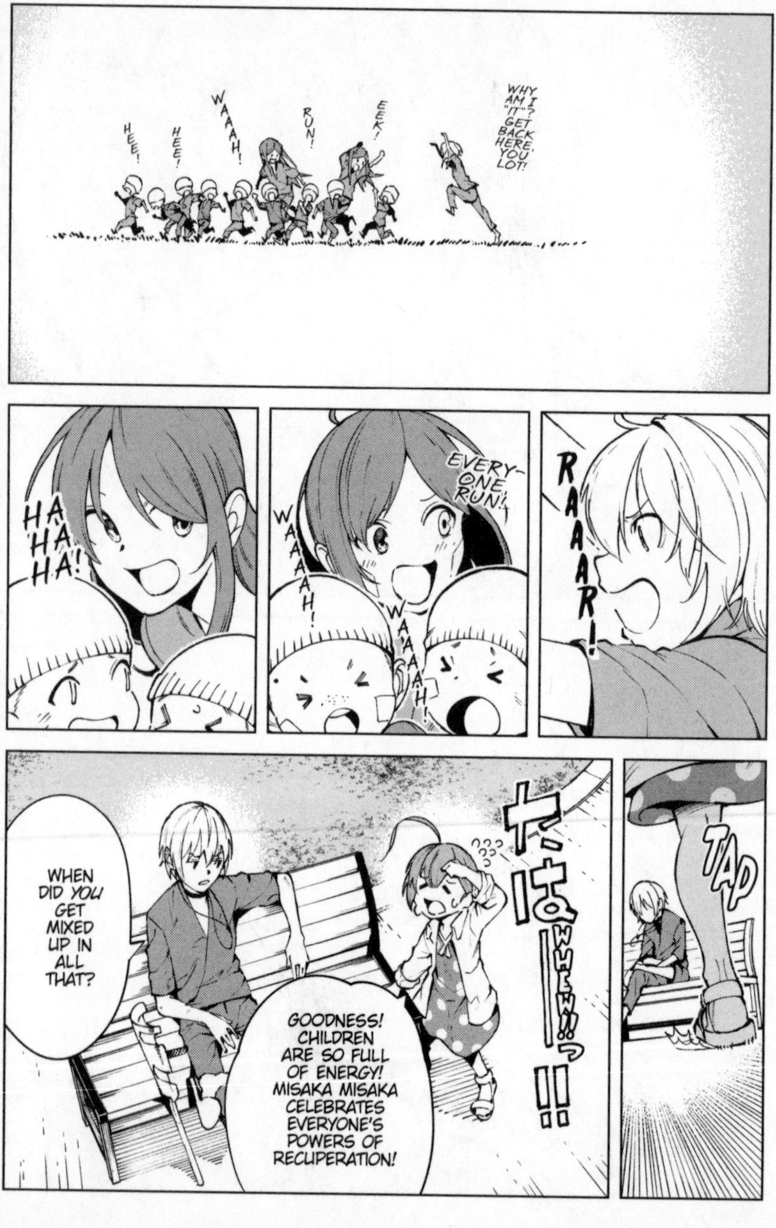

WHY AM I "IT"? GET BACK HERE, YOU LOT!
EEK!
RUN!
WAAAAH!
HEE!
HEE!
RAAAR!
EVERY-ONE, RUN!
WAAAAAH!
WAAAAH!
HA HA HA!
TAP
WHEW!!
GOODNESS! CHILDREN ARE SO FULL OF ENERGY! MISAKA MISAKA CELEBRATES EVERYONE'S POWERS OF RECUPERATION!
WHEN DID YOU GET MIXED UP IN ALL THAT?

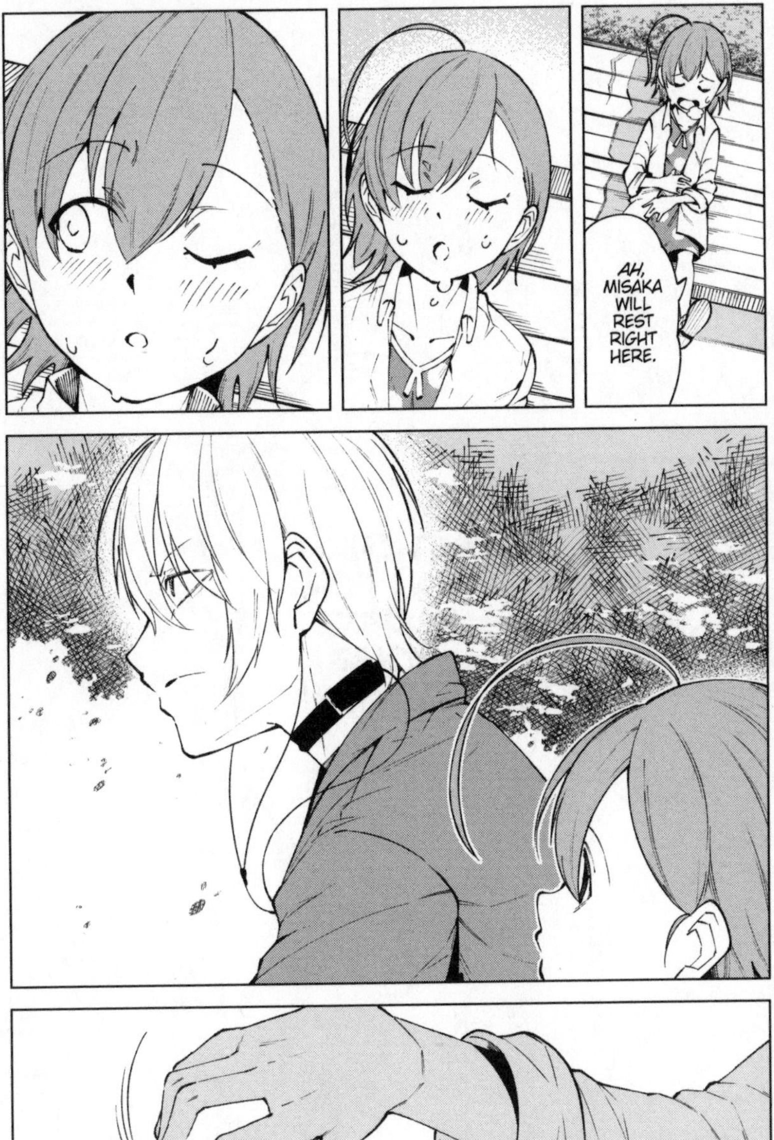
AH, MISAKA WILL REST RIGHT HERE.

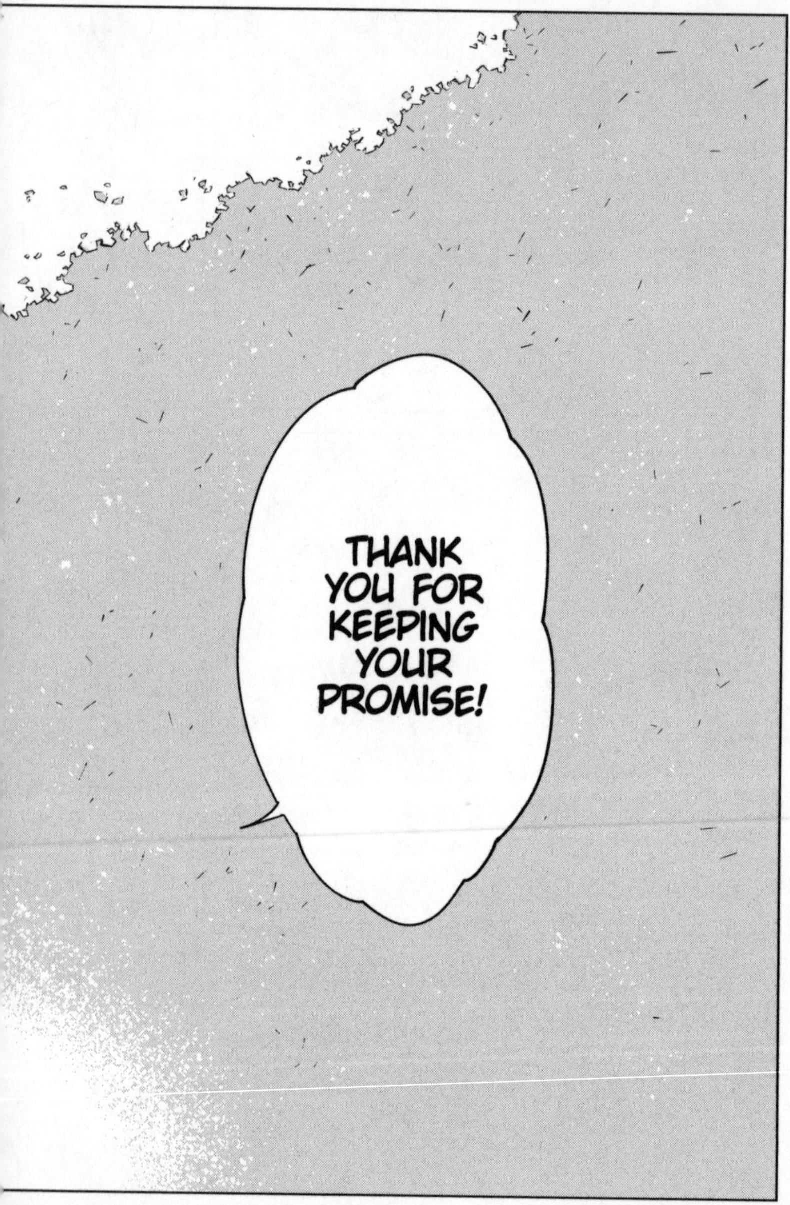
THANK YOU FOR KEEPING YOUR PROMISE!

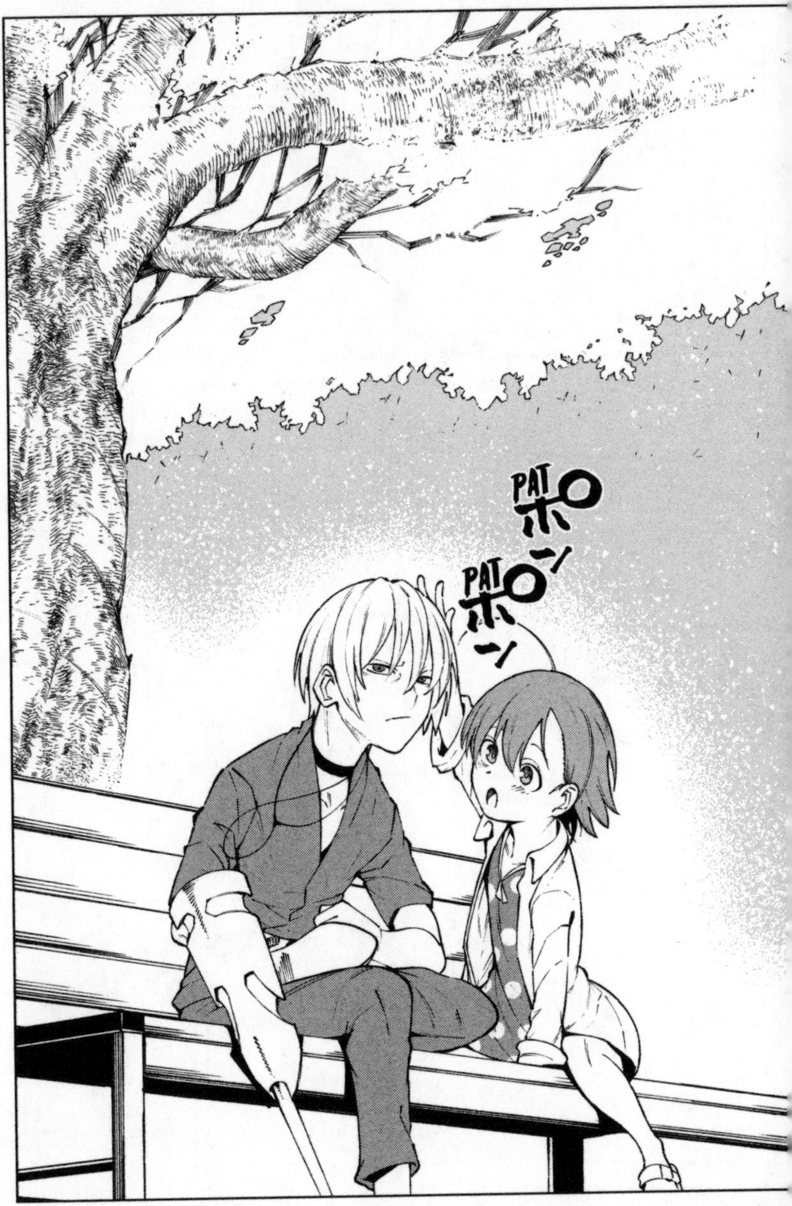
PAT ポン
PAT ポン

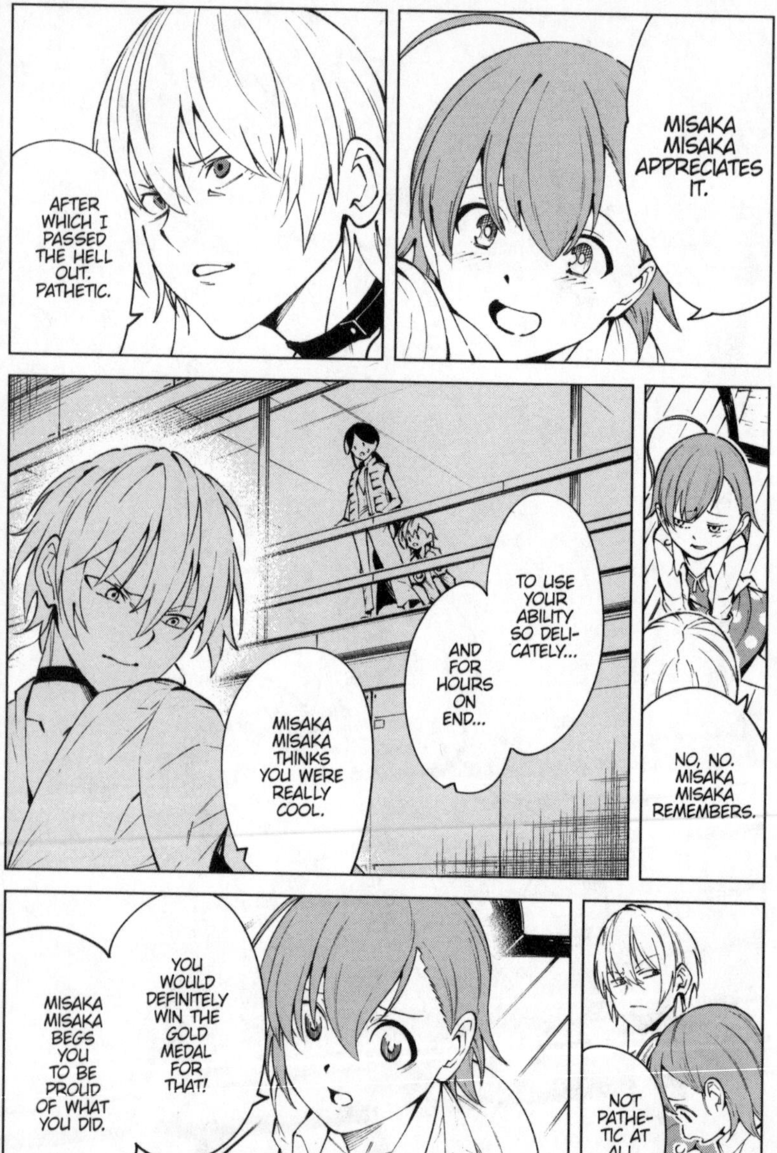
MISAKA MISAKA APPRECIATES IT.
AFTER WHICH I PASSED THE HELL OUT. PATHETIC.
NO, NO. MISAKA MISAKA REMEMBERS.
TO USE YOUR ABILITY SO DELICATELY...
AND FOR HOURS ON END...
MISAKA MISAKA THINKS YOU WERE REALLY COOL.
NOT PATHETIC AT ALL.
YOU WOULD DEFINITELY WIN THE GOLD MEDAL FOR THAT!
MISAKA MISAKA BEGS YOU TO BE PROUD OF WHAT YOU DID.

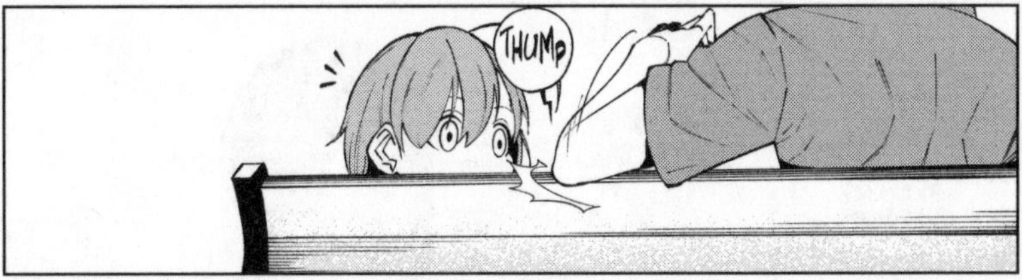
THUMP

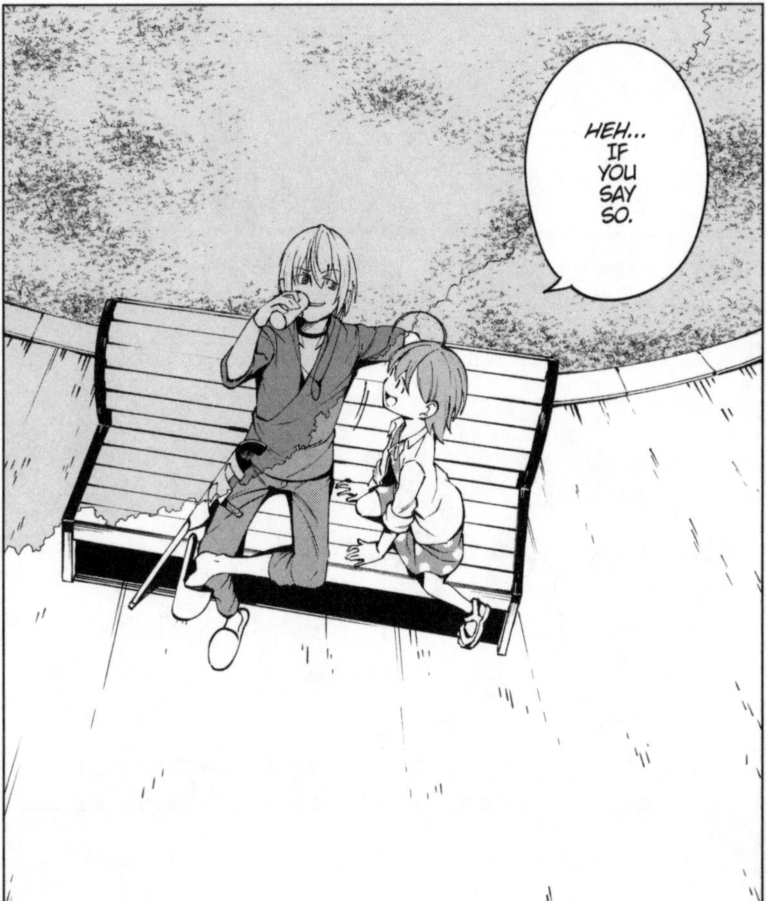
HEH... IF YOU SAY SO.

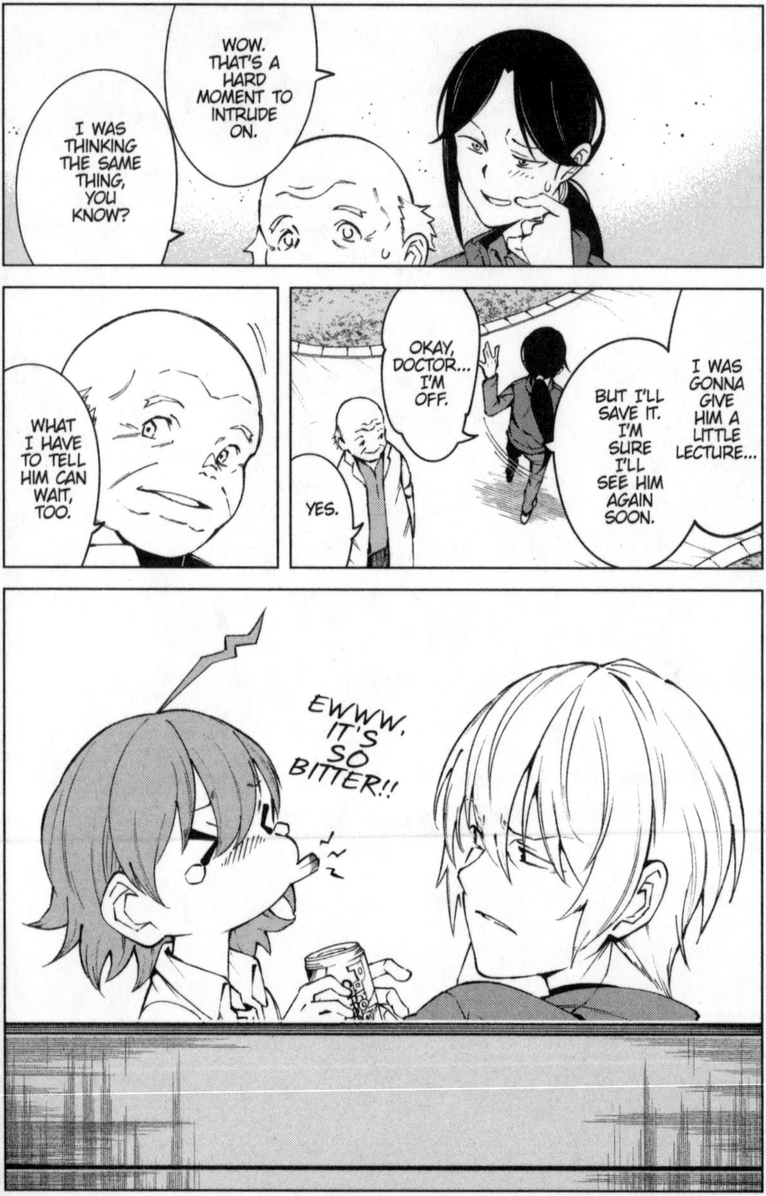
WOW. THAT'S A HARD MOMENT TO INTRUDE ON.
I WAS THINKING THE SAME THING, YOU KNOW?
I WAS GONNA GIVE HIM A LITTLE LECTURE...
BUT I'LL SAVE IT. I'M SURE I'LL SEE HIM AGAIN SOON.
OKAY, DOCTOR... I'M OFF.
YES.
WHAT I HAVE TO TELL HIM CAN WAIT, TOO.
EWWW, IT'S SO BITTER!!

a certain
SCIENTIFIC
ACCELERATOR

とある科学の一方通行 アクセラレータ

とある魔術の禁書目録 外伝

FINAL CHAPTER

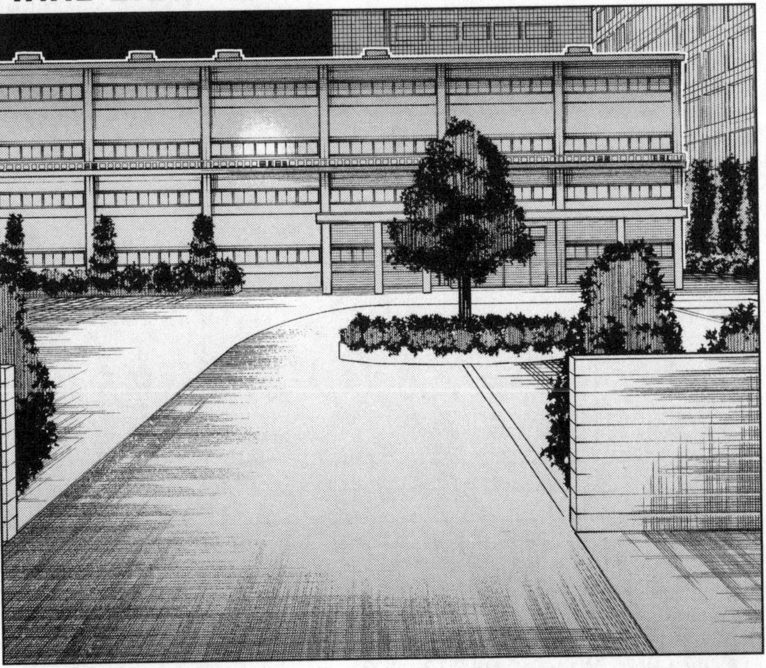

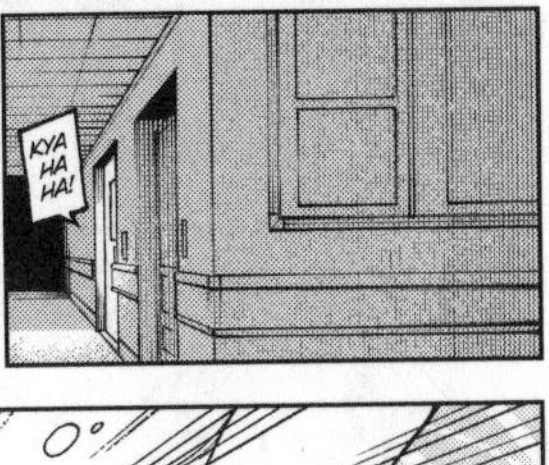
KYA HA HA!

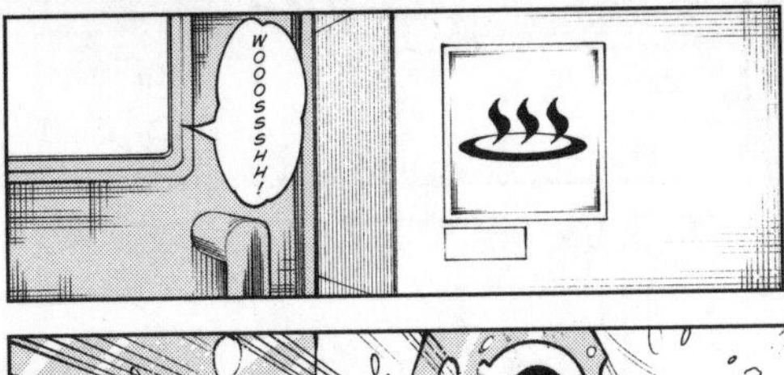
WOOOSSSHH!

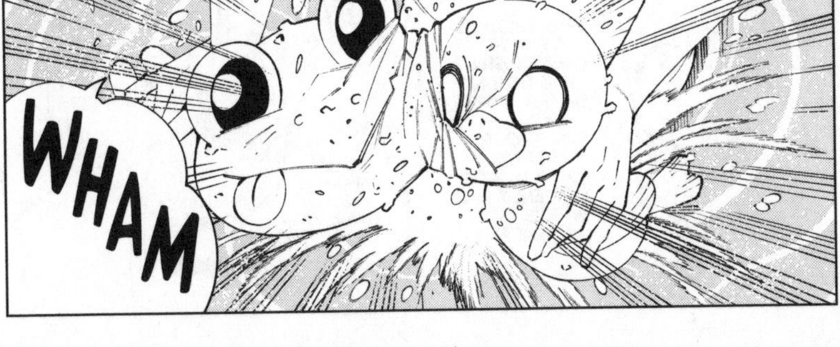
WHAM

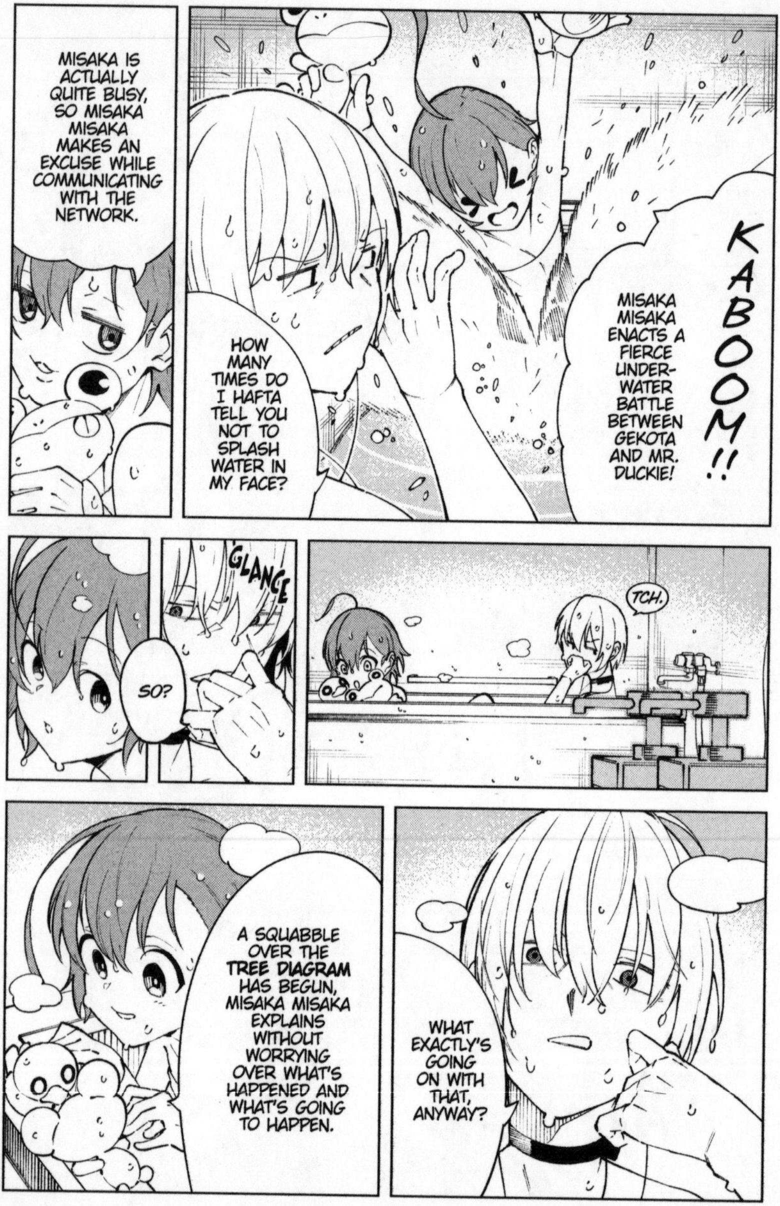
KABOOM!!
MISAKA MISAKA ENACTS A FIERCE UNDER-WATER BATTLE BETWEEN GEKOTA AND MR. DUCKIE!
HOW MANY TIMES DO I HAFTA TELL YOU NOT TO SPLASH WATER IN MY FACE?
MISAKA IS ACTUALLY QUITE BUSY, SO MISAKA MISAKA MAKES AN EXCUSE WHILE COMMUNICATING WITH THE NETWORK.
TCH.
GLANCE
SO?
WHAT EXACTLY'S GOING ON WITH THAT, ANYWAY?
A SQUABBLE OVER THE TREE DIAGRAM HAS BEGUN, MISAKA MISAKA EXPLAINS WITHOUT WORRYING OVER WHAT'S HAPPENED AND WHAT'S GOING TO HAPPEN.

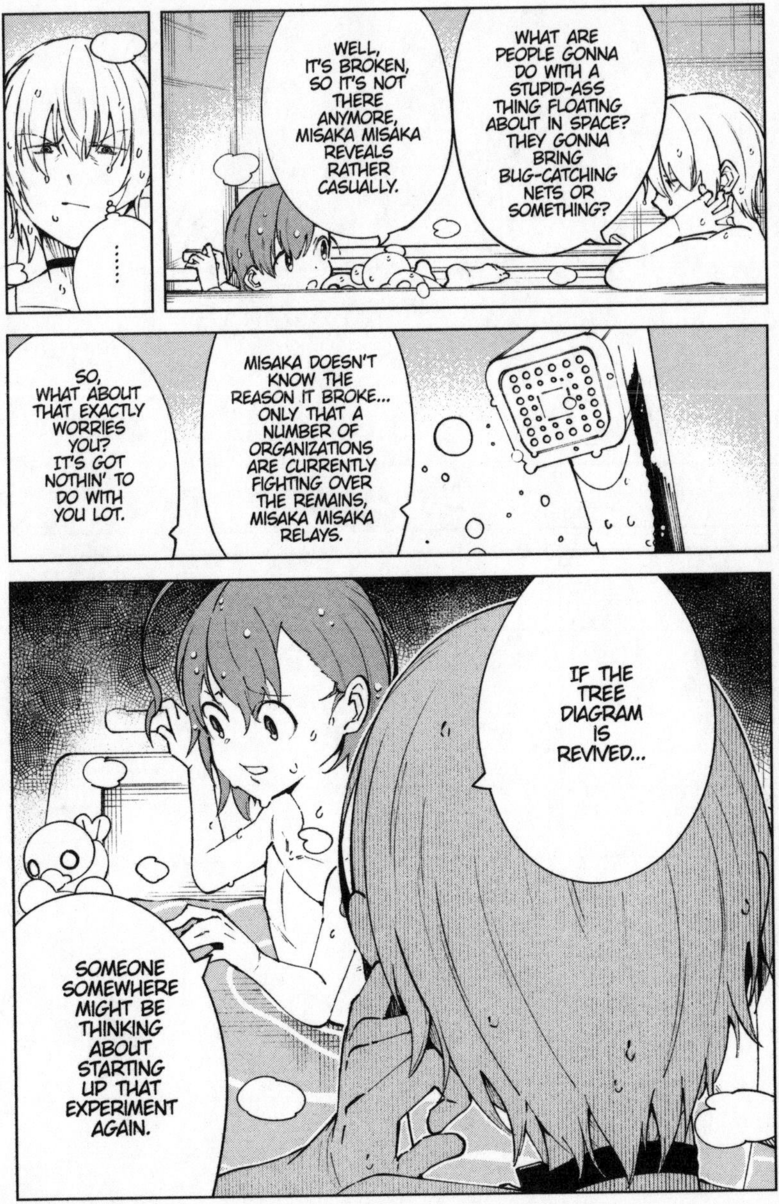
WHAT ARE PEOPLE GONNA DO WITH A STUPID-ASS THING FLOATING ABOUT IN SPACE? THEY GONNA BRING BUG-CATCHING NETS OR SOMETHING?
WELL, IT'S BROKEN, SO IT'S NOT THERE ANYMORE, MISAKA MISAKA REVEALS RATHER CASUALLY.
......
MISAKA DOESN'T KNOW THE REASON IT BROKE... ONLY THAT A NUMBER OF ORGANIZATIONS ARE CURRENTLY FIGHTING OVER THE REMAINS, MISAKA MISAKA RELAYS.
SO, WHAT ABOUT THAT EXACTLY WORRIES YOU? IT'S GOT NOTHIN' TO DO WITH YOU LOT.
IF THE TREE DIAGRAM IS REVIVED...
SOMEONE SOMEWHERE MIGHT BE THINKING ABOUT STARTING UP THAT EXPERIMENT AGAIN.

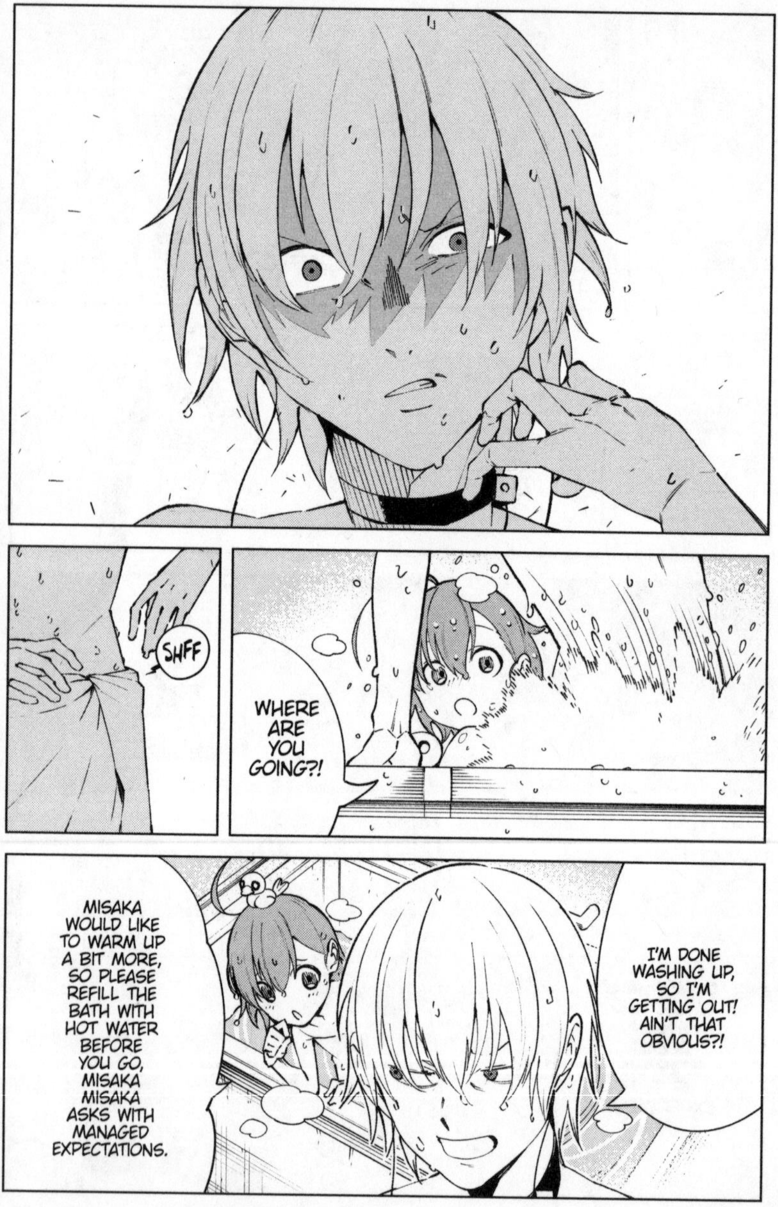
WHERE ARE YOU GOING?!
SHFF
I'M DONE WASHING UP, SO I'M GETTING OUT! AIN'T THAT OBVIOUS?!
MISAKA WOULD LIKE TO WARM UP A BIT MORE, SO PLEASE REFILL THE BATH WITH HOT WATER BEFORE YOU GO, MISAKA MISAKA ASKS WITH MANAGED EXPECTATIONS.

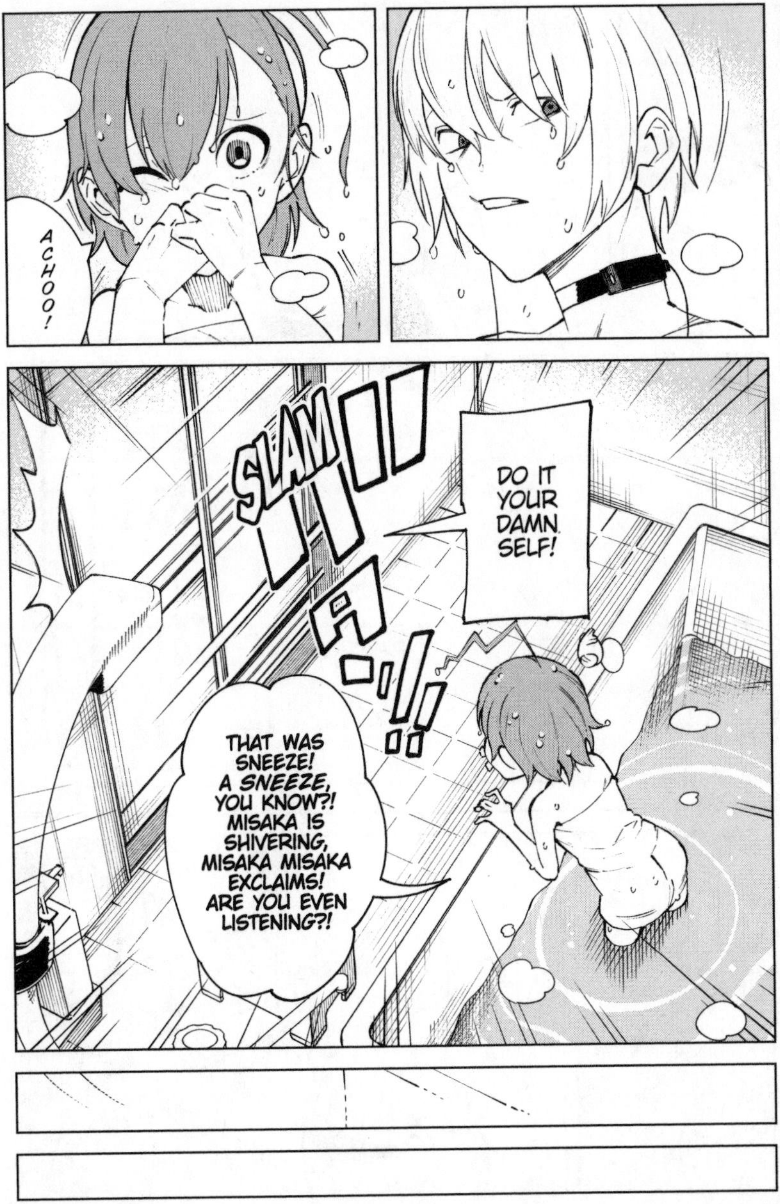
ACHOO!
DO IT YOUR DAMN SELF!
SLAM
A...!!
THAT WAS SNEEZE! A *SNEEZE*, YOU KNOW?! MISAKA IS SHIVERING, MISAKA MISAKA EXCLAIMS! ARE YOU EVEN LISTENING?!

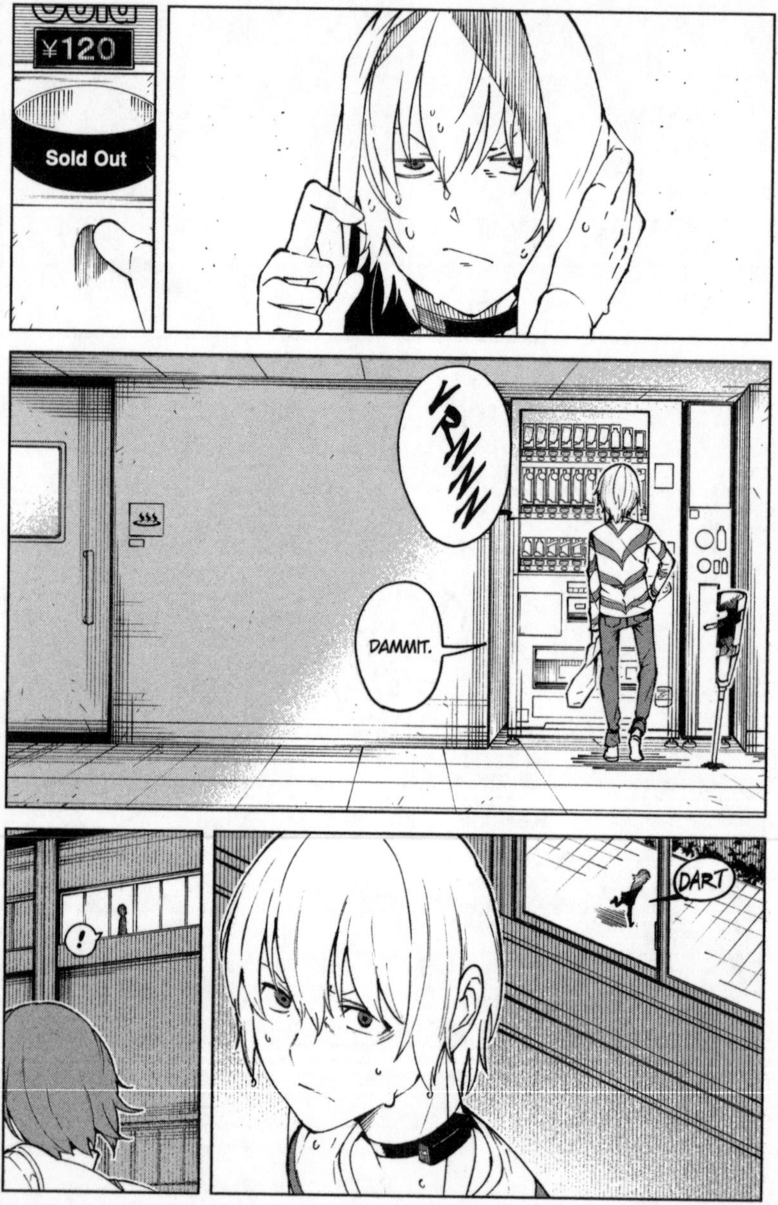

¥120
Sold Out
VRNNN
DAMMIT.
DART
!

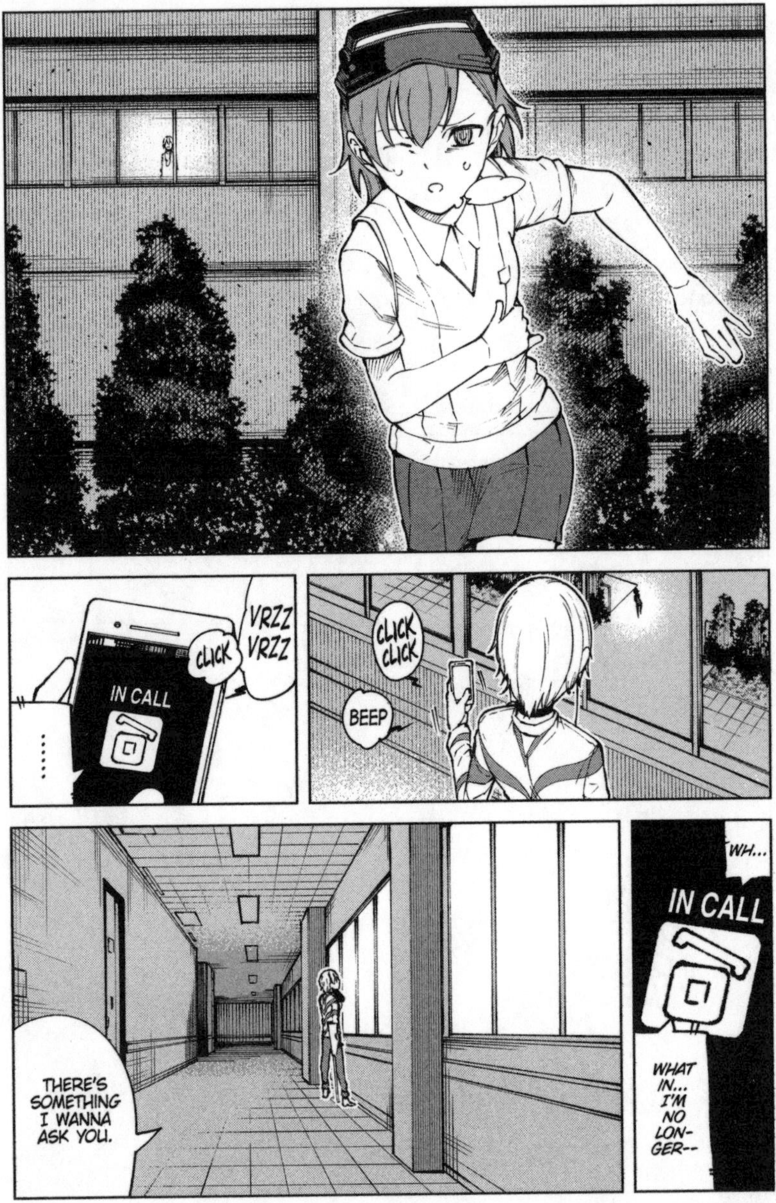
CLICK CLICK
BEEP
VRZZ VRZZ
CLICK
IN CALL
......
WH...
IN CALL
WHAT IN... I'M NO LONGER--
THERE'S SOMETHING I WANNA ASK YOU.

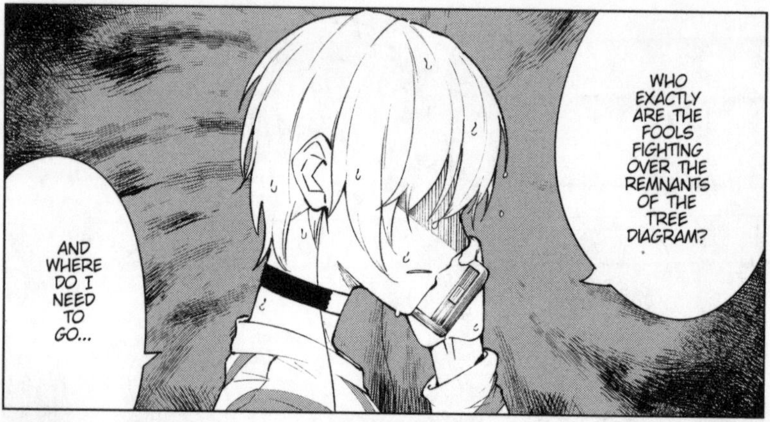
WHO EXACTLY ARE THE FOOLS FIGHTING OVER THE REMNANTS OF THE TREE DIAGRAM?
AND WHERE DO I NEED TO GO...
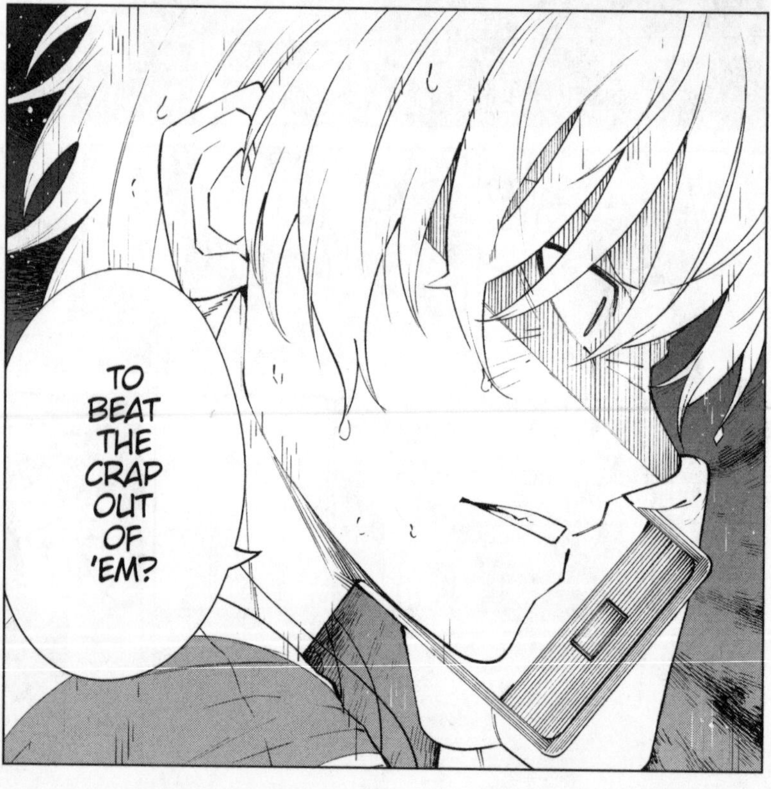
TO BEAT THE CRAP OUT OF 'EM?

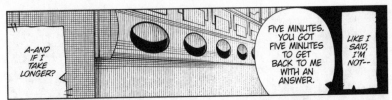

LIKE I SAID, I'M NOT--
FIVE MINUTES. YOU GOT FIVE MINUTES TO GET BACK TO ME WITH AN ANSWER.
A-AND IF I TAKE LONGER?
THEN I PAY YOU A VISIT. RIGHT AWAY.
GYAH! I'LL CALL YOU RIGHT BACK!
YEAH, YOU DO THAT.
CLICK
Call Ended

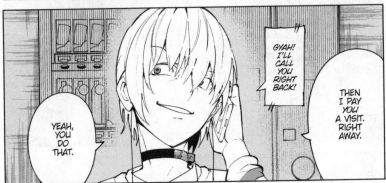

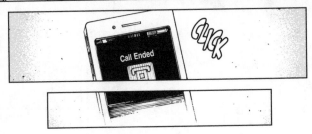

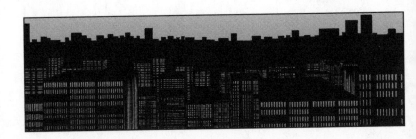

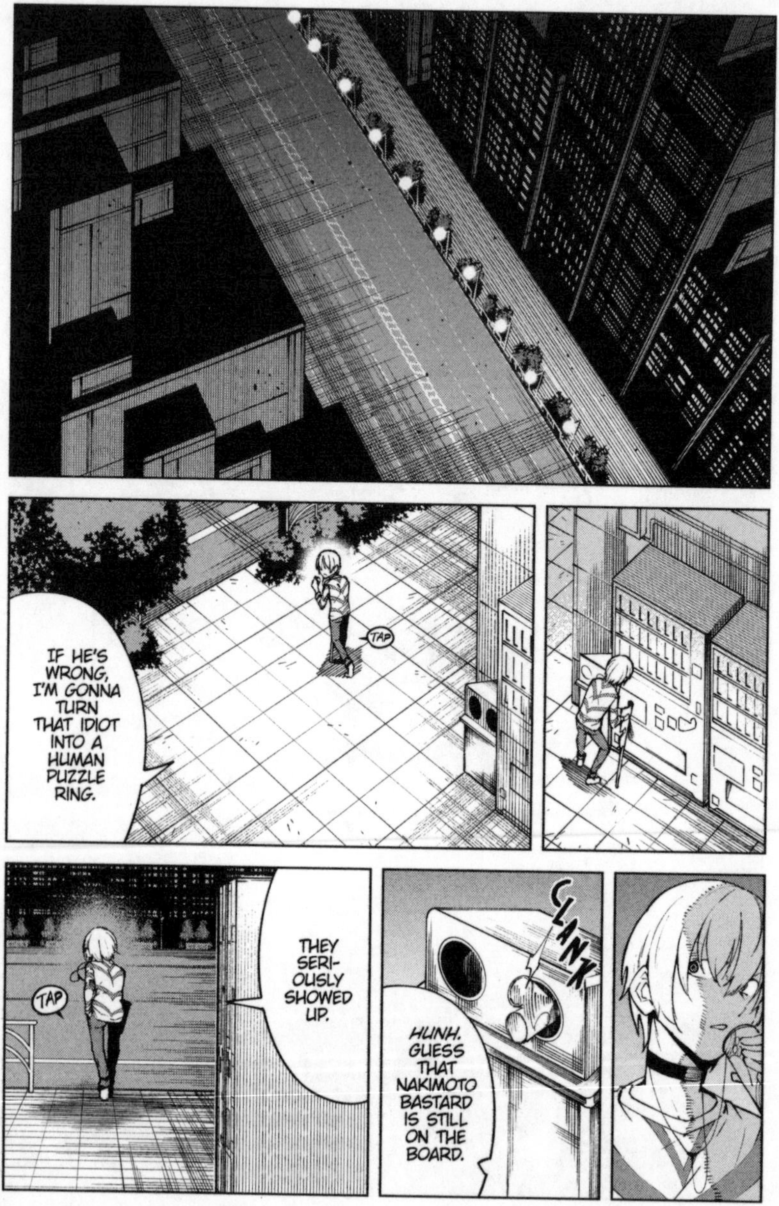
TAP
IF HE'S WRONG, I'M GONNA TURN THAT IDIOT INTO A HUMAN PUZZLE RING.
CLANK
HUNH. GUESS THAT NAKIMOTO BASTARD IS STILL ON THE BOARD.
THEY SERI-OUSLY SHOWED UP.
TAP

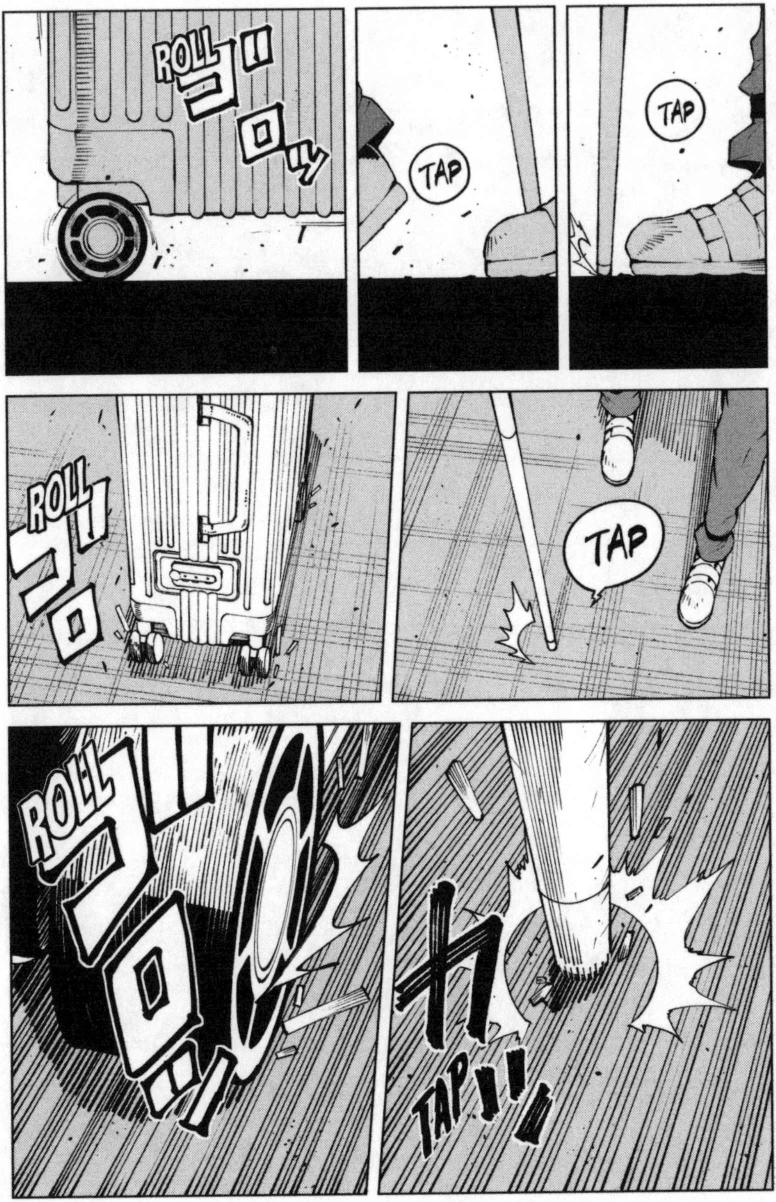
TAP
TAP
ROLL
TAP
ROLL
TAP!!
ROLL

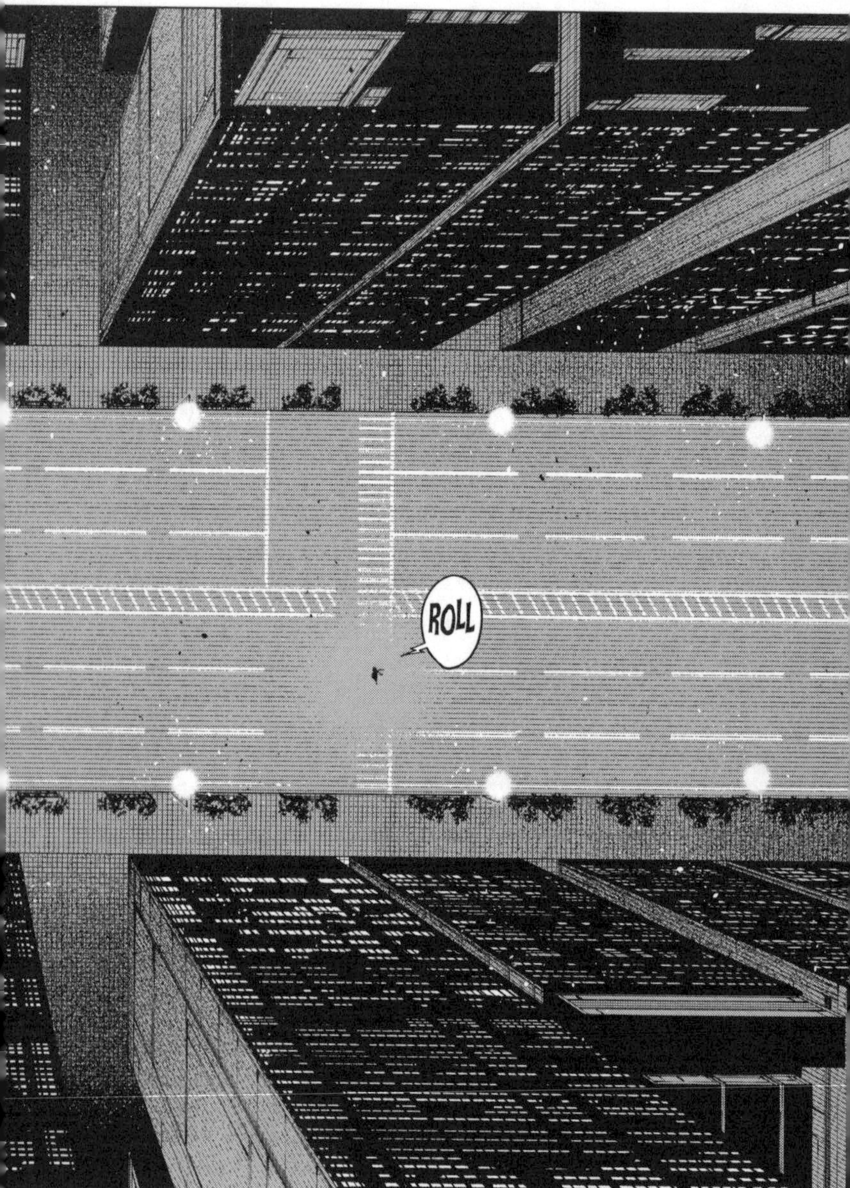
ROLL

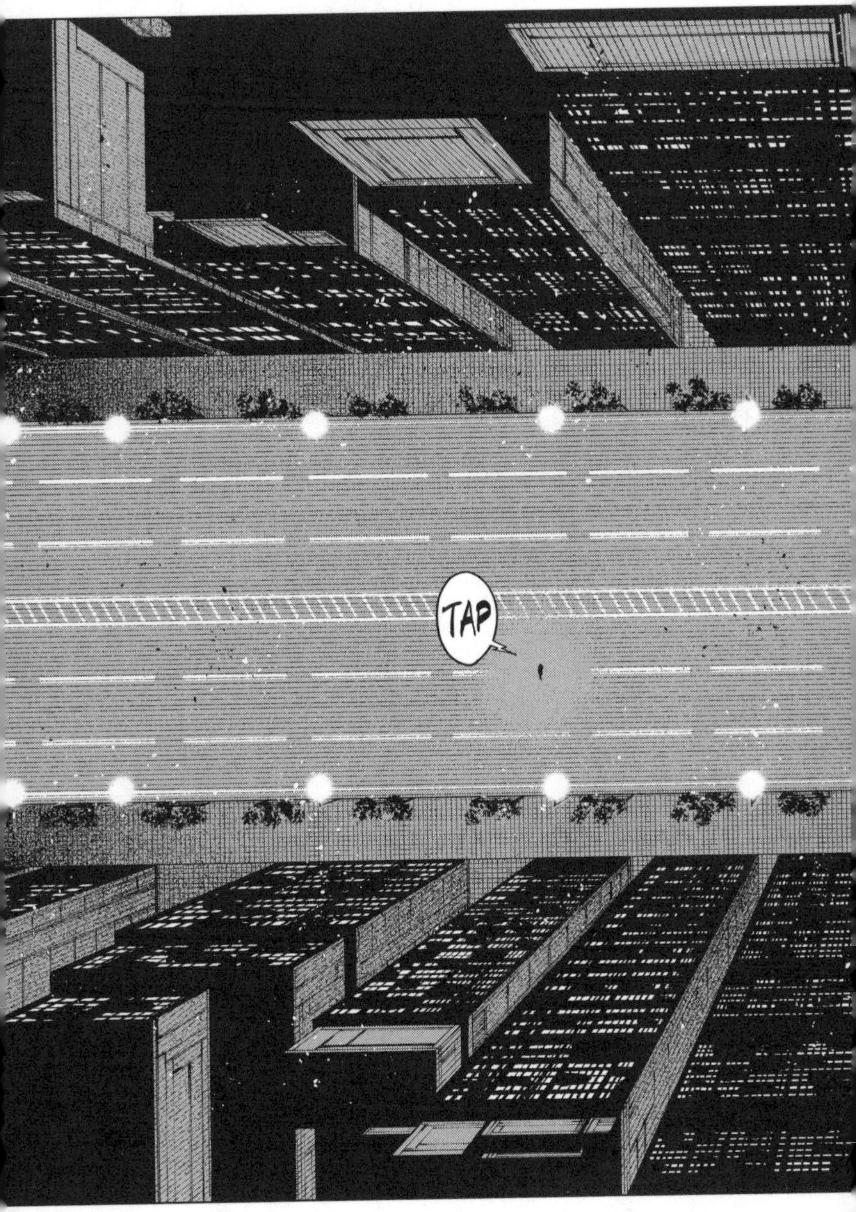
TAP

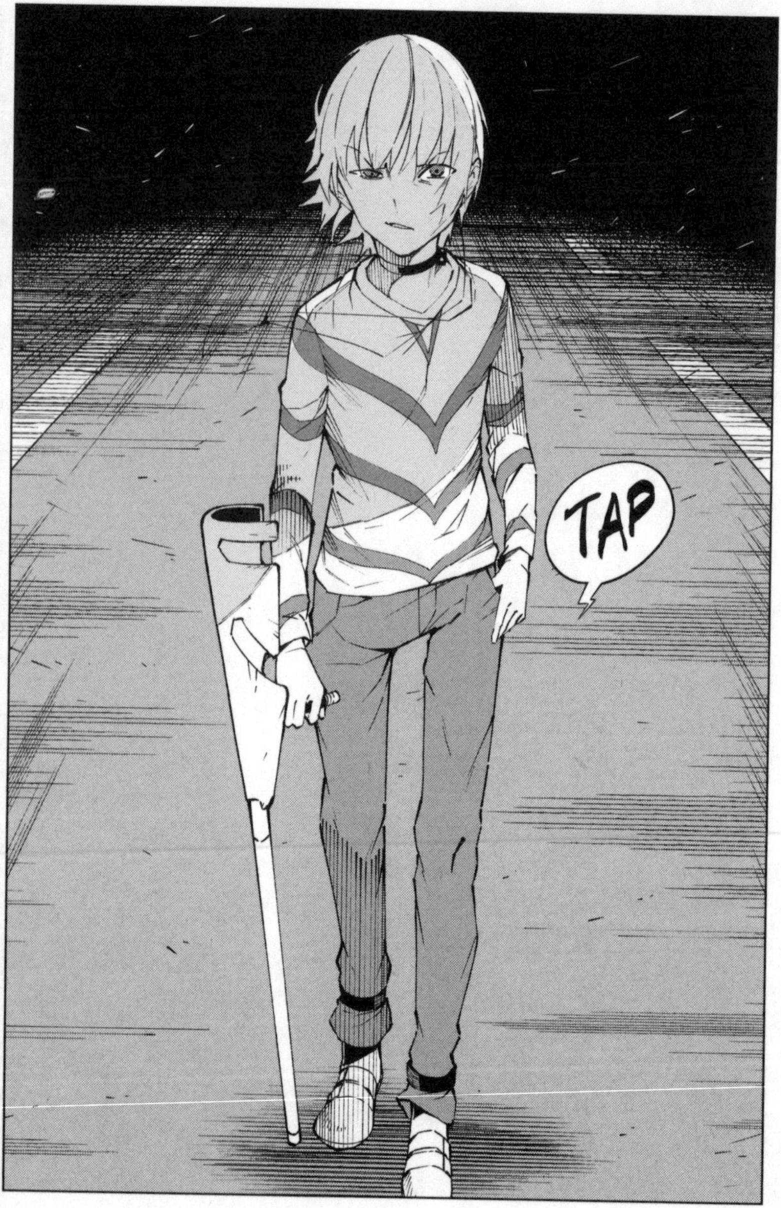
TAP

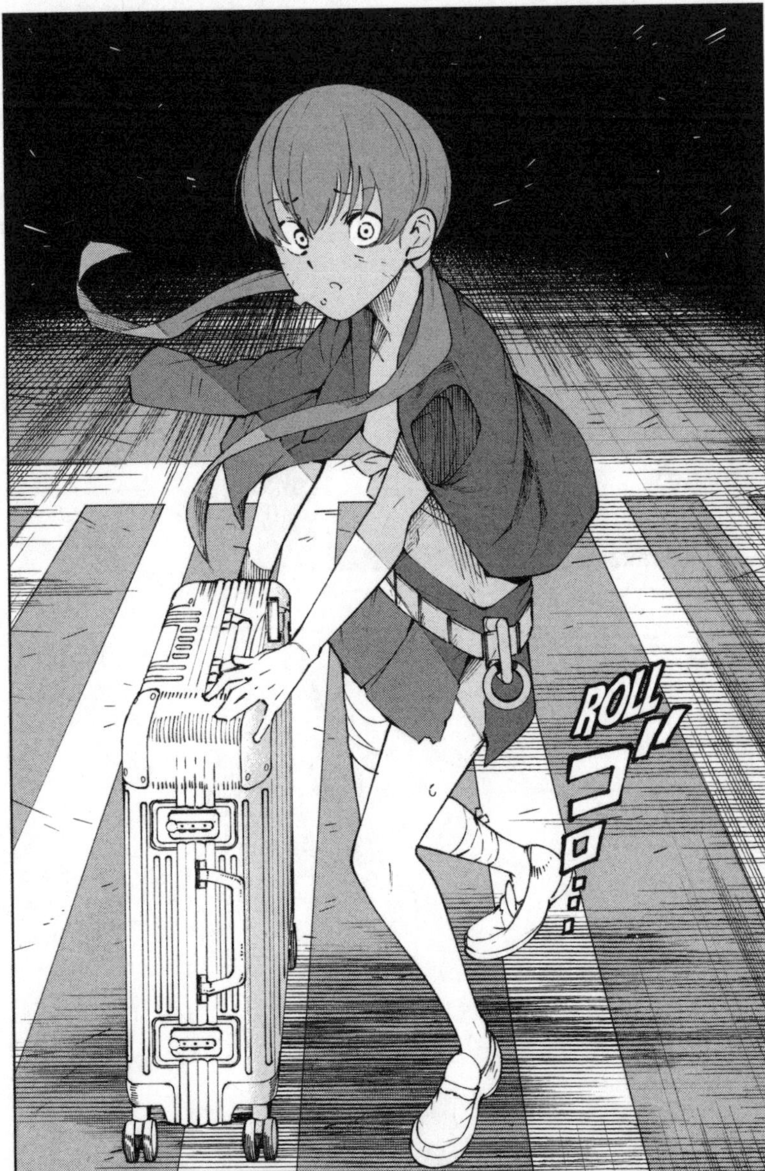
ROLL
ゴロロ…

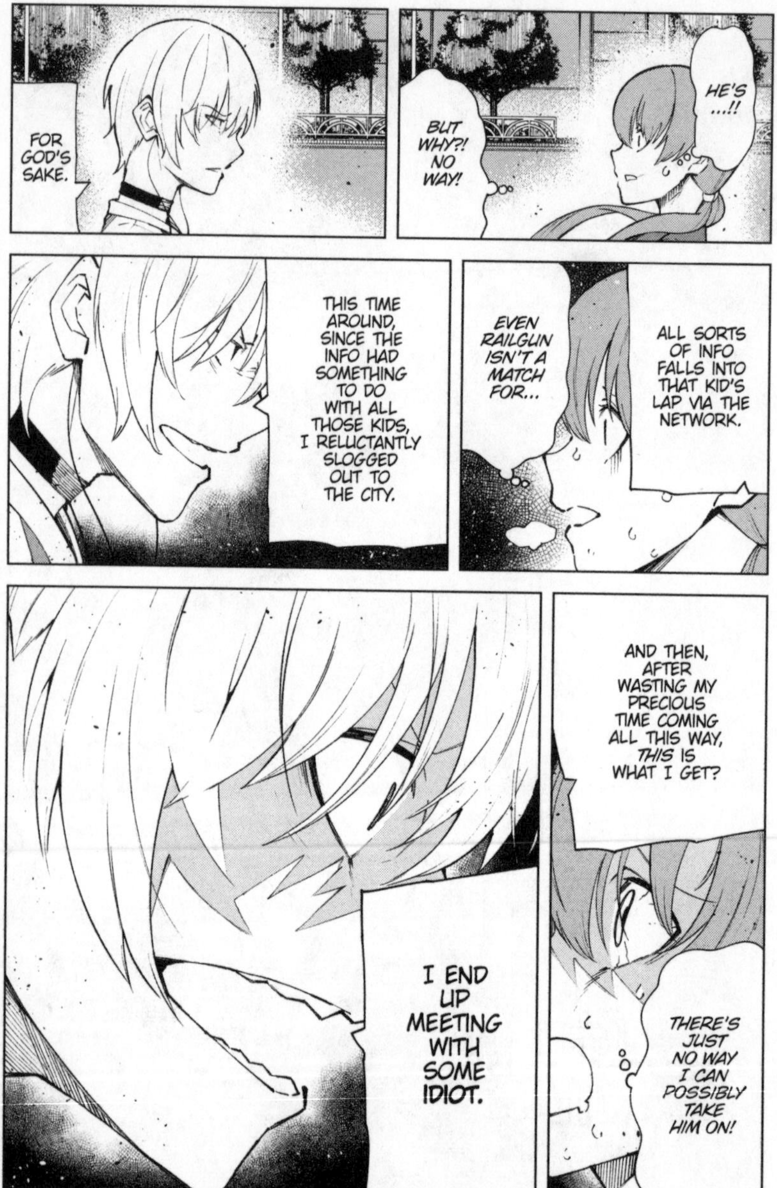
HE'S ...!!
BUT WHY?! NO WAY!
FOR GOD'S SAKE.
ALL SORTS OF INFO FALLS INTO THAT KID'S LAP VIA THE NETWORK.
EVEN RAILGUN ISN'T A MATCH FOR...
THIS TIME AROUND, SINCE THE INFO HAD SOMETHING TO DO WITH ALL THOSE KIDS, I RELUCTANTLY SLOGGED OUT TO THE CITY.
AND THEN, AFTER WASTING MY PRECIOUS TIME COMING ALL THIS WAY, THIS IS WHAT I GET?
THERE'S JUST NO WAY I CAN POSSIBLY TAKE HIM ON!
I END UP MEETING WITH SOME IDIOT.

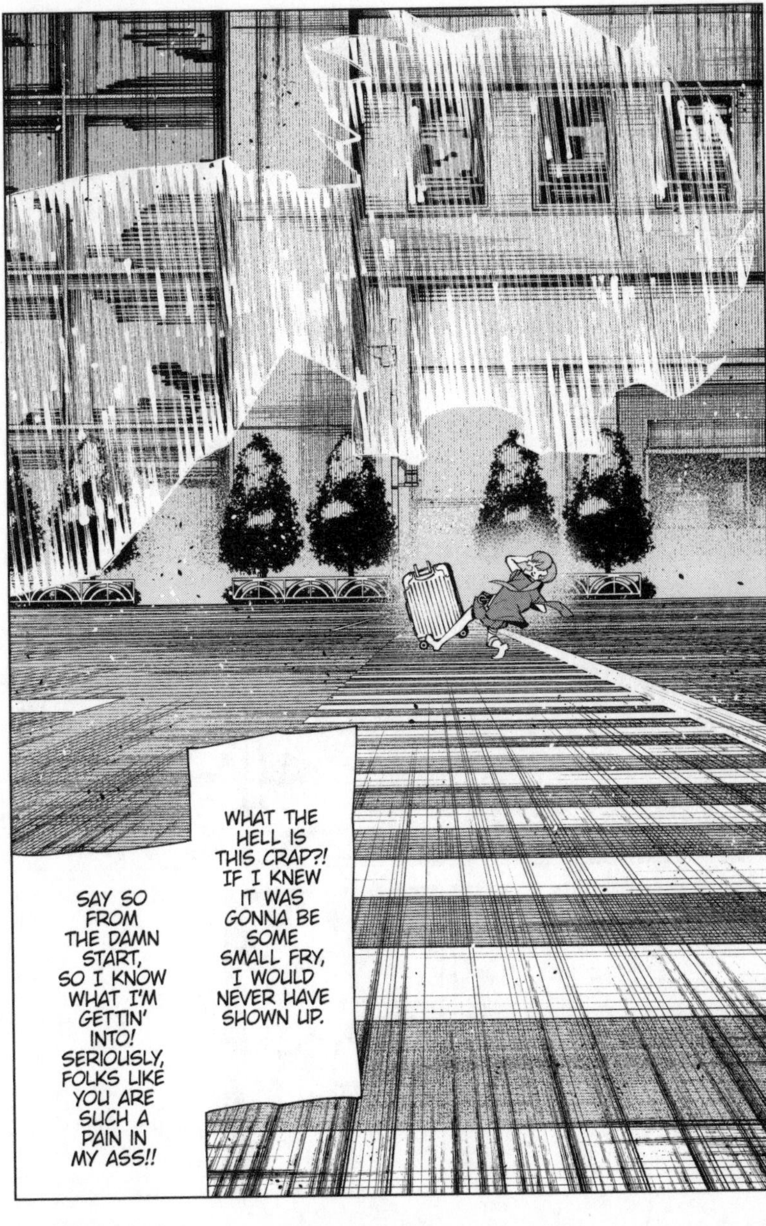
WHAT THE HELL IS THIS CRAP?! IF I KNEW IT WAS GONNA BE SOME SMALL FRY, I WOULD NEVER HAVE SHOWN UP.
SAY SO FROM THE DAMN START, SO I KNOW WHAT I'M GETTIN' INTO! SERIOUSLY, FOLKS LIKE YOU ARE SUCH A PAIN IN MY ASS!!

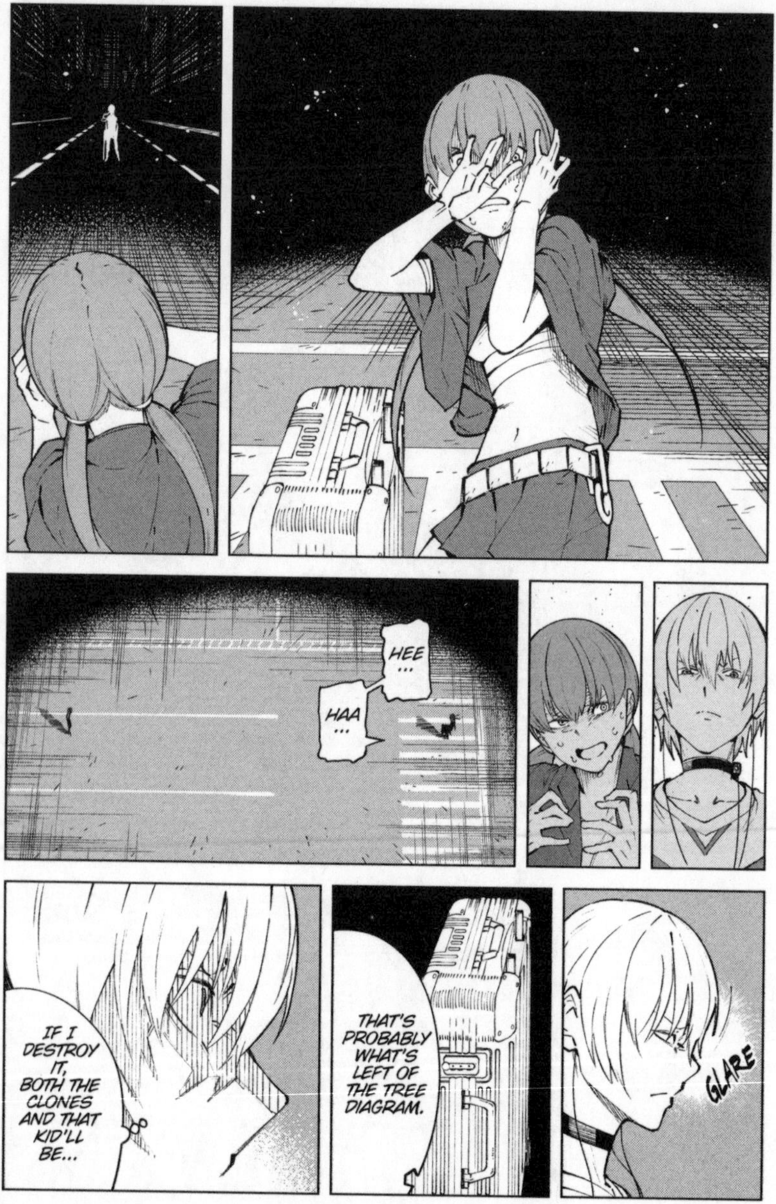
HEE...
HAA...
GLARE
THAT'S PROBABLY WHAT'S LEFT OF THE TREE DIAGRAM.
IF I DESTROY IT, BOTH THE CLONES AND THAT KID'LL BE...

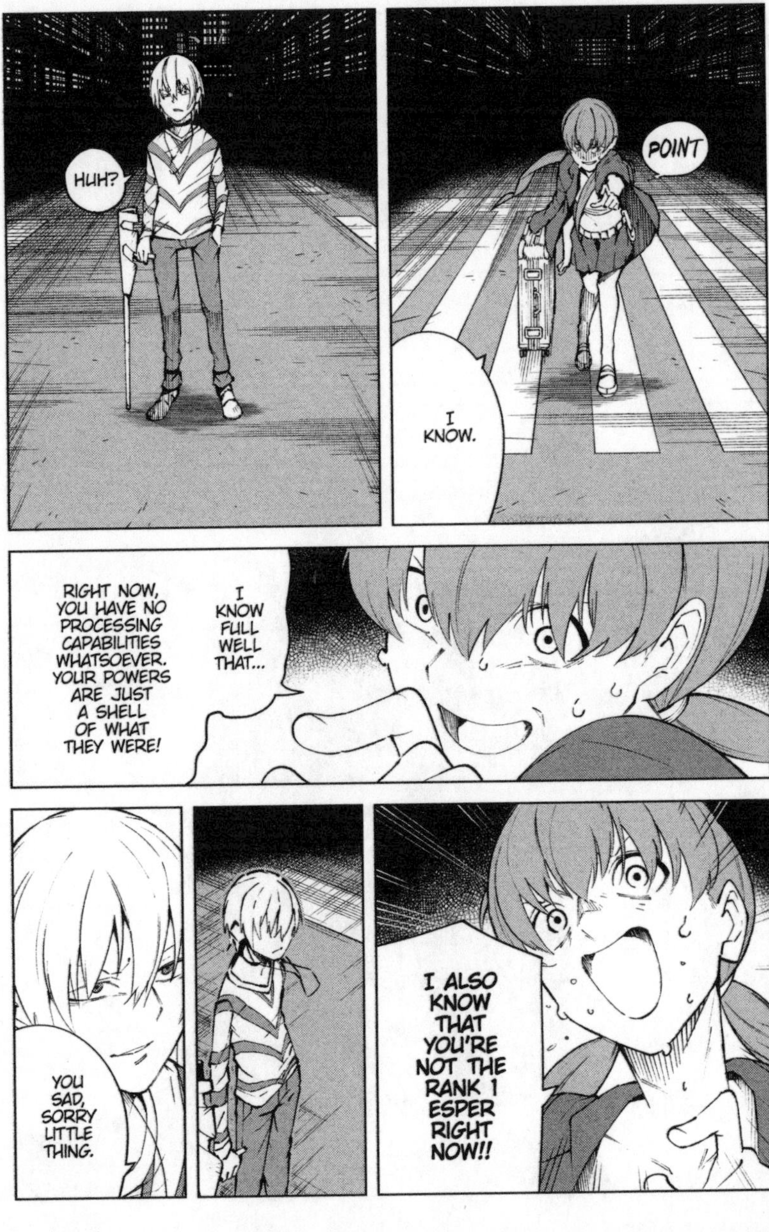
POINT
I KNOW.
HUH?
I KNOW FULL WELL THAT...
RIGHT NOW, YOU HAVE NO PROCESSING CAPABILITIES WHATSOEVER. YOUR POWERS ARE JUST A SHELL OF WHAT THEY WERE!
I ALSO KNOW THAT YOU'RE NOT THE RANK 1 ESPER RIGHT NOW!!
YOU SAD, SORRY LITTLE THING.

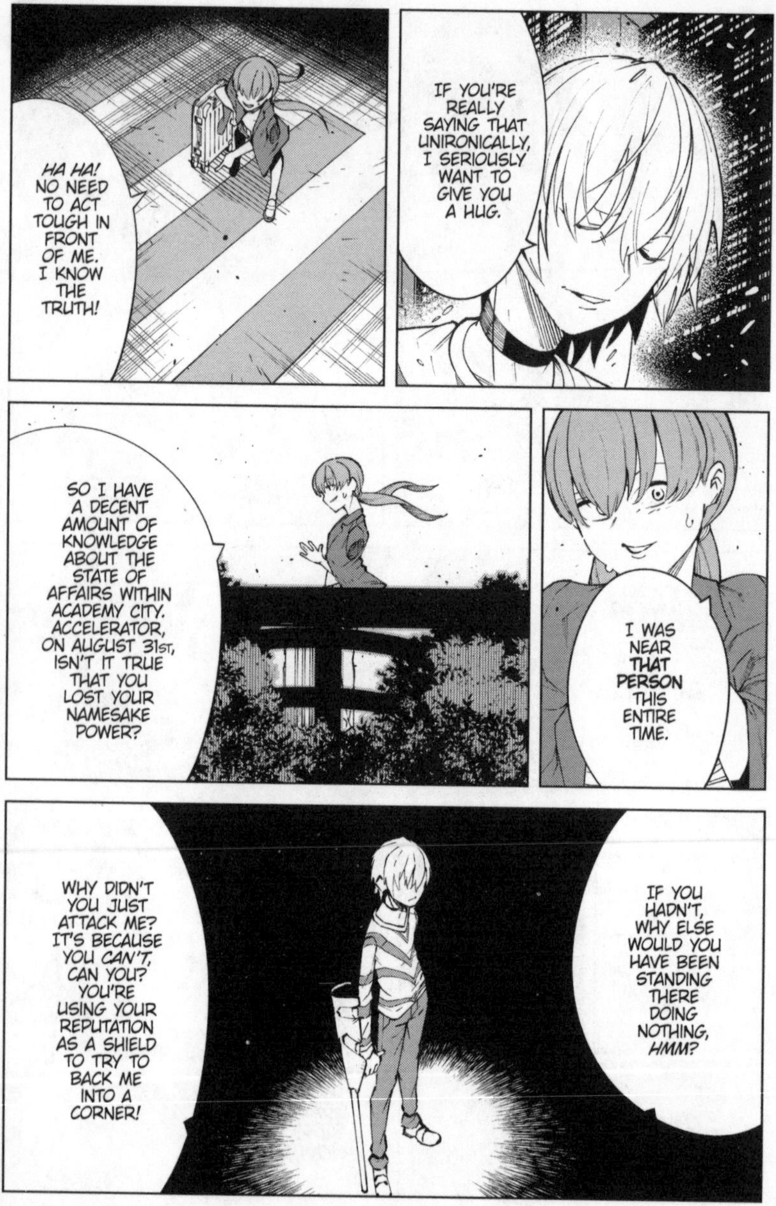
IF YOU'RE REALLY SAYING THAT UNIRONICALLY, I SERIOUSLY WANT TO GIVE YOU A HUG.
HA HA! NO NEED TO ACT TOUGH IN FRONT OF ME. I KNOW THE TRUTH!
I WAS NEAR **THAT PERSON** THIS ENTIRE TIME.
SO I HAVE A DECENT AMOUNT OF KNOWLEDGE ABOUT THE STATE OF AFFAIRS WITHIN ACADEMY CITY. ACCELERATOR, ON AUGUST 31ST, ISN'T IT TRUE THAT YOU LOST YOUR NAMESAKE POWER?
IF YOU HADN'T, WHY ELSE WOULD YOU HAVE BEEN STANDING THERE DOING NOTHING, *HMM?*
WHY DIDN'T YOU JUST ATTACK ME? IT'S BECAUSE YOU *CAN'T*, CAN YOU? YOU'RE USING YOUR REPUTATION AS A SHIELD TO TRY TO BACK ME INTO A CORNER!

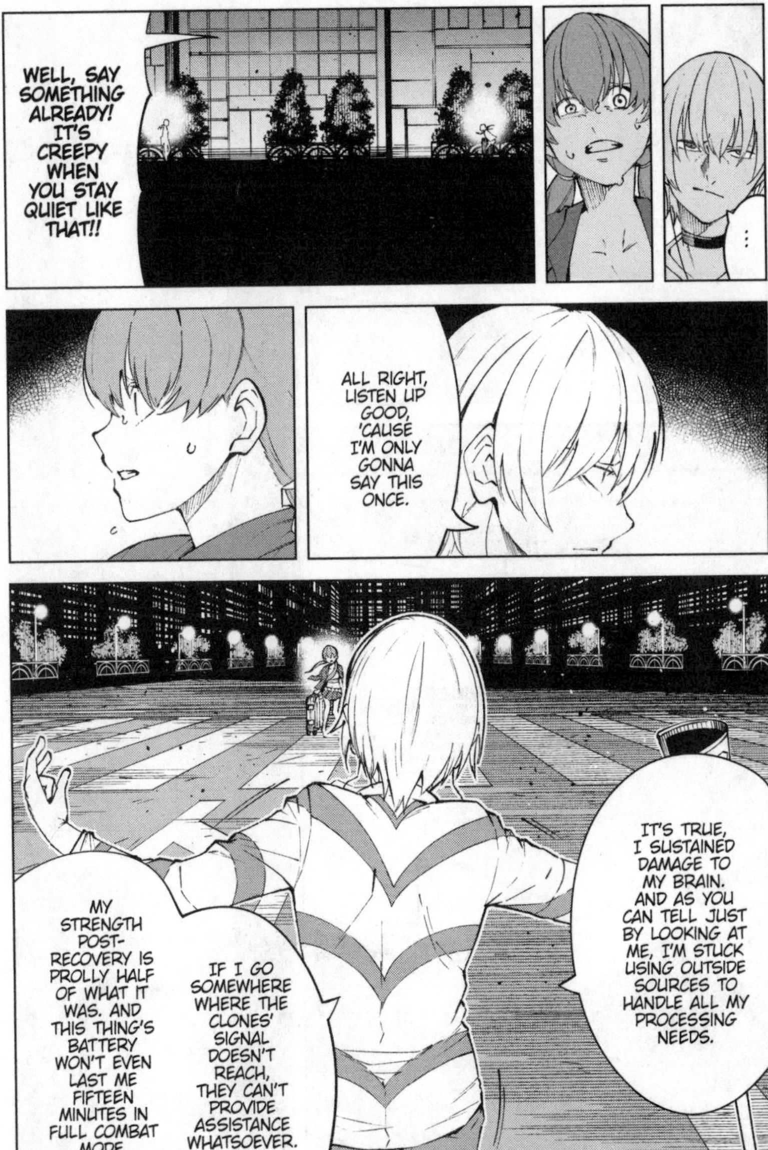
...
WELL, SAY SOMETHING ALREADY! IT'S CREEPY WHEN YOU STAY QUIET LIKE THAT!!
ALL RIGHT, LISTEN UP GOOD, 'CAUSE I'M ONLY GONNA SAY THIS ONCE.
IT'S TRUE, I SUSTAINED DAMAGE TO MY BRAIN. AND AS YOU CAN TELL JUST BY LOOKING AT ME, I'M STUCK USING OUTSIDE SOURCES TO HANDLE ALL MY PROCESSING NEEDS.
IF I GO SOMEWHERE WHERE THE CLONES' SIGNAL DOESN'T REACH, THEY CAN'T PROVIDE ASSISTANCE WHATSOEVER.
MY STRENGTH POST-RECOVERY IS PROLLY HALF OF WHAT IT WAS. AND THIS THING'S BATTERY WON'T EVEN LAST ME FIFTEEN MINUTES IN FULL COMBAT MODE.

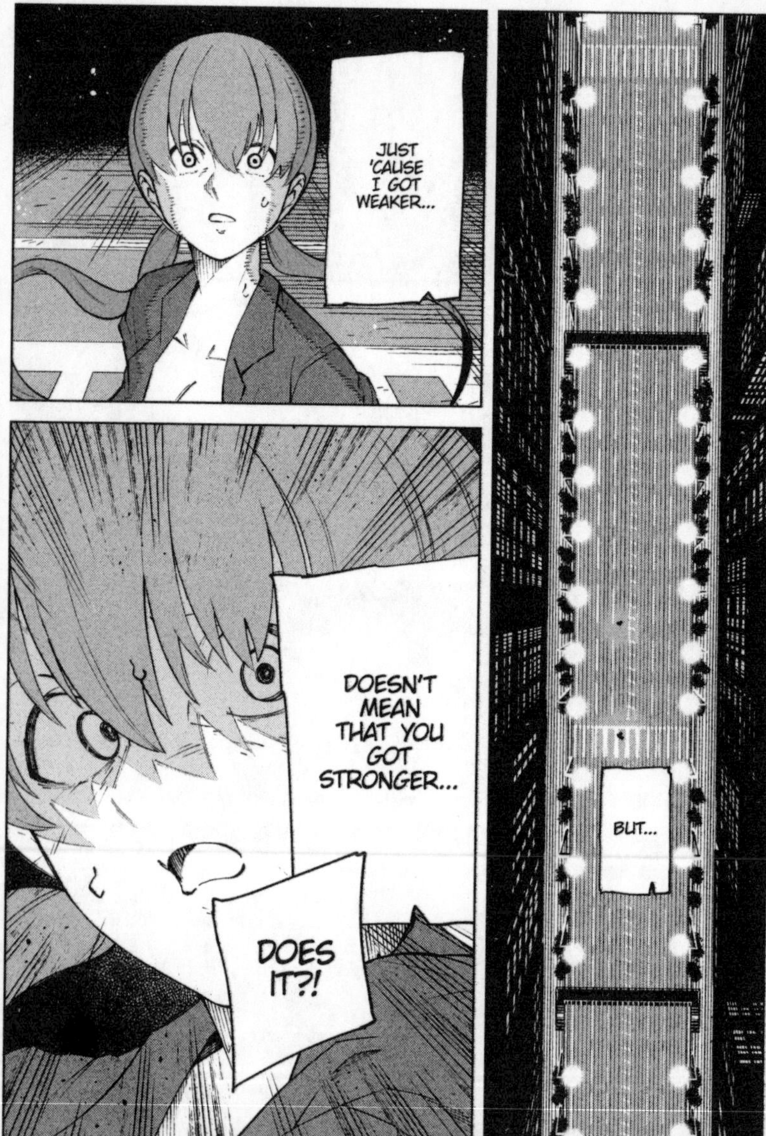
BUT...
JUST 'CAUSE I GOT WEAKER...
DOESN'T MEAN THAT YOU GOT STRONGER...
DOES IT?!

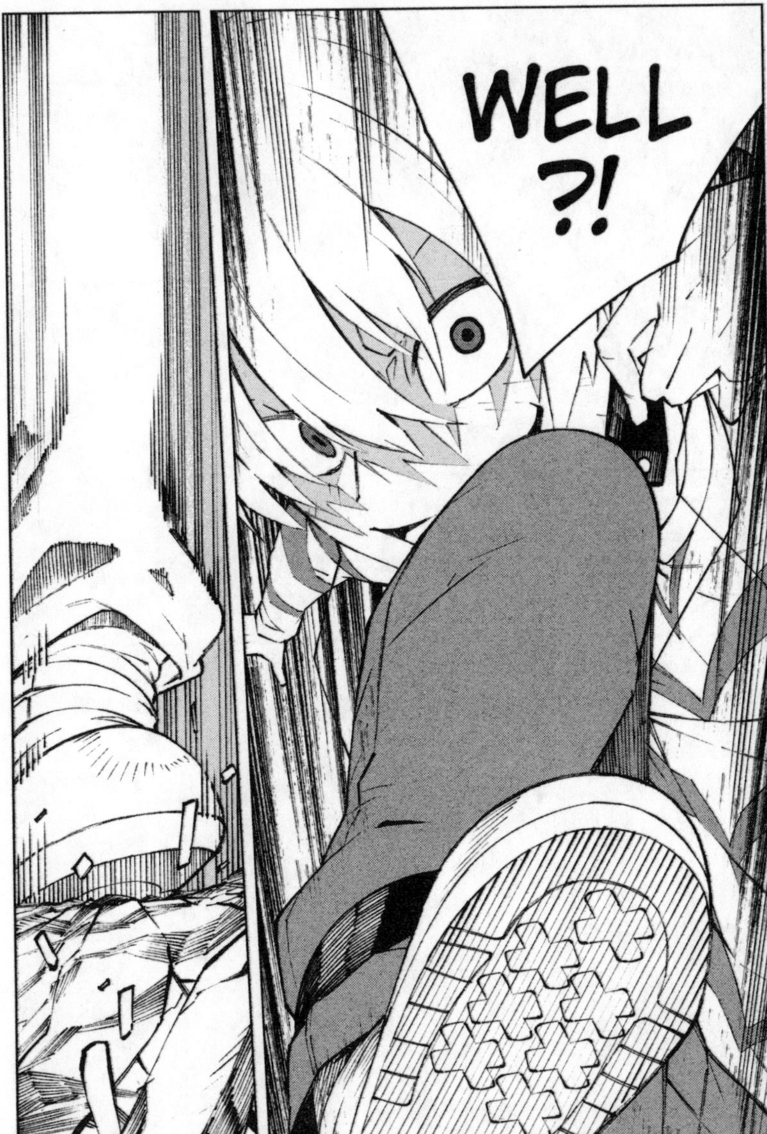
WELL ?!

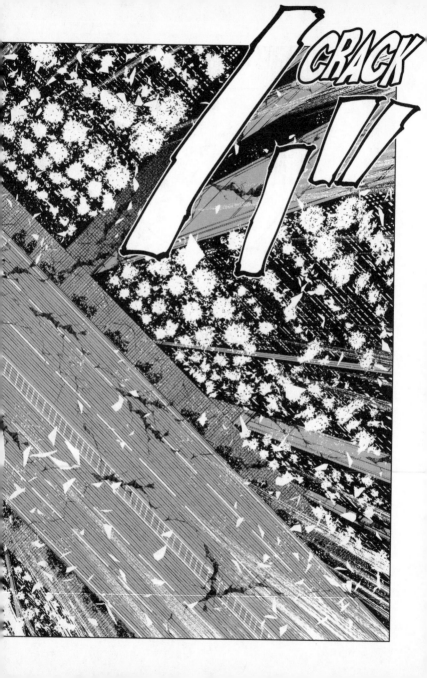

CRACK

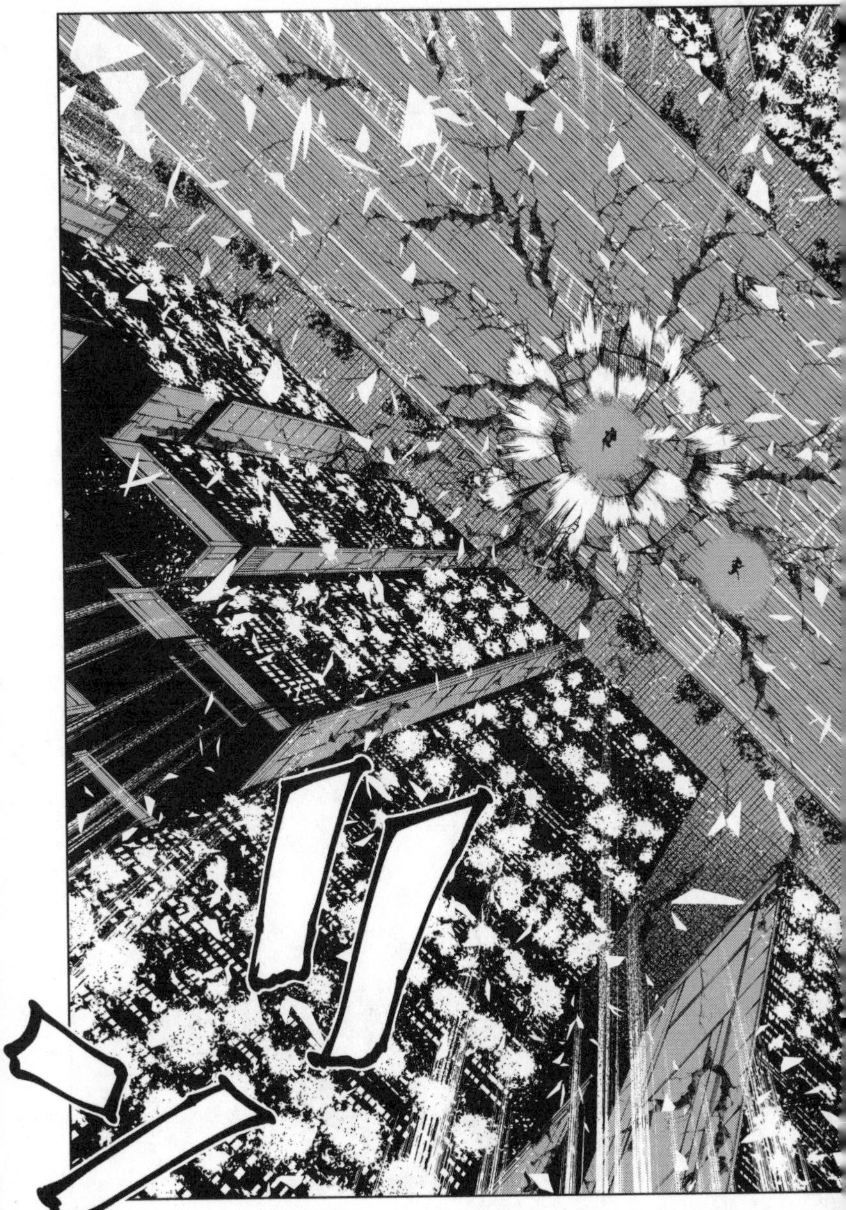

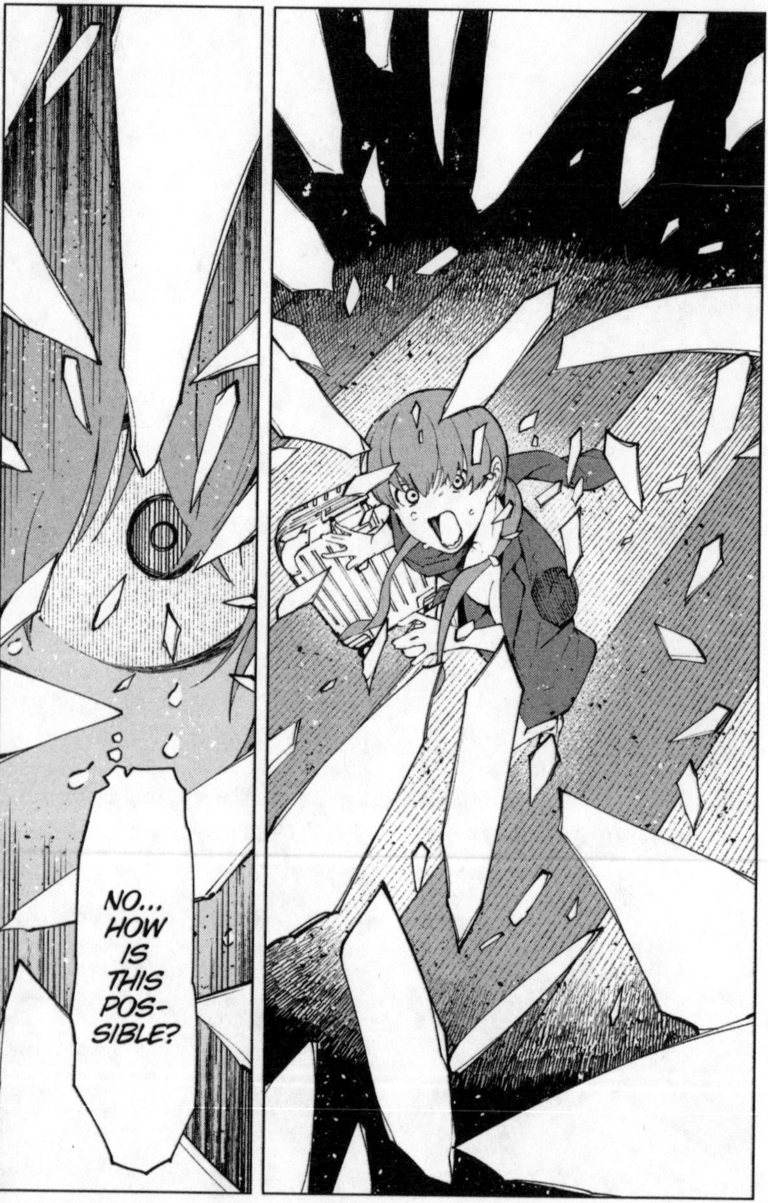
NO... HOW IS THIS POSSIBLE?

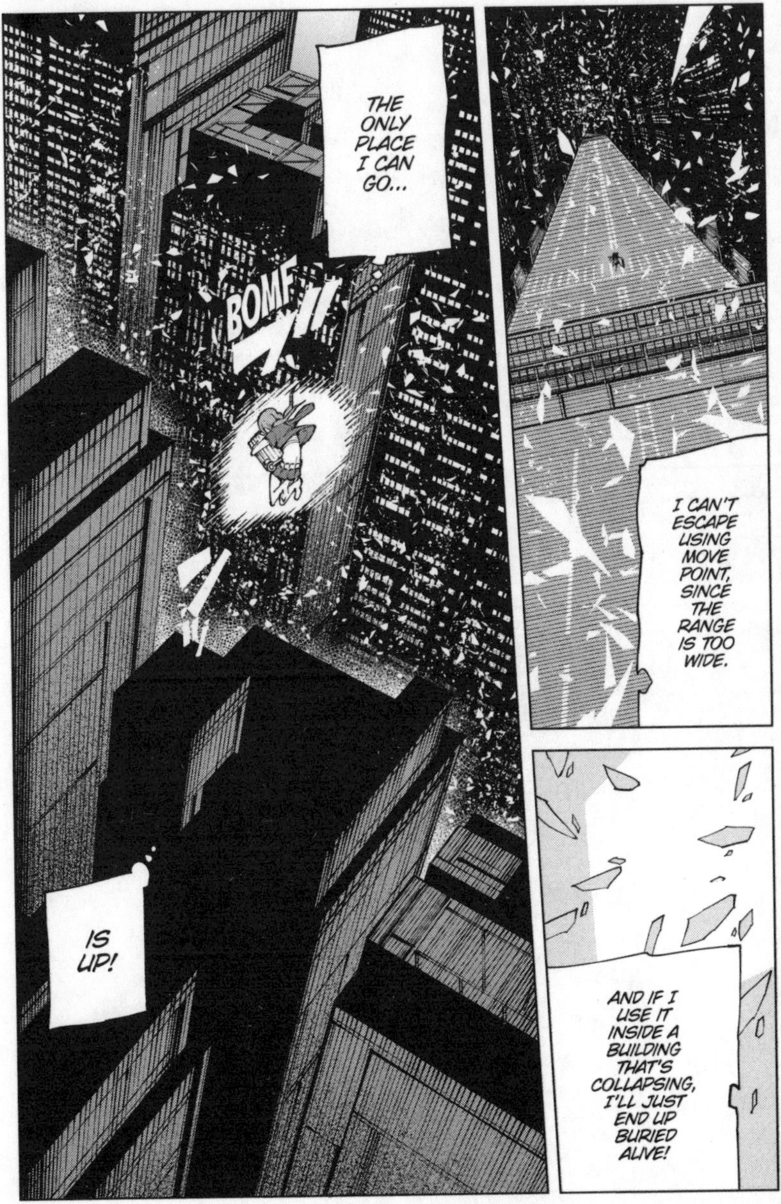
I CAN'T ESCAPE USING MOVE POINT, SINCE THE RANGE IS TOO WIDE.
AND IF I USE IT INSIDE A BUILDING THAT'S COLLAPSING, I'LL JUST END UP BURIED ALIVE!
THE ONLY PLACE I CAN GO...
BOMF
IS UP!

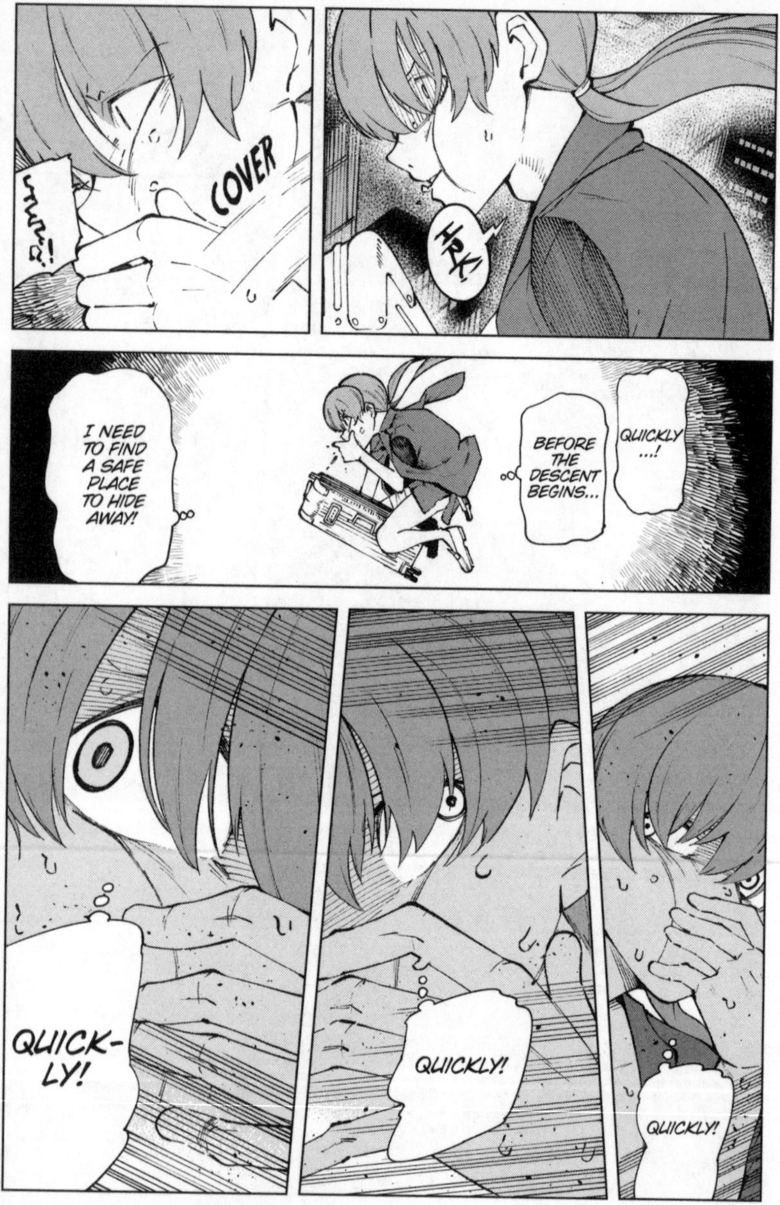
HRK!
COVER
QUICKLY ...!
BEFORE THE DESCENT BEGINS...
I NEED TO FIND A SAFE PLACE TO HIDE AWAY!
QUICKLY!
QUICKLY!
QUICK-LY!

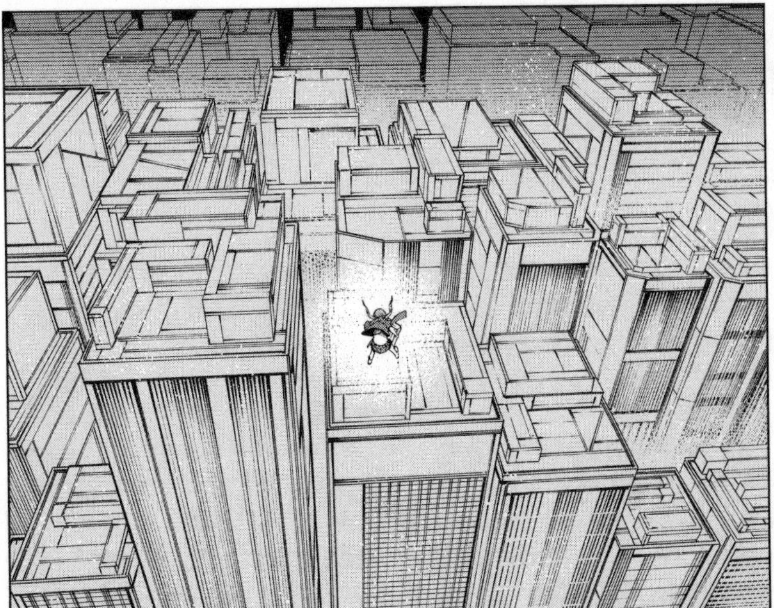
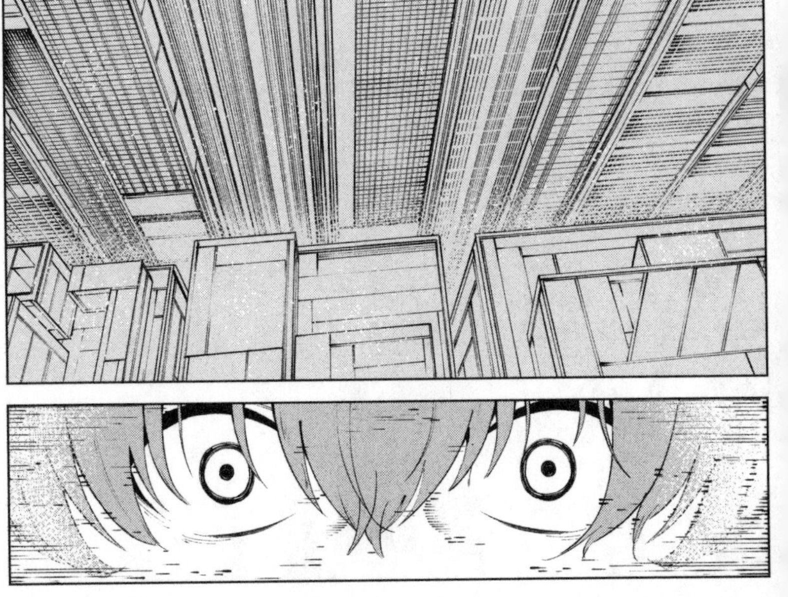

IT'S NO GOOD.

ACK...!

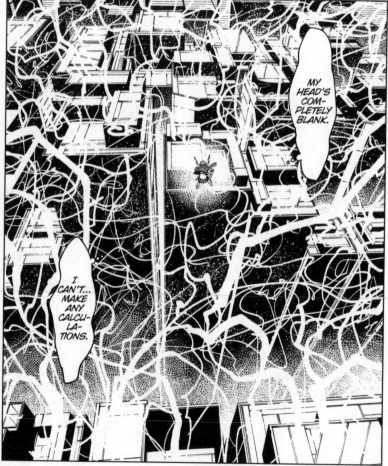

MY HEAD'S COMPLETELY BLANK.

I CAN'T... MAKE ANY CALCULATIONS.

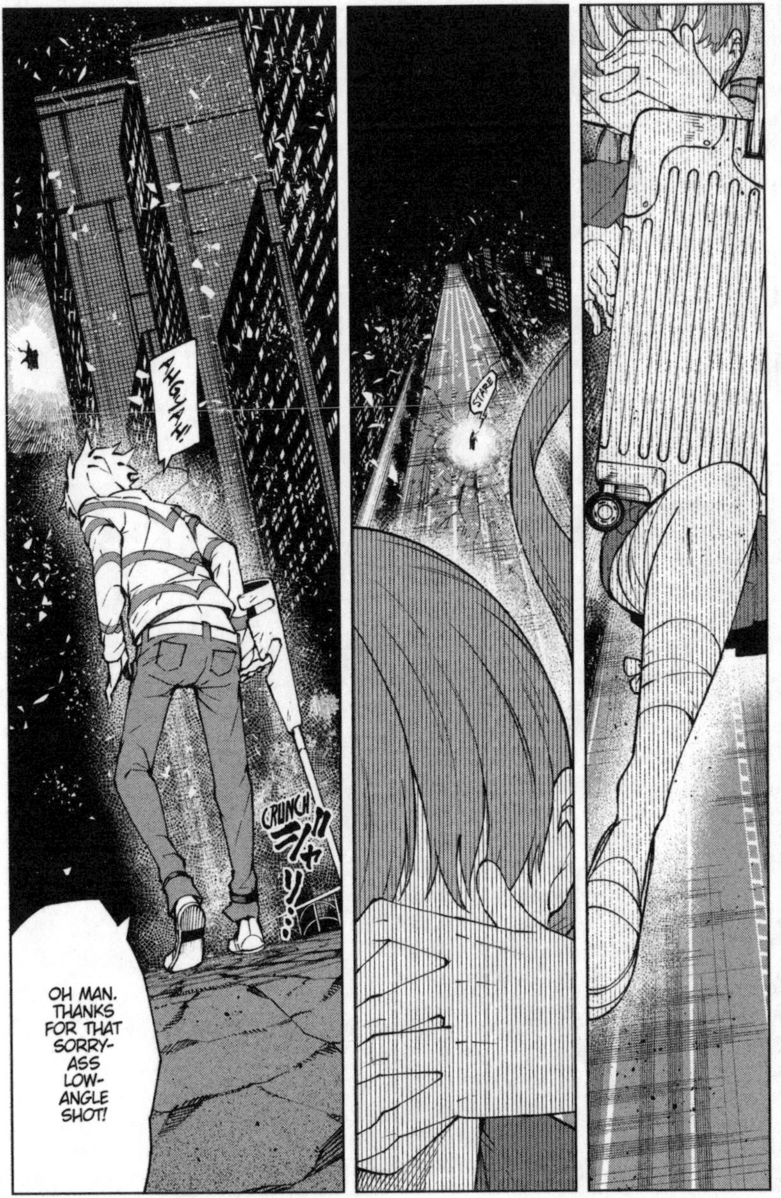
STARE
AHGUAH!!
CRUNCH
シャリ…
OH MAN. THANKS FOR THAT SORRY-ASS LOW-ANGLE SHOT!

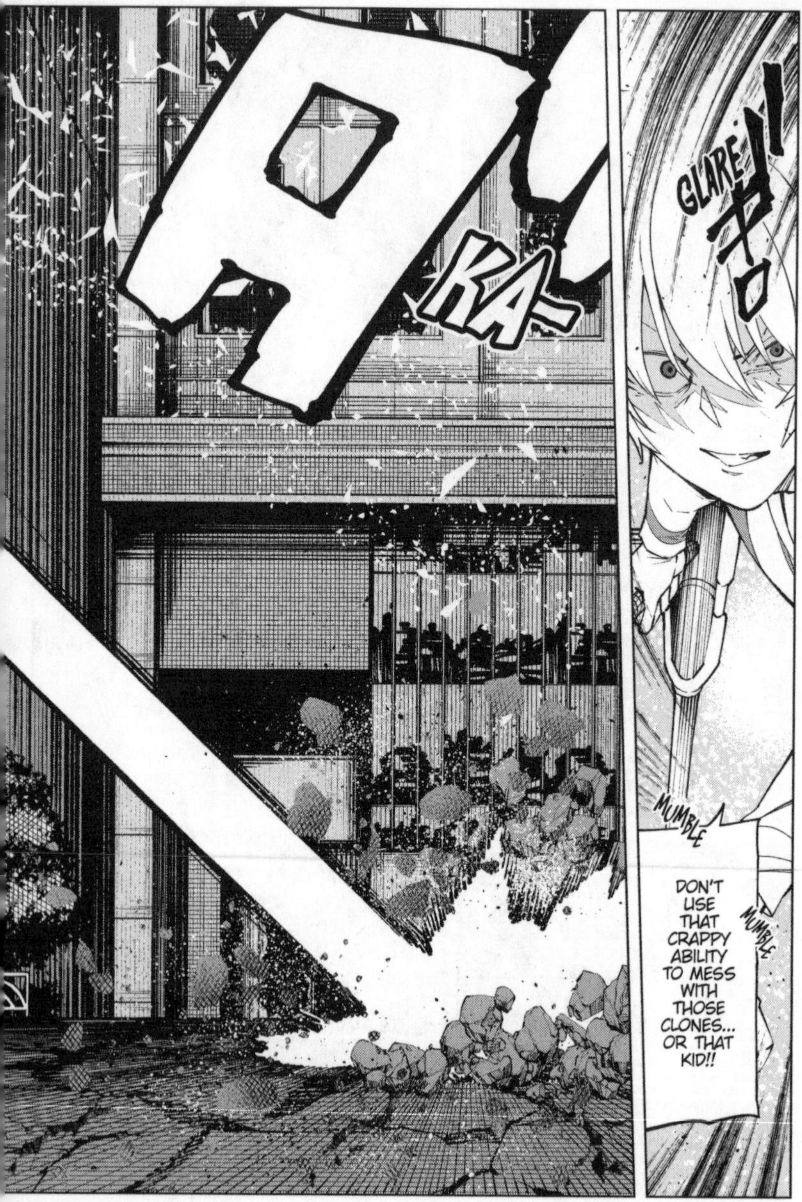
GLARE
MUMBLE
DON'T USE THAT CRAPPY ABILITY TO MESS WITH THOSE CLONES... OR THAT KID!!
MUMBLE
KA-

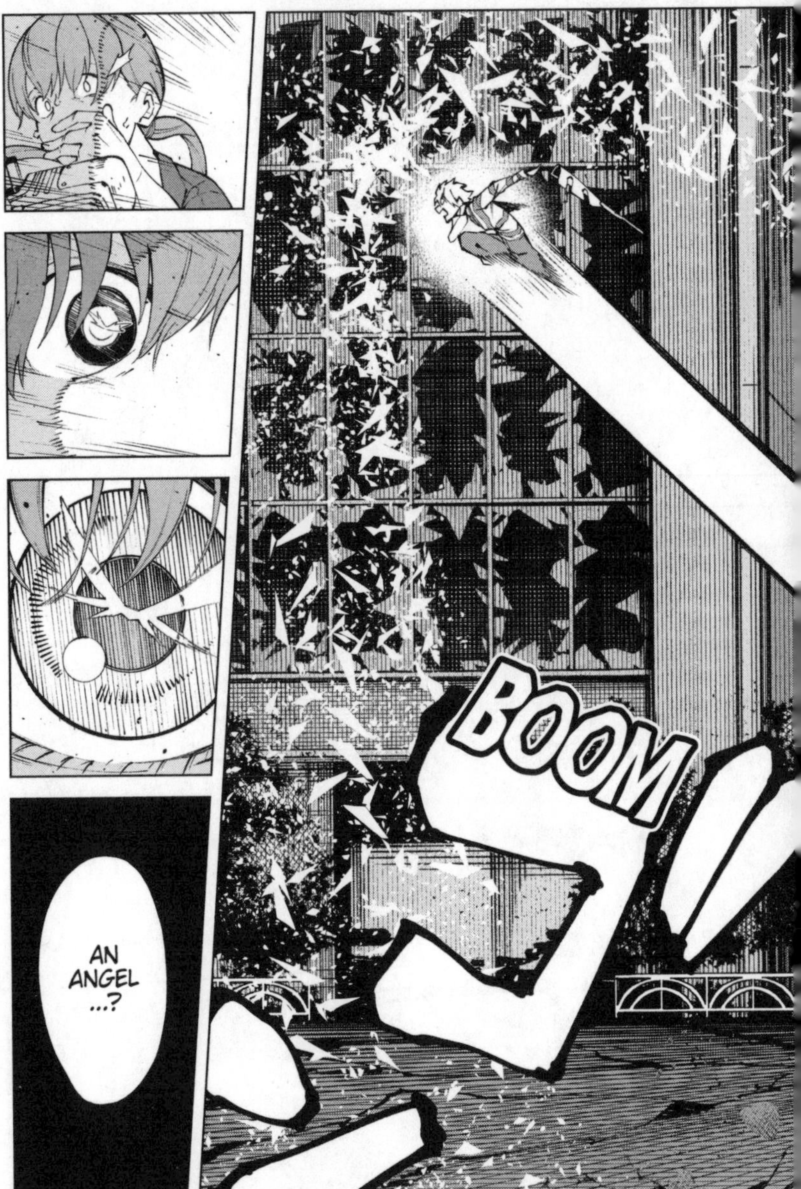
BOOM
AN ANGEL ...?

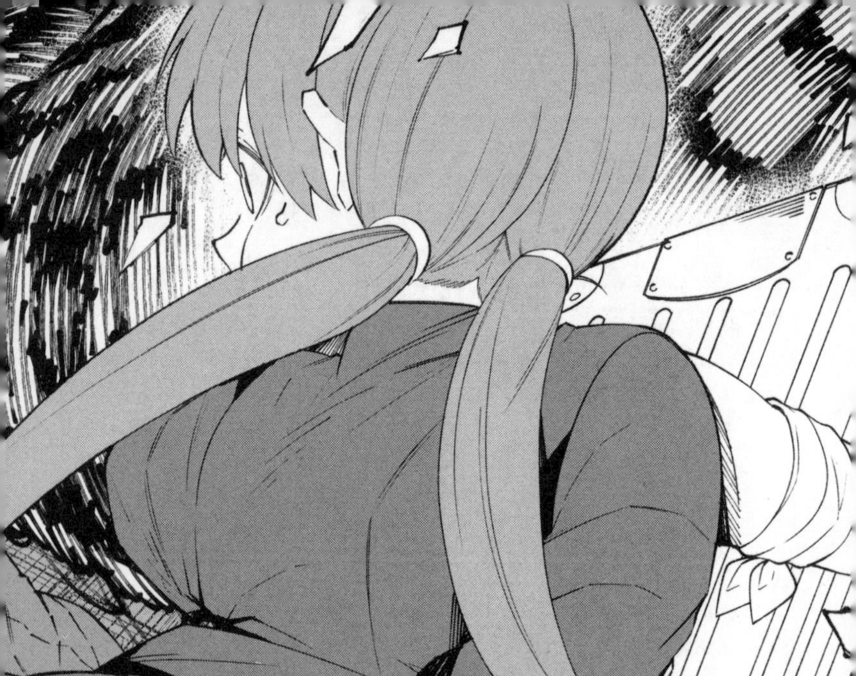

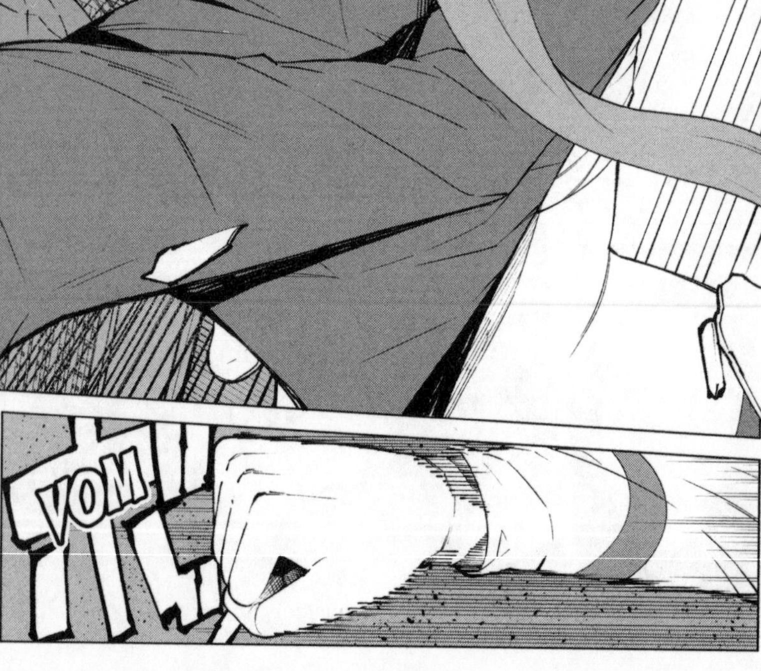
VOM

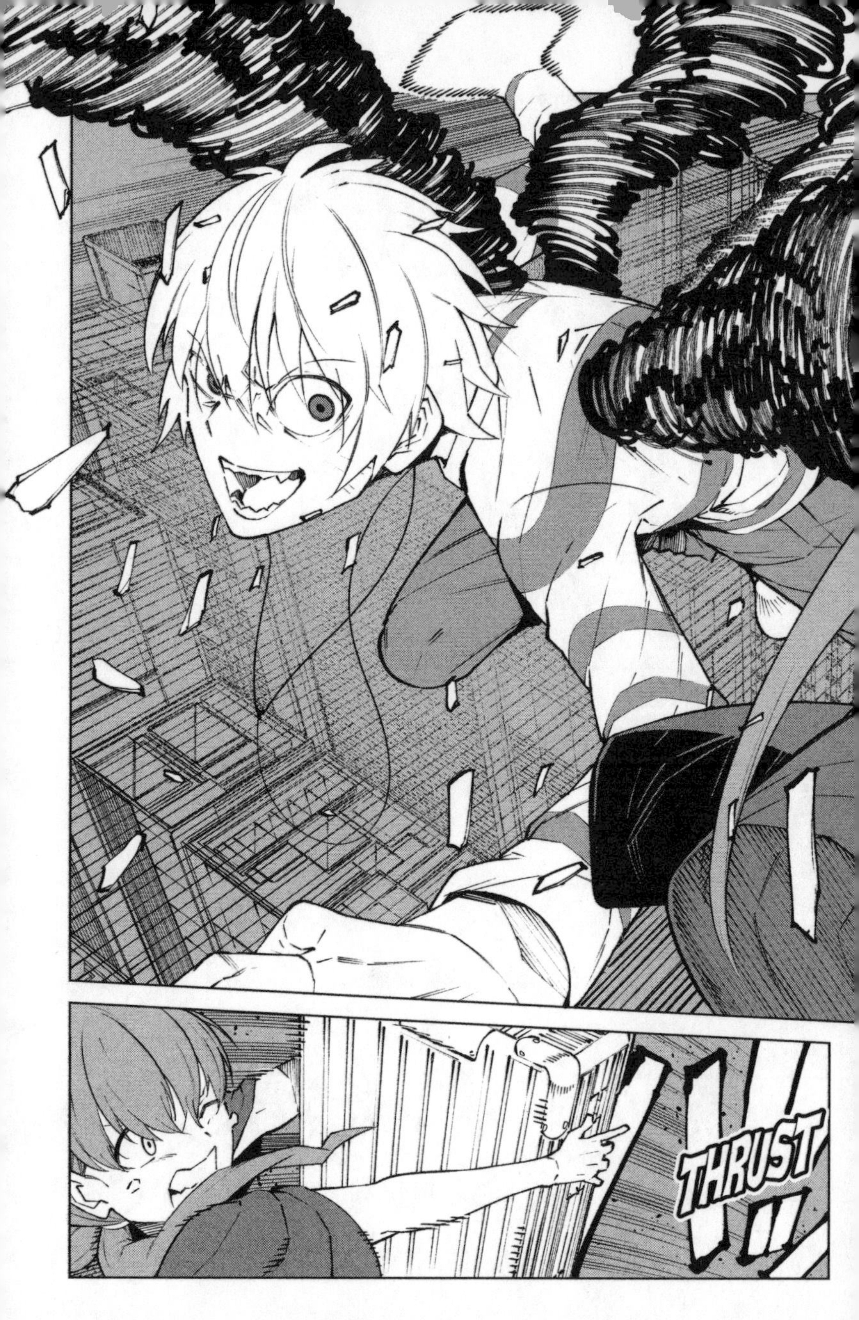
THRUST

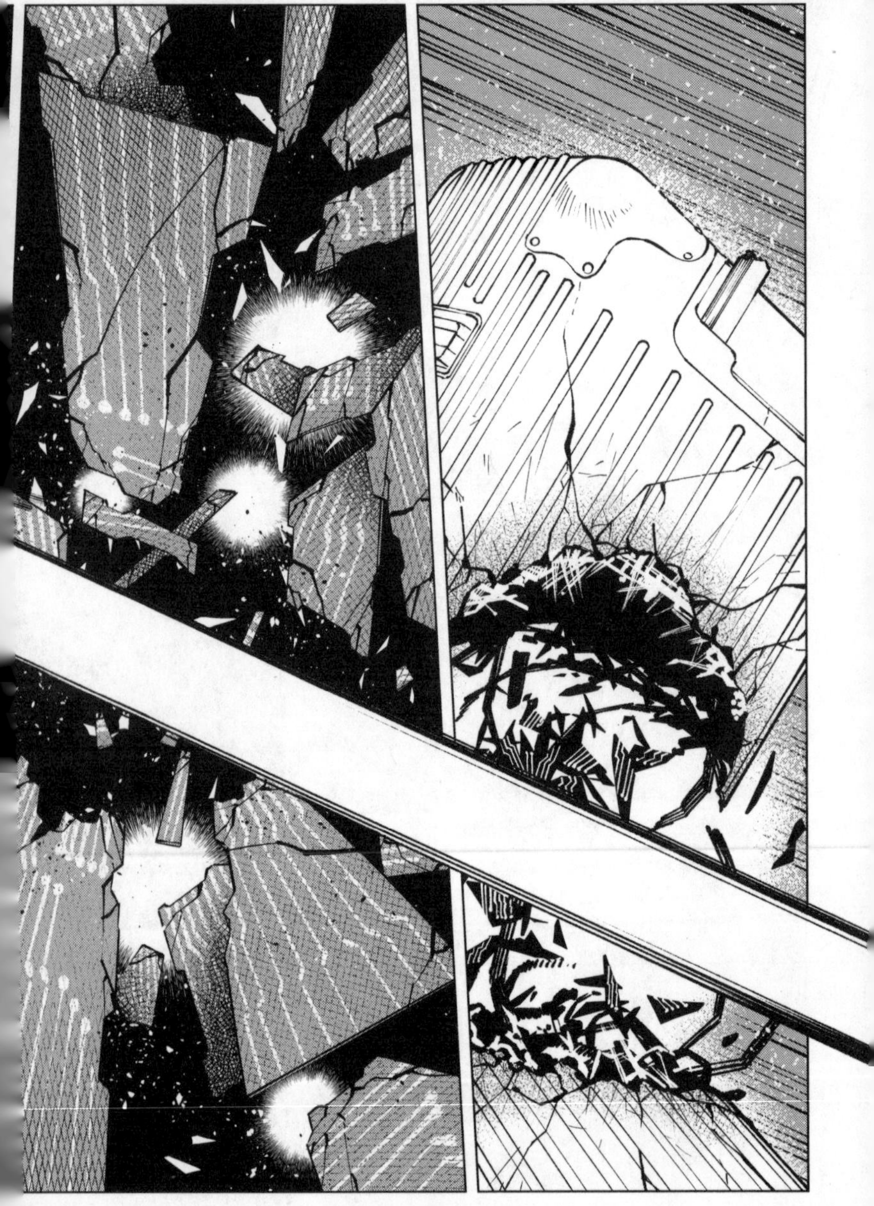

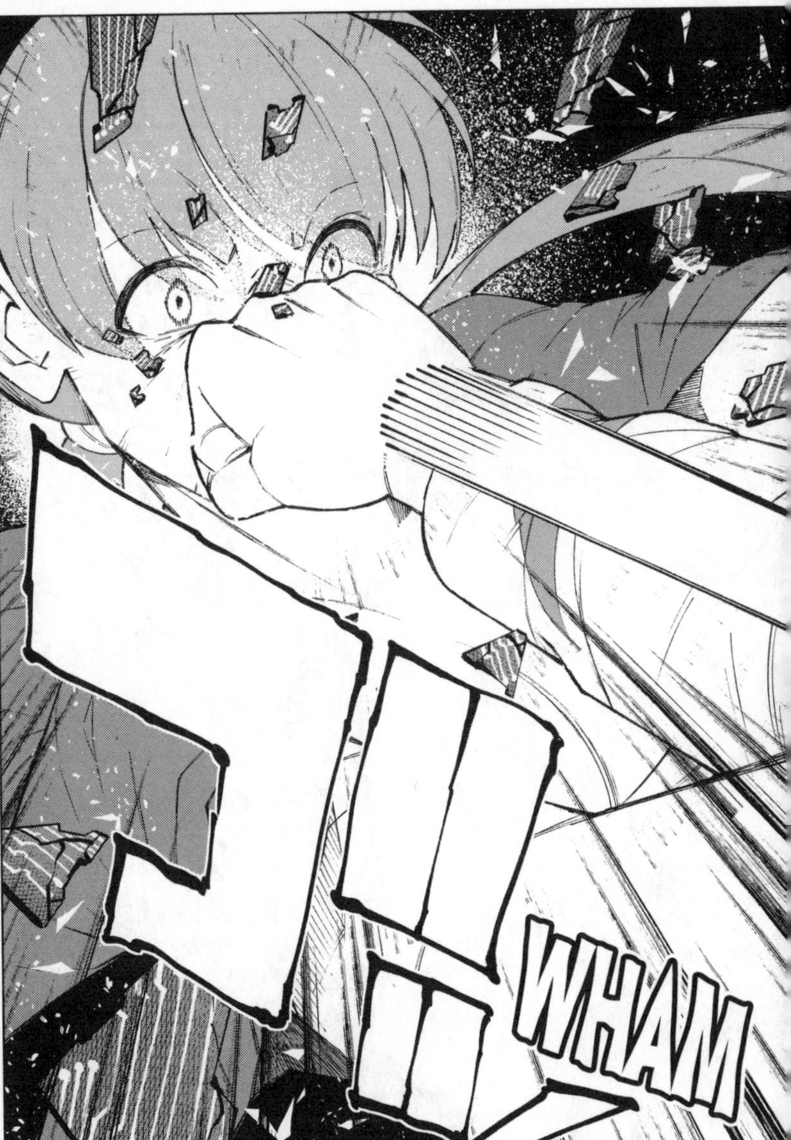
WHAM

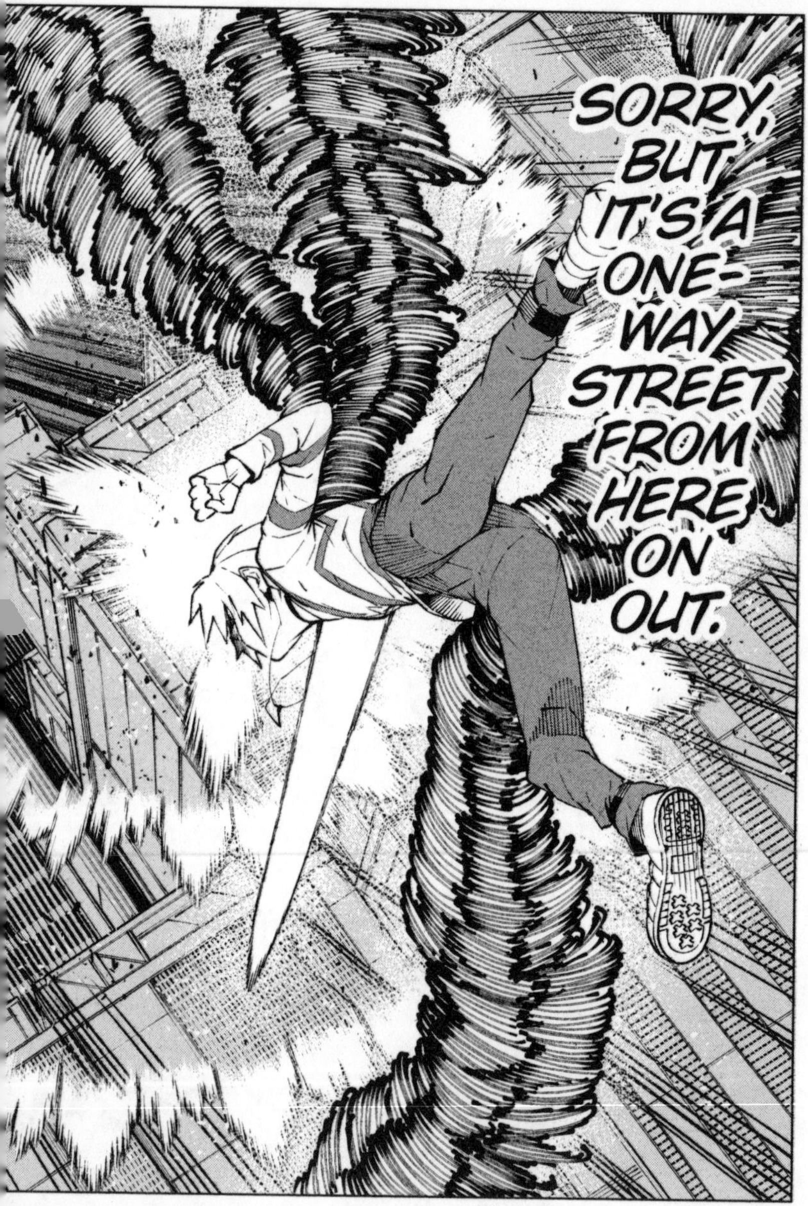
SORRY, BUT IT'S A ONE-WAY STREET FROM HERE ON OUT.

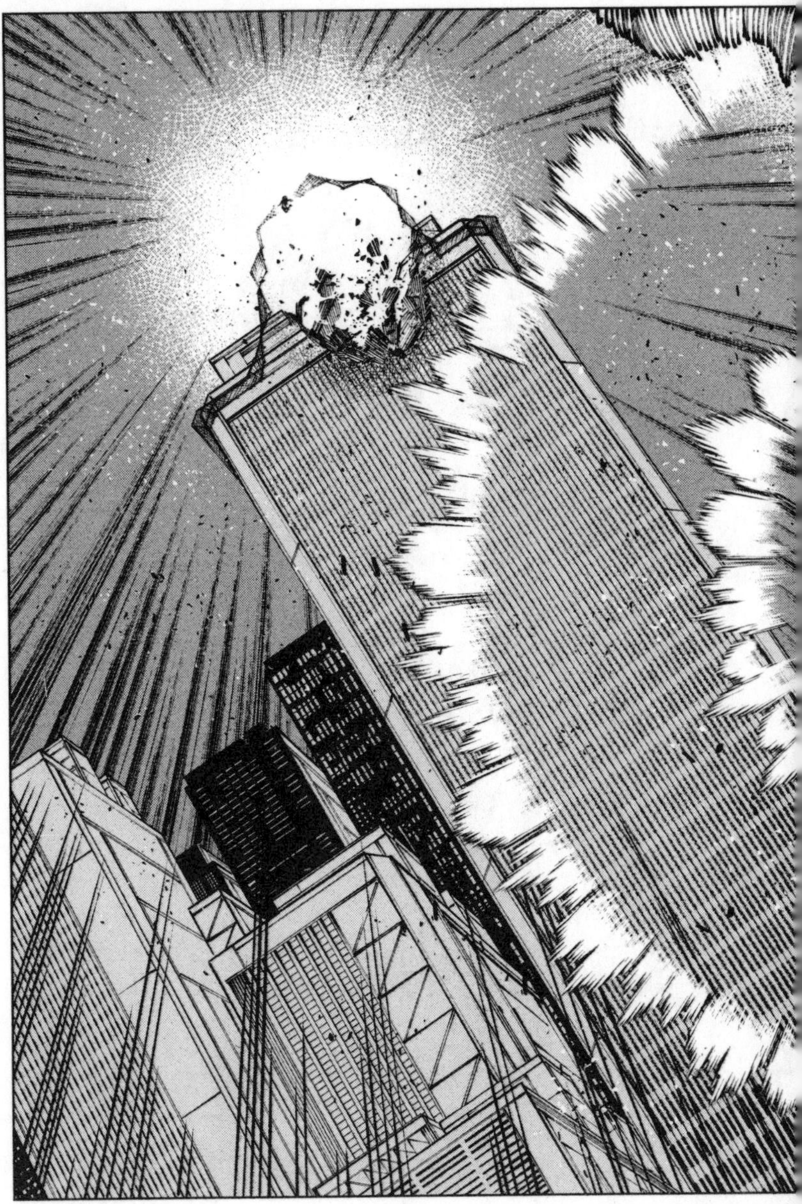

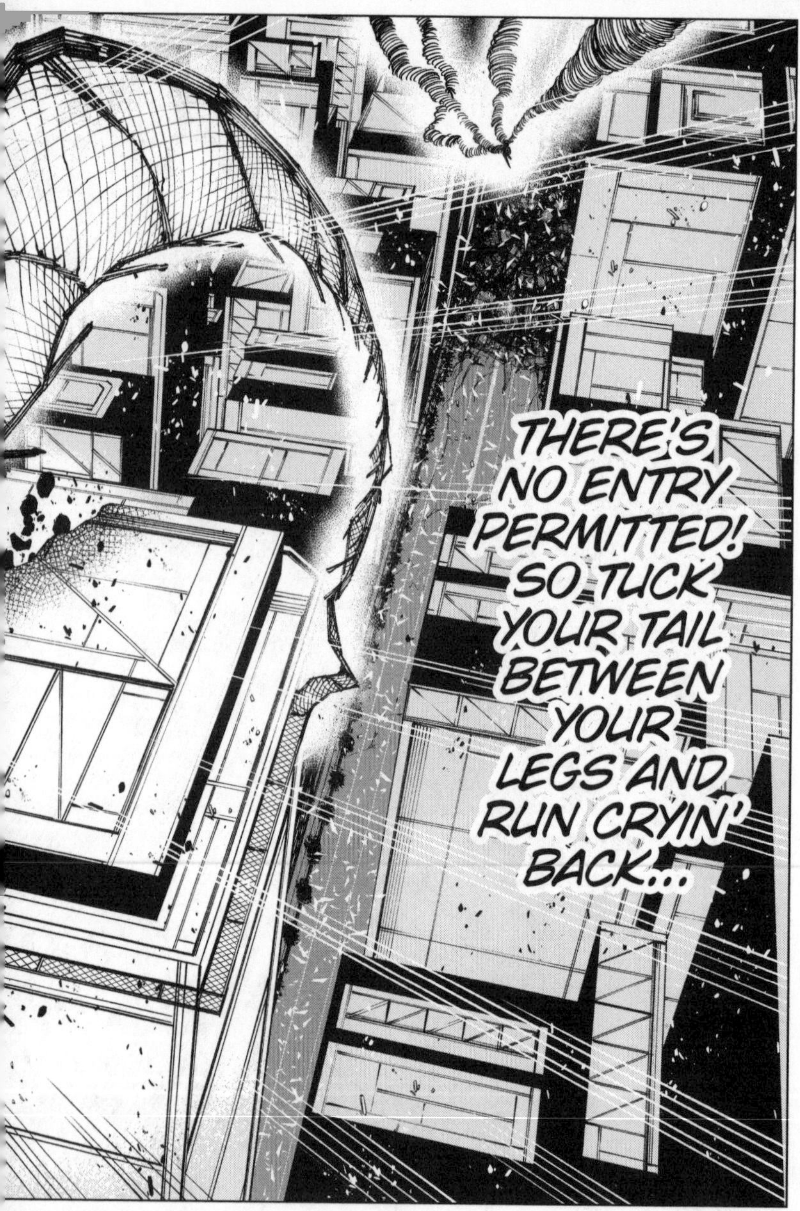
THERE'S NO ENTRY PERMITTED! SO TUCK YOUR TAIL BETWEEN YOUR LEGS AND RUN CRYIN' BACK...

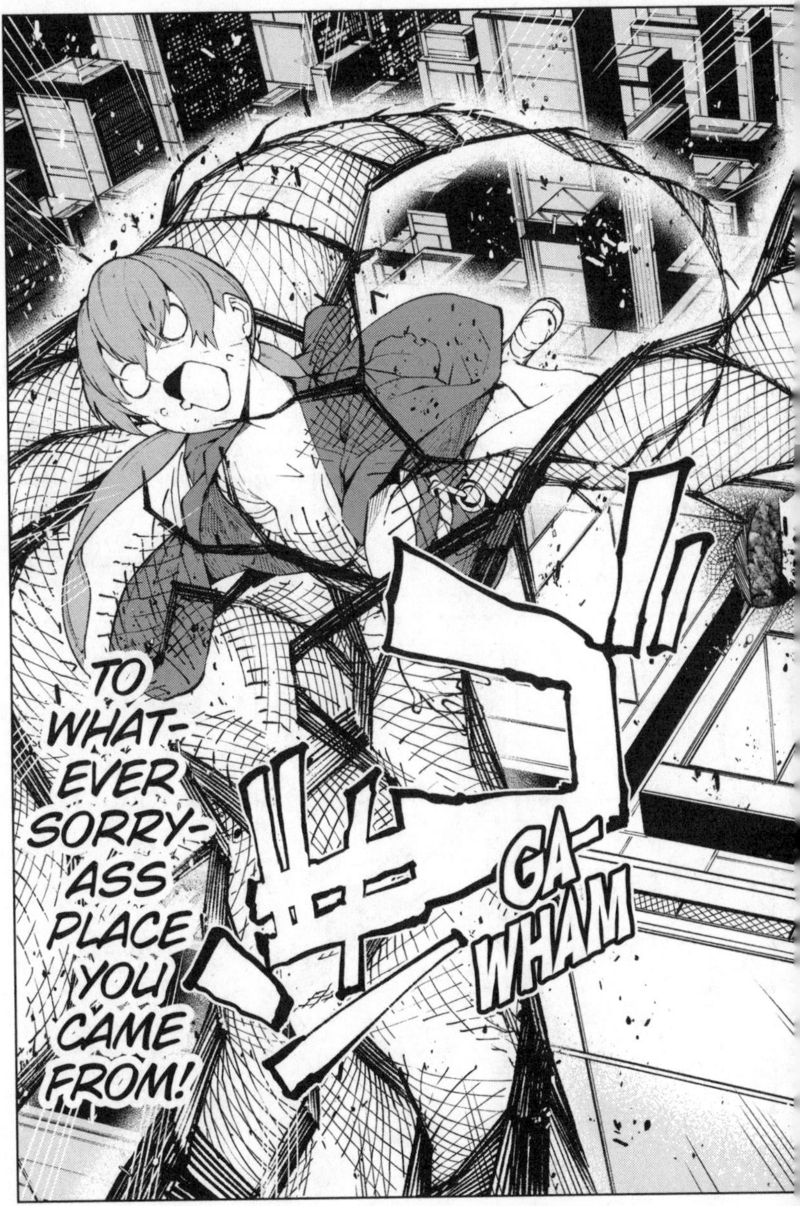
TO WHAT-EVER SORRY-ASS PLACE YOU CAME FROM!
GA-WHAM

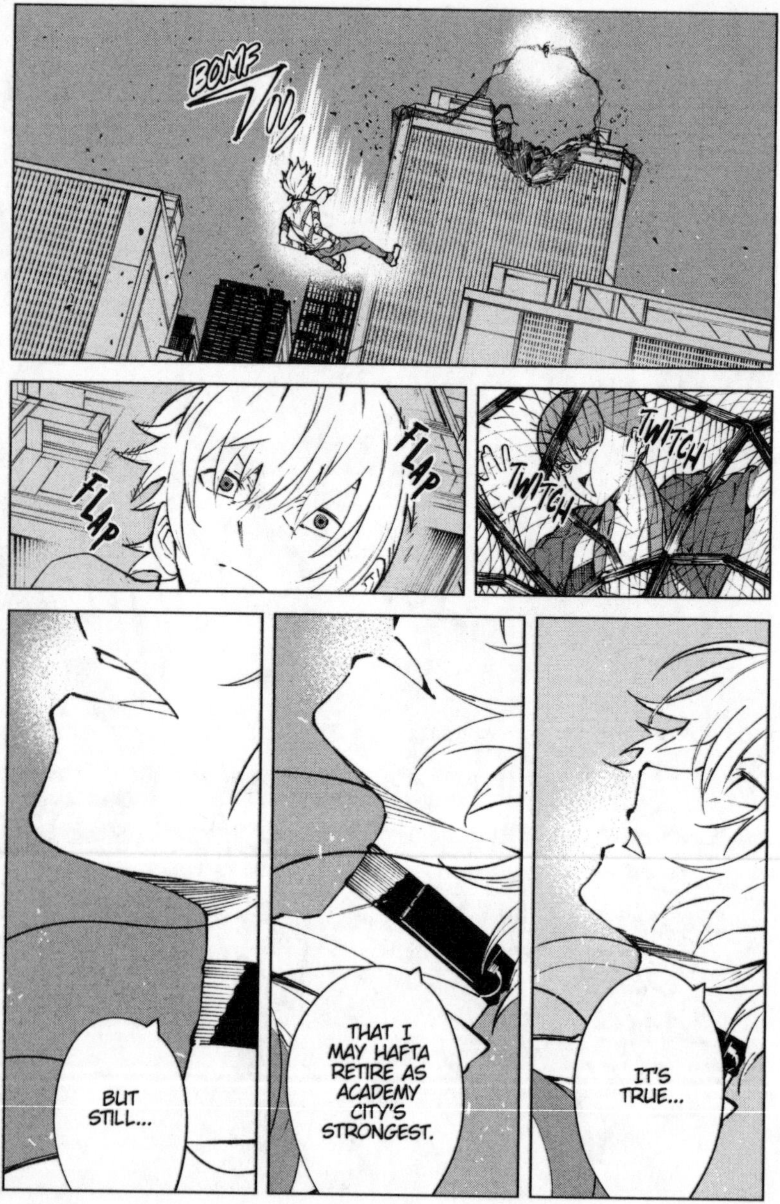
BOMF
TWITCH
TWITCH
FLAP
FLAP
IT'S TRUE...
THAT I MAY HAFTA RETIRE AS ACADEMY CITY'S STRONGEST.
BUT STILL...

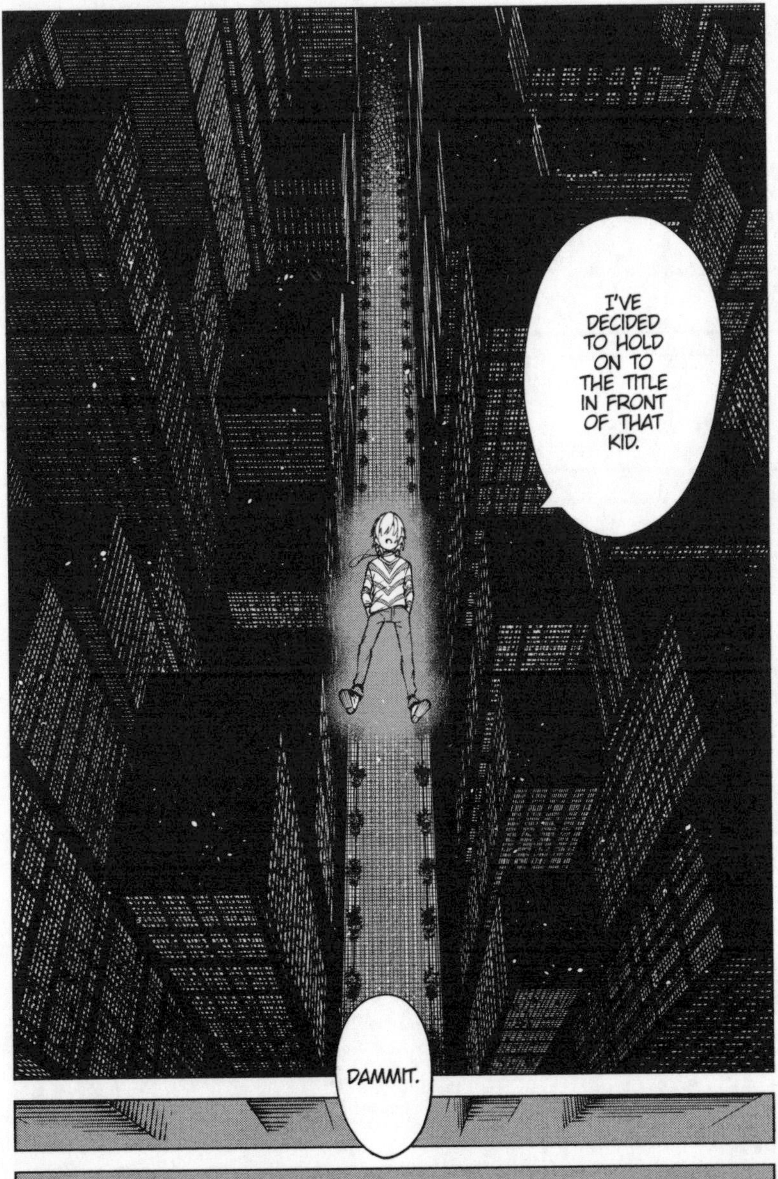
I'VE DECIDED TO HOLD ON TO THE TITLE IN FRONT OF THAT KID.
DAMMIT.

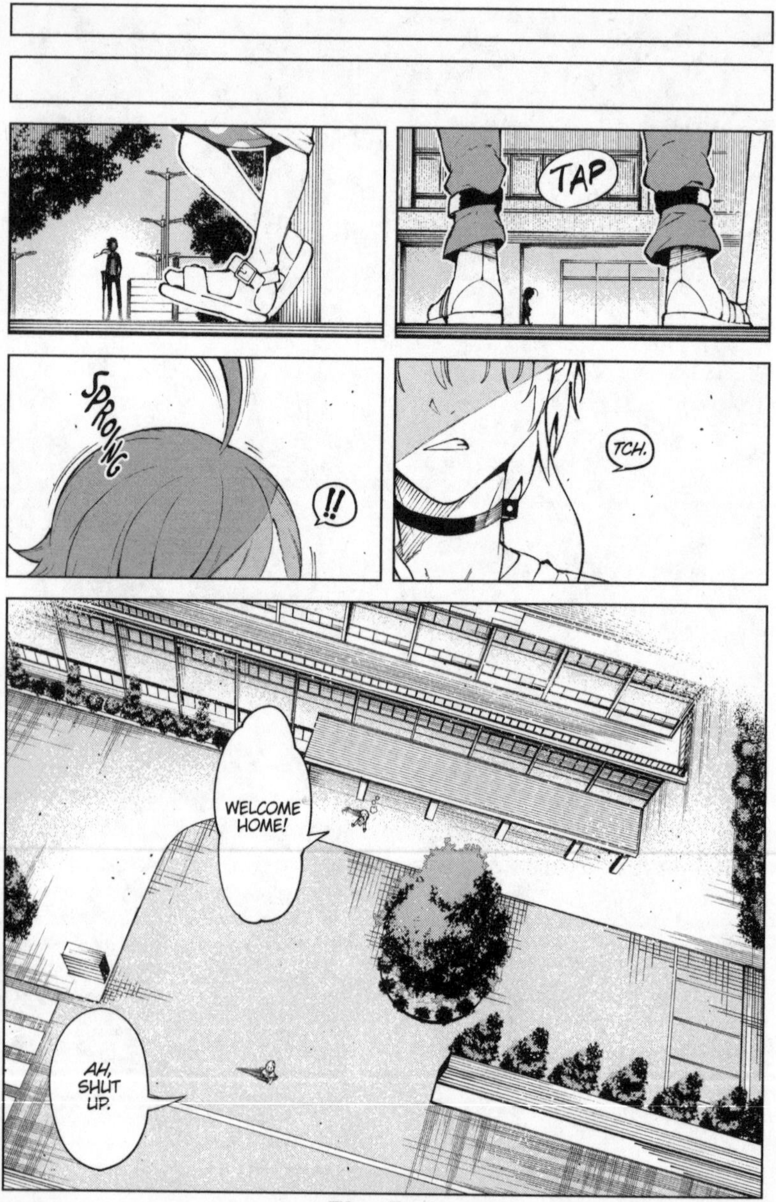
TAP
TCH.
SPROING
!!
WELCOME HOME!
AH, SHUT UP.

The End

AFTERWORD

Hello, everyone. It's me, Arata Yamaji.
Over approximately six years and twelve volumes, so very much has happened.
Since I'm no good at writing, I'll convey my joy and thanks in itemized form.

> I successfully won the competition for a spin-off comicalization of a work I'd read and watched. I was so surprised, I puked.

> I was told it would be turned into an anime by a wonderful production company. I fell over.

> The opening theme was given to The Sixth Lie-san, whom I adore. I was so happy that I dashed into my neighborhood forest, where I was chased by bees.

> The ending theme was given to sajou no hana-san, whom I also adore. I climbed to the highest spot in the giant park in my neighborhood and bowed in a direction that sajou no hana-san might be in.

> Chapter 58 in Volume 11 was dedicated to the members of The Sixth Lie and Chapter 59 in Volume 12 to the members of sajou no hana as a thank-you. How many chains are there? And what is the string extending from Last Order's little finger entwined with? I don't have enough space to confirm the answers here, but both illustrations have a trick to them, so please look closely.

> During the preview of the first episode, the movie theater's schedule read "Screen 7: A Certain Scientific Accelerator Advance Screening," and I felt happiness well up within me.

> The Sixth Lie and sajou no hana's live show was really great. The power of song is just incredible.

> The anime was wonderful. After I watched the final episode, I went and hid in the toilet so my wife wouldn't see me crying.

> I had fun with the battle against Musujime-san in the final chapter of the manga, and I thought I was able to draw it quite coolly.

> Thank you to Kamachi-san, the editors, and everyone involved in the comicalization of this work.

> Thank you to everyone involved in making this work into an anime.

> Thank you to all the readers who made it this far.

> I'm writing an afterword, so I'm glad that I was able to finish this properly.

> **Finally, to Accelerator and Last Order and everyone else who appeared in this work, thank you.**

2020.07.06. ARATA YAMAJI.

SEVEN SEAS ENTERTAINMENT PRESENTS

a certain SCIENTIFIC ACCELERATOR
volume 12

story by KAZUMA KAMACHI / art by ARATA YAMAJI

TRANSLATION
Nan Rymer

ADAPTATION
Maggie Danger

LETTERING AND RETOUCH
Roland Amago
Bambi Eloriaga-Amago

COVER DESIGN
Nicky Lim

EDITOR
Peter Adrian Behravesh

PREPRESS TECHNICIAN
Rhiannon Rasmussen-Silverstein

PRODUCTION ASSOCIATE
Christa Miesner

PRODUCTION MANAGER
Lissa Pattillo

MANAGING EDITOR
Julie Davis

ASSOCIATE PUBLISHER
Adam Arnold

PUBLISHER
Jason DeAngelis

SEP 0 - 2021

A CERTAIN SCIENTIFIC ACCELERATOR VOL. 12
TOARU MAJUTSU NO INDEX GAIDEN TOARU KAGAKU
NO ACCELERATOR VOL.12
©Kazuma Kamachi / Arata Yamaji 2020
First published in 2020 by KADOKAWA CORPORATION, Tokyo.
English translation rights arranged with KADOKAWA CORPORATION, Tokyo.

Seven Seas press and purchase enquiries can be sent to Marketing Manager Lianne Sentar at press@gomanga.com. Information regarding the distribution and purchase of digital editions is available from Digital Manager CK Russell at digital@gomanga.com.

ISBN: 978-1-64505-827-4

Printed in Canada

First Printing: June 2021

10 9 8 7 6 5 4 3 2 1

FOLLOW US ONLINE: www.sevenseasentertainment.com

READING DIRECTIONS

This book reads from *right to left*, Japanese style. If this is your first time reading manga, you start reading from the top right panel on each page and take it from there. If you get lost, just follow the numbered diagram here. It may seem backwards at first, but you'll get the hang of it! Have fun!!

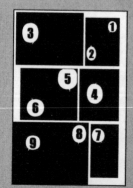